100 GREATEST U.S. COINS

FOURTH EDITION

Complete With Market Values

Jeff Garrett

with Ron Guth

Foreword by Mark Salzberg

Whitman
Publishing, LLC
PUBLISHING SINCE 1934

www.whitman.com

Whitman Publishing, LLC
Atlanta, GA

100 GREATEST U.S. COINS

FOURTH EDITION

Whitman Publishing, LLC
PUBLISHING SINCE 1934
www.whitman.com

© 2015 Whitman Publishing, LLC

3101 Clairmont Road • Suite G • Atlanta GA 30329

100 GREATEST is a registered trademark of Whitman Publishing, LLC.

Correspondence concerning this book may be directed to the publisher,
Attn: 100 Greatest U.S. Coins, at the address above.

ISBN: 0794842755
Printed in the United States of America.

If you enjoy the fascinating history and color images of the *100 Greatest U.S. Coins*, you will also enjoy the other books in this collection, including *100 Greatest Ancient Coins*, *100 Greatest American Currency Notes*, *100 Greatest American Medals and Tokens*, *100 Greatest U.S. Modern Coins*, *100 Greatest U.S. Error Coins*, and *100 Greatest American Stamps*.

For a complete catalog of numismatic reference books, supplies, and storage products,
visit Whitman Publishing online at www.whitman.com

CONTENTS

CREDITS AND ACKNOWLEDGMENTS

The authors acknowledge the following:

David W. Akers
John Albanese
Michael Berkman
Q. David Bowers
Kenneth Bressett
Steve Contursi
Adam Crum
John Dannreuther

William Gale
Ben Garrett
Mary Lynn Garrett
Morgan Garrett
Kent Gulley
Maggie Guth
Ron Guth
James L. Halperin

John B. Hamrick
Larry Hanks
Haley Hardy
Robert Harwell
Brian Hendelson
Steve Ivy
David Lange
Robert B. Lecce

Lee S. Minshull
Paul Montgomery
Charles Moore
Douglas Mudd
Tom Mulvaney
Gregory J. Rohan
Mark Salzberg
Scott Schechter

Max Speigel
Harvey G. Stack
Saul Teichman
Douglas A. Winter

Professional Numismatists Guild Voter Acknowledgments

The Professional Numismatists Guild, founded in 1955, is one of the leading numismatic societies in the United States. Initially, membership in the PNG was by invitation. Today a dealer may apply to join, but must demonstrate that he or she brings expertise to the society and must be elected by a majority of members. The PNG is committed to educational outreach programs that benefit the numismatic industry and has hosted seminars and sponsored scholarship essay contests to help educate the public about coins. For more information about this fine organization, visit www.pngdealers.com.

100 Greatest U.S. Coins Fourth Edition Voter List

Gary Adkins
John Albanese
Buddy Alleva
Thomas Caldwell
Brett Charvelle
Adam Crum
John Dannreuther

John Feigenbaum
Pierre Frike
Michael R. Fuljenz
William Gale
Ira M. Goldberg
Lawrence Goldberg
Kent Gulley

James L. Halperin
John Hamrick
Larry Hanks
Robert Harwell
Brian Hendelson
Todd Imhof
Victor Ingraffia

Steve Ivy
Larry Lee
Brett Leifer
Kevin Lipton
Lee S. Minshull
Michael Moline
Paul Nugget

Andrew Pappacoda
Joseph Peralla
Daniel Ratner
Greg Roberts
Maurice Rosen
Thomas Smith
Barry S. Stuppler

Additional Voters From the First, Second, and Third Editions

David W. Akers
Dan Avena Jr.
Dan Avena Sr.
Robert L. Avena
Loren D. Barnett
Lee J. Bellisario
David A. Berg
Harlan J. Berk
Brad Bohnert
Nick Brown
John Stanford Brush
Mrs. C.E. Bullowa
William A. Burd
Robert H. Campbell
Jason Carter
Michael Casper
Mark Crane
Allan Davisson
Klaus Degler
Thomas M. Denley

Silvano Di Genova
John Donnelly
William Dominick
Sheridan Downey
Ronald R. Drezwucki Jr.
Kathleen Duncan
Joel T. Edler
Arthur L. Friedberg
Kent Morris Froseth
Stephen J. Gehringer
Dennis M. Gillio
Mark E. Goldberg
Frank Greenberg
John B. Hamrick
Gene L. Henry
George B. Humphreys
Steve Ivy
Harry E. Jones
Don Kagin
Don Ketterling

Bruce Kutcher
Harry Laibstain
Robert B. Lecce
Julian M. Leidman
Jonathan Lerner
Edwin Leventhal
Stuart Levine
Robert Levinson
James Long
Samuel Lopresto
Chris Victor McCawley
Daryl Mercer
Wayne Miller
Warren T. Mills
Paul Montgomery
Richard T. Munzner
Richard N. Nachbar
Chris Napolitano
Thomas W. Noe
Casey Noxon

Dean Oakes
David Olmstead
Joel D. Perlin
Peter R. Pienta
Diane Piret
Richard H. Ponterio
Robert Rhue
Brad Rodgers
Gregory J. Rohan
John N. Rowe
Mark Salzberg
Mary Sauvain
Byrd Saylor III
Glenn Schinke
Anthony Michael Scirpo
Leonard Shafer
Van Simmons
Larry Gerald Spence
Harvey G. Stack
Robert L. Steinberg

Michael R. Storeim
Anthony J. Swiatek
Anthony Terranova
Rick Tomaska
Mark B. Todd
Jacob Jay Van Grover
Fred Weinberg
Harold B. Weitz
Larry Whitlow
Paul R. Whitnah
Dale L. Williams
Douglas A. Winter
David Wnuck
John J. Woodside
Gordon Wrubel
William J. Youngerman

Collector Jack Collins spent more than 30 years cataloging and tracking each of the known examples of the 1794 silver dollar and found just 100 different specimens. Today, there are believed to be approximately 130, and each is appreciated for its own unique qualities.

This is a book filled with treasures. A significant number of the most valuable coins in the world are classic U.S. coins, and almost all of those are in this book. In the great scheme of things, however, they aren't valuable enough.

The 250 highest prices paid for U.S. coins at auction total just less than $250 million in value. In context, that is a bit less than the sales price of the most valuable painting ever sold, Paul Cezanne's *The Card Players*, and the top ten most valuable paintings ever sold traded for a combined $1.4 billion. Are the greatest coins really that different from works of art?

Here, among the pages of *100 Greatest U.S. Coins*, we can explore this special intersection of coins and art. Coins are displayed with large-format images and appreciated as beautiful objects. Beside them, text probes further and illustrates why these coins merit our adoration. Indeed, it is a numismatic museum in a single volume.

Of course, collectors are not satisfied with merely gazing upon artifacts. They also must possess them, grouping them together to tell a curated story. All collectors feel this way, which partly explains why this book fits equally well on the shelves of both the most advanced, astute collectors and those of the novices who are only beginning to explore the hobby of coin collecting. For both groups, these coins provoke the same response: a desire to learn more about them and a desire to own them.

On the topic of ownership, the book again engages collectors of all levels, as the wide range of coins within this book includes several that are obtainable with a relatively small budget. For example, included on the list are coins like the 1909-S V.D.B. Lincoln cent. Despite its place as one of the most important coins of the 20th century, an example can still be had for less than $1,000. It is accessible to so many collectors.

And not only is it affordable, but the 1909-S V.D.B. can also be bought and sold, in any grade, any day of the week, with a single phone call. The collector of this coin benefits from some of the unique features of the rare coin marketplace. Price guides are plentiful, and dealers make markets with tight buy-sell spreads. Independent, expert certification is easy to use and very affordable—and comes with a guarantee of authenticity.

This contrasts sharply from what we think about the art market, in which collectors and dealers can pay very different prices, and concerns about authenticity weigh heavily. The coin market seems to have "figured it out." It has alleviated the major deficiencies of other collectibles markets.

In further support of that idea, coins themselves have some distinct advantages. They are portable and a great store of wealth, and they have a good track record. All the same, an example of every coin included in the *100 Greatest U.S. Coins* available to collectors could be bought for less than the price of one great modern painting or sculpture.

That being said, this may be changing. For example, consider specifically the 1794 silver dollar, the first coin of that denomination struck. Here we find that individual specimens, singular examples of the issue, are sought out by collectors because of their aesthetic qualities, provenance, and other features. An effort has been made to catalog the entire extant population of more than 125 examples.

Now, each coin is unique, even though multiples exist. The highest-quality pieces are marketed using 10,000-word auction descriptions and condition census rosters that rank the individual coin among the best that are known. And the values vary from $100,000 well into the millions. Much like art, coins are now often sold with their unique and individual merits at the fore.

Coin collections too are morphing. Art collections usually consist of what collectors want to look at and live with on the walls of their homes. The shape, form, and size of art collections can be loosely defined by overarching themes like time period, style, or geography guiding purchases. Historically, coin collections were viewed rigidly.

Today, however, we don't always conceive of a coin collection as being a complete set of a particular series, or a type set with one of every design of a denomination. Instead, just as coins are evaluated individually, a collection can be an individual assemblage of important coins that all meet personalized criteria. Many collectors refer to a "box of twenty," 20 coins that comprise the core of a collection and reflect the goals, aesthetics, and interests of the collector. Similar trends can be observed in other collectible fields, including comic books, ancient coins, and currency.

In the field of U.S numismatics, without question, *100 Greatest U.S. Coins* has been a contributing factor to this developing phenomenon. The coins that are included in the book are what we understand to be perennially important, those that have shaped our hobby and will influence its future. Regardless of how interests shift, like masterworks of art, these are the coins that form the foundation and will never go out of fashion.

Mark Salzberg
Sarasota, Florida

Foreword author **Mark Salzberg** is chairman of Numismatic Guaranty Corporation (NGC), the world's largest third-party coin grading service. A life-long numismatist, Salzberg has personally graded nearly all of the significant rarities and collections to come to market in the past 25 years. He is widely recognized for his grading expertise and is a central figure in promoting coin certification both in the United States and abroad.

In recognition of his achievements, the American Numismatic Association gave Salzberg the ANA Presidential Award in 1998 and named him Numismatist of the Year in 2006. He continues to give back to the industry through his sponsorship of the Smithsonian's Legendary Coins & Currency exhibit and support of the American Numismatic Association.

I t truly goes without saying that beauty is in the eye of the beholder. The same can also be said of something as subjective as selecting what might be called the 100 greatest U.S. numismatic treasures. In this book, you will begin a tour through the vast medley of coin delicacies that have thrilled collectors of all ages and levels of interest. These are the gems that we all long to see, savor, study, or own. The authors have done a superb job of presenting them in a fashion that shows the importance of each item and why they deserve to be ranked among the pantheon of "greats."

The inclusion of coins discussed here (and in earlier editions of the compilation) was recommended by a select panel of several hundred prominent numismatists. Each offered suggestions about the coins they deemed worthy of special attention based on the popularity, value, and historical

Not all of the 100 Greatest U.S. Coins are unique specimens confined to one collection. A lucky numismatist could potentially find a 1955 Doubled-Die Obverse Lincoln cent in their pocket any day!

importance of each item. Each coin was then carefully researched and described by the authors in a narrative that is sure to capture the reader's imagination and interest.

Few people, regardless of their involvement in the coin hobby, will ever get the opportunity to actually see or handle some of these rare and valuable coins. Yet that should not dissuade them from learning about the existence of such remarkable items, nor of longing to find one in an unexpected place or by some quirk of fortune. As will be seen, not every one of the 100 examples is a classic coin of antiquity. Some actually circulated in the recent past and might have been used or saved by a relative.

Take, for instance, the very popular 1955 Doubled-Die Obverse Lincoln cent (No. 74 in the rankings). Its existence was not widely known until two or three years after it was minted. Examples may still be lurking somewhere, waiting to be discovered by someone who has learned about the unusual Mint error through this book. While one may never get to hold or even see some of the great rarities presented herein, they can enjoy a vicarious thrill in viewing the magnificent enlarged color photographs of each item.

Those who have previously enjoyed the earlier editions of this classic work by authors Jeff Garrett and Ron Guth will be happy to find a plethora of new material in this expanded fourth edition. The enhanced introduction has been expanded to cover more of the romance and accounts of numismatic history of the country. This new coverage has also been augmented with numerous illustrations of coins, tokens, personalities, and related items. Readers will also find useful the expanded glossary, which features many additional words that have been added to clarify current numismatic jargon. Others will find their interest drawn to reviewing the valuation updates that track the steady increases in prices of rare coins over the past 25 years.

Whatever your interest in U.S. numismatic history, it is bound to be stimulated and inspired through the stories of these great coins in this truly great book.

Kenneth Bressett
Colorado Springs, Colorado

Kenneth Bressett has actively promoted the study and hobby of numismatics for more than 50 years. His published works on the subject cover a wide range of topics and extend from short articles to standard reference books on such diverse areas as ancient coins, paper money, English, and U.S. coins.

Throughout his career he has worked as an author, editor, and publisher of books and products for coin collectors. He has also taught the subject to hundreds of students through courses at Colorado College and other places. From 1983 to 1988, he served the American Numismatic Association as Director of Coin Authentication

and Educational Programs. Subsequently he served on the ANA Board of Governors, and as Vice President and President.

Bressett was appointed to the U.S. Assay Commission in 1966 by President Lyndon Johnson and in 1996 was made a member of the Citizens Commemorative Coin Advisory Committee. He has received numerous awards in recognition of his service and dedication to numismatics, including election to the National Numismatic Hall of Fame, the American Numismatic Association Medal of Merit, and the Ferran Zerbe award.

Jeff Garrett began his coin collecting the all-American way, with Lincoln cents. In 1969, a family friend gave him a Lincoln cent board. Since then, coins have been the focus of his life. Growing up in the Tampa Bay area in Clearwater, Florida, Garrett became very active in several local clubs, serving as a junior officer of the Clearwater Coin Club in the 1970s. He was mentored at an early age by many of the area's dealers, among them Ed French and Jeff Means. Garrett attended his first American Numismatic Association convention in 1974 in Miami with Ed French and has not missed one since. He has been a member of the ANA for more than 25 years, with life membership number 3124.

At the age of 17, Garrett was offered a position with Florida Coin Exchange, one of the dominant firms of the day. Two years later, he became a partner. In 1984, Garrett founded Mid-American Rare Coin Galleries, which continues to operate today. He is also co-owner of the Sarasota Rare Coin Gallery. During the 1980s, he was a partner in Mid-American Rare Coin Auctions, which sold many important collections and earned Catalog of the Year in 1986 from the Numismatic Literary Guild. Several years later, Garrett organized the Bluegrass Coin Club in Lexington, Kentucky. Because local coin clubs were so important in his early life, Garrett wanted to foster the same atmosphere of enthusiastic collectors that he enjoyed as a youth. Today the club is very healthy, with more than 30 members in attendance each month.

Today, Garrett describes his expertise as being a "dealer's dealer." With a network of professionals he has established over 25 years, he helps with financing, research, and acquisitions sales. Over the course of his career, Garrett has handled nearly every United States rarity. During the American Numismatic Association convention in 2003, he was one of the experts called upon to authenticate the long-lost 1913 Liberty Head nickel. In 2004 he handled one of the greatest gold collections ever assembled, the famed Dukes Creek set of Georgia gold, a collection that sold for nearly $4 million.

Another important aspect of his career is his membership in the Professional Numismatists Guild, to which he has belonged since 1982. Today, Garrett is a former president of the prestigious organization. In 2003, the PNG awarded him the Abe Kosoff Founder's Award, that organization's highest honor, for work promoting the hobby and organization. More recently, Garrett has been serving as a governor of the American Numismatic Association, and is now vice president of the organization.

In 2003 the first edition of *100 Greatest United States Coins* was given the Best Book award by both the Numismatic Literary Guild and the Professional Numismatists Guild. Although he spends most of his time buying and selling coins, Garrett enjoys research and the study of rare coins. He is coauthor of *The Official Red Book of Auction Records* and is also coauthor of the award-winning *Encyclopedia of U.S. Gold Coins 1795–1933*, a project done in cooperation with the Smithsonian Institution. Garrett is currently the valuations editor for *A Guide Book of United States Coins* (the Red Book), published annually by Whitman.

Living in Lexington, Kentucky, he enjoys golf, travel, and spending time with his family: his wife Mary Lynn, their daughter Morgan, and their son Ben, who runs his own rare-coin business in Sarasota, Florida.

Ron Guth is a recognized authority on U.S. and German coins. He is a licensed Certified Public Accountant who has been involved professionally in numismatics for more than 40 years as a collector, dealer, researcher, and writer. His books and articles have earned numerous awards, including the American Numismatic Association's Heath Literary and the Olga & Wayte Raymond awards, the Numismatic Literary Guild's Best Numismatic Investment Book and Best Book of the Year awards, and the Professional Numismatic Guild's Best Book of the Year Award. The American Numismatic Association awarded Ron the prestigious President's Award in 2003 and the Numismatist of the Year Award in 2014 for his many contributions to numismatics.

Ron is president of PCGS CoinFacts, a division of Collectors Universe. He and his wife Maggie have been married for more than 35 years and have three children and three grandchildren. They live close to the ocean in San Diego, California, where they enjoy sailing, rowing, biking, cooking, and being grandparents.

One of the first questions new collectors ask is "What is the greatest U.S. coin?" The answer to that question is not as simple as one might think. Because we all come from different backgrounds and our experiences in numismatics are different, our answers to that question will also be different. For example, the person who has collected Lincoln cents will probably choose one of the rare dates in that series, perhaps the one coin he or she still needs to complete the set—because, to that collector, that is the greatest coin. Another person might choose the most *valuable* coin—or the rarest coin—or the coin with the most beautiful design. One of the reasons *100 Greatest U.S. Coins* was written is to help answer the question of what is the most valuable coin. That is the question that is almost always asked when the subject of rare coins comes up in conversation with non-collectors. Many are stunned to find out that a rare coin sold for more than $7 million at auction. The natural question is "How can it be worth so much?" When you tell them the history of the 1933 double eagle, with its intrigue, drama, and legal battles, they start to understand how the item can be so coveted.

Beyond its intrinsic worth as a high-denomination gold coin, the 1933 Saint-Gaudens double eagle is made all the more valuable by its stunningly beautiful appearance and incredible backstory.

WHAT MAKES A COIN GREAT?

Greatness is subjective. Much of greatness depends on personal tastes and preferences. However, greatness also depends on objective factors, characteristics that can be measured against each other and from one coin to another. All of the great coins listed in this book will have at least one of the following characteristics:

Rarity—Great coins are rare, meaning that only a few were made or, in some instances, only a few survived. Many of the coins in this book are unique; others are so rare that they are almost impossible to obtain because they come to market so infrequently. However, others are rare only in the context of their series, and for some "popular rarities," such as the 1909-S V.D.B. Lincoln cent, tens of thousands survive.

Value—Great coins are generally expensive, but not necessarily so. The 1787 Fugio cent (available in Choice Uncirculated condition for less than $6,000) ranks near the 1861 Paquet Reverse double eagle (valued at $2 million) in the 100 Greatest U.S. Coins list!

Quality—Great coins are usually in exceptional condition. However, high quality does not necessarily mean perfection. For example, the finest 1802 half dime is only About Uncirculated.

Popularity—Great coins are appreciated by a large audience. Some coins may be rare and valuable, but the voting for the 100 Greatest U.S. Coins illustrated how much of a popularity contest this really was. Why else would the 1909-S V.D.B. cent, of which thousands exist, rank higher on the list (No. 23) than the unique 1870-S half dime (No. 58)?

Beauty—Great coins are aesthetically pleasing. For example, part of the allure of the 1872 Amazonian gold pattern set (No. 16) is the sheer beauty and uniformity of the designs and the soft, mellow color of the gold in which they were struck.

History—Great coins have a story to tell. Who can resist the incredible story of the 1804 silver dollars, how they were first made in 1834, how some of them traveled from the Far East to Europe and back to America? Or the fascinating history behind the 1792 silver-center cent and how the early Mint worked so hard to produce new coins for a new country? These stories and many more are at the heart of why most of the coins in 100 Greatest U.S. Coins have made the list. These are certainly not the 100 rarest coins, but the coins that most capture the imagination. In many cases, they are coins that have not even been seen in person, but are known only in reference books. We have attempted not only to create a list, but also to give the readers the background stories that make these coins so fascinating.

HISTORY OF UNITED STATES COINAGE

Although colonial coins are for the most part not represented in this book, they are a very important part of coinage and the early history of the United States. The earliest coins to circulate in the colonies and the young United States were actually world coins such as the Spanish milled dollar. These are sometimes referred to as "Pillar dollars." Many of the shipwrecks found in the last couple of decades contained coinage that had circulated at the time the ships sank. It is not unusual for sunken ships from as late as the 1840s and 1850s to have nearly as many world coins as U.S. coins on board. Coins from South America and beyond circulated freely in this country for many years after the first U.S. coins were struck in 1792. The most frequently seen coins in the early years of our country were Spanish 8-real pieces, English guineas, German thalers, Dutch ducats, and many others. Furs and tobacco were also commonly accepted in trade. Hard currency was usually in short supply, as England made little effort to supply the colonies with enough gold and silver coinage.

Spanish 8-real pieces (or "Pillar dollars," top) and English guineas (bottom) were among the world coins that circulated in the colonies and early United States.

From left to right, Willow Tree, Oak Tree, and Pine Tree coins are some of the first to be minted in what would later become the United States. All were dated 1652, but their production continued for at least three successive decades. Struck in multiple denominations, one shilling coins are shown here.

By the mid-1600s, the first coins minted for the colonies in America were struck in Massachusetts. In 1652, John Hull began the production of New England shillings, sixpence, and three-pence coins. They are very simple in design, with one side being stamped NE and the other with Roman numerals for the denomination. These are all very rare and seldom seen on the market, bringing healthy six-figure prices when offered. Shortly thereafter, the design improved with the production of Willow Tree, Oak Tree, and finally Pine Tree coinage. Although these coins are all dated 1652, they were struck for at least three decades after that. Examples of Pine Tree coinage were widely circulated, and are today still quite affordable.

Eventually many more coins were struck by private firms to fill the need for hard currency. Around 1659, Lord Baltimore had several denominations struck in England for use in what is now Maryland. Mark Newby imported coins from Ireland for use in the province of New Jersey in 1682. Today these are known as "St. Patrick" coinage. An extensive series of coins was produced in England by William Wood starting in 1722. These circulated rather widely, and today can be purchased for a few hundred dollars in most cases. During the 18th century, several individuals were responsible for other copper coins that circulated in colonial commerce, many of which were actually struck in England but shipped to the colonies. These include Kentucky, Myddelton, and Franklin Press tokens. Other interesting coins were produced by J. Chalmers, John Higley, Standish Barry, and even Ephraim Brasher, who produced the famous Brasher doubloons.

The Articles of Confederation, adopted in 1781, stipulated that Congress should have the sole right to regulate and value coins struck by its own authority or by that of respective states. States therefore had the right to strike coinage with the approval of Congress. New Hampshire was the first to strike coins, but very few were made, and they are now extremely rare. From 1785 to 1788, Vermont, Connecticut, New Jersey, and Massachusetts all produced coins or had them struck by private contractors. There are dozens of striking variations, with some struck in large quantities. Some are extremely rare and highly collectible. Others are quite common and easily purchased.

The Libertas Americana medal, although not an actual coin, is also a very important piece of early U.S. numismatics. That medal graces the cover of another book in the 100 Greatest series, *100 Greatest American Medals and Tokens,* by Katherine Jaeger and Q. David Bowers. Its design inspired the use of the liberty cap on coinage of the new republic. Benjamin Franklin (U.S. commissioner to France at the time) proposed the concept and mottoes for the piece, which was made in Paris. French artist Esprit-Antoine Gibelin sketched the design, and the dies were made by Augustine Dupré. The medal depicts the mythical subject of the infant Hercules strangling two serpents, symbolizing the young nation of the United States defeating the British armies at Saratoga and Yorktown. Minerva symbolizes the United States' crucial ally France, as with shield and spear she holds the British lion at bay. The medal is one of the most beautiful items of U.S. numismatics. Franklin presented gold versions of the medal to the king and queen of France. Silver

The famous Libertas Americana medal is closely linked to the United States' early coinage.

versions were presented to French ministers, and copper examples were also struck. The gold medals are unknown today, possibly melted for their gold content during the French Revolution.

One of the greatest collections ever assembled of colonial coins and currency was put together by John J. Ford Jr. His holdings of early Americana were simply staggering. The rare coin auction house Stack's in New York City sold his collection over a period of a few years, producing some of the finest rare-coin auction catalogs ever produced. Those catalogs today are probably the best source of information on colonial and early U.S. coinage, medals, tokens, and paper money.

The first federally authorized coin was the Fugio cent (No. 36). For that reason, and its close association with Benjamin Franklin, it qualifies as one of the 100 Greatest U.S. Coins. The coin was struck privately by contract with the government. On March 3, 1791, Congress passed a resolution that a mint should be established. President Washington was authorized to make preparations for the production of coins. The next year, on April 12, 1792, a bill was passed providing "that money of account of United States should be expressed in dollars or units, dismes (later, dimes) or tenths, cents or hundredths, and milles or thousands; a disme being the tenth part of a dollar, a cent the hundredth part of a dollar, a mille the thousandth part of a dollar." Denominations established were as follows: the copper half cent, copper cent, silver half disme, silver disme, silver quarter dollar, silver half dollar, silver dollar, gold quarter eagle, gold half eagle, and gold eagle.

The first director of the Mint was David Rittenhouse, a well-known scientist of the day. He was appointed by President George

Washington. The first Mint was established in Philadelphia in mid-1792. The very first coin struck by the new U.S. Mint was the famous 1792 half disme, another member of the 100 Greatest U.S. Coins list (No. 12). One of the reasons this coin is so desirable is its close ties to George Washington. Only 1,500 coins were struck, and it is thought that Washington provided some of the silver needed to make the coins. The popular legend of the 1792 half disme is that they were struck from Martha Washington's silverware. It is very likely that there is some truth to the story. Although the 1792 half disme is very rare, it is the most commonly seen of all 1792 coins. Several coins were saved at the time of issue, and there are a few incredible gem examples known. Perhaps Washington or Jefferson presented these to close associates who saw the wisdom of saving such an important relic for future generations. If only coins could talk!

Several other pattern coins were produced in 1792, but in very small numbers. These are all very rare, and each is on the list of 100 Greatest U.S. Coins. These include the 1792 silver-center cent (No. 40), the 1792 Birch cent (No. 25), the 1792 disme (No. 20), and the 1792 quarter dollar (No. 72).

The first U.S. coins reflected the nation's youth and the inexperience of the new U.S. government. The concept of liberty and freedom appears on our country's first coins in the form of a young woman. On the half cent, a liberty cap (also called a Phrygian or freedman's cap) atop a staff reinforces the concept of liberty, while the chain on the back of the cent symbolizes the unity of the first states. Striking the first coinage was a very important step for the new nation, as this privilege is reserved to sovereign entities, not colonial subjects.

David Rittenhouse was appointed the first director of the U.S. Mint by President George Washington in 1792. The first coin produced at the Mint was the 1792 half disme (No. 12 in the 100 Greatest U.S. Coins).

The year 1793 saw the first regular-issue Mint coinage. The first year, only half cents and large cents were struck. The very first delivery to the treasury on March 1, 1793, consisted of 11,178 copper cents. For the year 1793, a total of 35,334 half cents and 110,512 cents was produced. The first silver (in the form of French coins worth $80,715) was deposited by the bank of Maryland on July 18, 1794. A Boston merchant deposited the first gold (in the form of ingots) on February 12, 1795. In 1794, the first silver coins were struck, including 86,416 half dimes (not dismes, as the term had changed by this time), 23,464 half dollars, and 1,758 dollars. The next year the first gold coins were struck, including 8,707 half eagles and 5,583 eagles. Today these early issues are among the most sought-after U.S. coins ever minted. The combination of history—the connection with our founding fathers—rarity, and beauty makes these coins all highly collectible. Several of the coins made the 100 Greatest U.S. Coins list, including the famous Chain cent (No. 13), the 1794 silver dollar (No. 9), and the 1795 "Nine Leaves" eagle (No. 78). Prices for these have soared since the first edition of this book was published in 2003. With renewed interest in U.S. history and the tremendous growth in national wealth, these early artifacts of our country's founding will probably continue to increase in price and popularity.

Although the production of U.S. coinage had begun, the volume of coins produced was still insufficient for the needs of our growing economy. Foreign coins continued to circulate until well into the 19th century. The U.S. Mint produced relatively ample supplies of coins in the early history of its operation, but coins were often melted or shipped overseas for their bullion value. The price of silver to gold was valued in a ratio of about 15 to 1. If the price of gold increased or the ratio fluctuated, many coins met their fate in the melting pots. A large majority of the early U.S. gold coins were destroyed after 1834, when the standard weight of gold coins was reduced. This would be a continuing theme in U.S. economic history, culminating in the recall of gold from U.S. citizens in 1933 and the melting of vast numbers of U.S. gold coins well into the 1930s. The gold at Fort Knox is the result of this final melt.

The 1793 Flowing Hair, Chain Reverse cent (or simply "Chain cent") is valued at $100,000. By comparison, the same coin was valued at $25,000 when the first edition of this book was published just a little more than a decade ago.

The coinage laws of 1834, which reduced the weight of standard gold, had the effect of putting the United States on the gold standard. Many new types were created, including what are now called the Classic Head quarter eagle and half eagle. Branch mints were established in 1838 in Dahlonega, Georgia; Charlotte, North

Artist Natalie Hause's *First United States Mint,* a recreation of Edwin Lamasure Jr.'s depiction of the nation's first mint buildings.

Carolina; and New Orleans, Louisiana. Many of the gold coins produced at these mints are very popular with collectors today. Several of the 100 Greatest U.S. Coins are found in this category, including the 1861-D gold dollar (No. 39), the only coin that was struck exclusively by the Confederate government. The production of eagles began again in 1838 after a pause in production since 1804. This series is also laden with rarities, including the famous 1875 eagle, with a mintage of only 100 coins.

As the only U.S. coin struck under Confederate control for which there is no federal counterpart, the 1861-D Indian Princess Head gold dollar is a historic oddity—not to mention a highly sought-after coin. (shown enlarged)

The next major development in U.S. coinage was the discovery of gold in California in 1848. Two new denominations were created: gold dollars and double eagles. The tiny gold dollar was struck from 1849 until 1889. Double eagles ($20 gold coins), were produced from 1849 until the final recall of gold in 1933. The double eagle series is full of major rarities, starting with the unique (and possibly most valuable) U.S. coin, the 1849 double eagle. The series ends with the 1933 double eagle (which until recently held the record for the highest auction price of a U.S. coin). Both of these items made the Top 10 on the list of 100 Greatest U.S. Coins (at No. 5 and No. 4, respectively). There are several other double eagles on the list as well. Large numbers of private gold coins were struck in California as well. Many rare and famous issues include Miners Bank $10 gold coins, Pacific Company $10 gold coins, Dubosq & Company $5 and $10 gold coins, Baldwin & Company $5 and $10 gold coins, and many other very interesting issues.

Liberty Seated coinage began in 1837, when half dimes and dimes were struck with the new design by Christian Gobrecht. Subsequently, Liberty Seated quarter dollars were struck starting in 1838, and Liberty Seated half dollars in 1839. The design lasted until 1891. This series is also full of major rarities. Some of the 100 Greatest U.S. Coins include the unique 1870-S half dime (No. 58), the unique 1873-CC "No Arrows" dime (No. 65), the 1866 "No Motto" patterns (Nos. 46, 48, and 83), the 1873-CC "No Arrows" quarter (No. 75), and the 1870-S silver dollar (No. 29). Other interesting developments in the mid-19th century included the three-cent postage rate, which resulted in the coinage of three-cent silver coins in 1851. Gold coins in the $3 denomination were produced starting in 1854. The 1875 $3 coin is a great coin (No. 59), with a mintage of just 20; it was one of the first numismatic items to sell for more than $100,000 at auction.

The year 1857 saw the end of half cents and large cents. The Coinage Act of 1857, reformed copper coinage. The new law reduced the size of the cent to its current size from that of a coin approximately the size of a half dollar. The first small cent produced was the 1856 Flying Eagle cent. About 1,000 of these were struck, and today this popular item makes the 100 Greatest U.S. Coins list as well (No. 57). The first small cents were actually

copper-nickel and quite thick. It was not until 1864 that the copper cent made its debut. The composition remained the same (except for minor alloy changes) until copper-plated zinc made its debut in 1982. The Lincoln cents, designed by Victor David Brenner, were first struck in 1909. One of the most popular and least expensive coins on the 100 Greatest U.S. Coins list is the 1909-S V.D.B. cent (No. 23). When these were first struck, the designer's initials were quite prominent on the reverse below the wreath. The initials were dropped in the second half of 1909. The 1909-S V.D.B. cent can be purchased in Mint State for around $2,000, though the price may increase with the anniversary of the Brenner design and the major redesign of the Lincoln cent authorized by Congress.

Although they are technically patterns, the $4 gold pieces of 1879 and 1880 ("Stellas," No. 18) are among the most sought-after U.S. gold coins. The coins were envisioned as the United States' answer to various foreign gold coins that were frequently seen on the international market. Stellas were intended to compete with British sovereigns, Italian 20-lire pieces, and Spanish 20-peseta coins. The idea never caught on, however, and very few of these interesting coins were ever minted. The coins were made in two versions: the Flowing Hair and Coiled Hair types. Even the common (by Stella standards) Flowing Hairs of 1879 now sell for at least $100,000. Coiled Hair Stellas have sold for more than $1 million.

In 1878, one of the most popular coins of all time was created. The resumption of silver dollars was authorized in the 1878 Bland-Allison Act, and George T. Morgan designed the new dollar. The coins were struck at the Philadelphia, San Francisco, New Orleans, Carson City, and Denver mints. Hundreds of millions were struck from 1878 to 1921 (despite coinage of silver dollars being suspended from 1904 until 1921). The two most famous Morgan dollars are the 1893-S and 1895. Both are on the 100 Greatest U.S. Coins list (No. 38 and No. 30, respectively).

Under the provisions of the Pittman Act of 1918, the Mint melted 270,232,722 silver dollars. This still left millions of silver dollars in the vaults of the federal government. In the early 1960s, one of the rarest Morgan dollars was considered to be the 1903-O, which sold for more than $1,500 at the time. In November of 1962, bags of the 1903-O dollars showed up from the vaults of the Philadelphia Mint. For the next couple of years, hundreds of millions of silver dollars were released by the federal government. By 1965, the price for a 1903-O Morgan dollar had fallen to $5. During the 1970s, millions more Carson City silver dollars were sold by the federal government. These are sometimes referred to as "Nixon dollars," as President Richard Nixon's name is found on the original packaging the government used to ship the coins. Morgan silver dollars are now one of the most widely collected series. Their large size and relative availability make them ideal

The Flying Eagle cent was the first small cent produced in the United States. The design was only used for three years, as the Indian Head cent debuted in 1859. (shown enlarged)

coins for those new to the hobby. The series is full of rarities, however, and putting together a complete set in Mint State would require a large investment.

In 1892, the dime, quarter, and half dollar were redesigned by Charles E. Barber. The Barber series continued until 1916. Of the series, the greatest rarity is the 1894-S dime (No. 7). Only 24 were struck, and today it is considered a landmark rarity. Other important coins include the 1896-S and 1901-S Barber quarters. Other than the 1894-S dime, the Barber series is very collectible, and within the reach of most advanced numismatists.

President Theodore Roosevelt was very dissatisfied with the artistic qualities of our nation's money. In 1906, he began a campaign to enlist his personal friend Augustus Saint-Gaudens, the United States' greatest sculptor at the time, to completely overhaul the designs for coinage. Saint-Gaudens is best known today as the artist who created the Sherman Victory monument in Central Park. He was a superb sculptor, and a visit to his home and museum in Cornish, New Hampshire, is a must for anyone serious about his coinage or art. Saint-Gaudens's struggle to produce a coin that would be true art, but also practical to make, is the stuff of legend. This struggle, though, produced some of the finest numismatic items ever crafted by any government. The MCMVII (1907) Indian Head double eagle pattern is our favorite coin. More about this coin (ranked No. 6) can be found in the text of this book. The MCMVII (1907) Ultra High Relief double eagle (No. 3) is another magical item. The coin is completely sculptural, and ranks as one of the most beautiful coins produced since ancient times. Greek coinage and sculpture were very influential in Saint-Gaudens's works. He also designed the very popular Indian Head eagle coinage of 1907 to 1933. The highlights of this series include the 1907 Rolled Edge and the 1933 eagles (both of which are on the 100 Greatest U.S. Coins list, at No. 37 and No. 41, respectively). For those interested in the coinage of Augustus Saint-Gaudens, we highly recommend Michael F. Moran's book *Striking Change: The Great Artistic Collaboration of Theodore Roosevelt and Augustus Saint-Gaudens*. It provides an in-depth look at the struggles Saint-Gaudens experienced while creating these magnificent coins.

Just 24 examples of the 1894-S Barber dime were struck. It, along with the 1804 silver dollar and 1913 Liberty Head nickel, comprise a "holy trinity" of rarity and desirability in numismatics. (shown enlarged).

President Theodore Roosevelt's determined efforts to realize more beautiful U.S. coinage led to a collaboration with artist and sculptor Augustus Saint-Gaudens and some of the most beautiful numismatic rarities, including the 1933 eagle and double eagle.

In 1916, the dime, quarter, and half dollar likewise saw major redesigns, this time with a different design for each denomination. Adolph Weinman created the popular Mercury (or Winged Liberty Head) dime and Liberty Walking half dollar in 1916. The 1916-D dime (No. 68) is considered the key to the dime series, and the 1921-S half dollar is the most expensive of the series in Mint State. Hermon A. MacNeil designed the lovely Standing Liberty quarter; the 1916 is the rarest of the issue (and also in the 100 Greatest U.S. Coins list, at No. 43).

The year 1909 saw the first shift away from the use of Liberty on our coinage in favor of deceased presidents. The trend began with the debut of the Lincoln cent in 1909. In 1932, George Washington's bust replaced the Standing Liberty design on the quarter. The year 1938 saw Thomas Jefferson take the place of the American Indian on the Buffalo nickel. Franklin Roosevelt soon replaced the Mercury design on our dimes. Eventually, the figure of Liberty was replaced on all U.S. coinage with a man or woman of historic or political significance. The United States celebrated its 200th anniversary of independence by issuing the 1975 and 1976 quarter dollar, half dollar, and silver dollar with Bicentennial designs. The success of these circulating commemoratives set the stage for the 50 State Quarters® Program, which began in 1999. The U.S. Mint now regularly releases new commemorative coins and special issues. The collection of so-called modern coins has risen sharply in recent years. The most positive aspect of the modern coin market is that many new collectors are introduced to the amazing world of numismatics.

For those with an interest in the fascinating subject of coinage and U.S. commerce, the first book to purchase would most certainly be *A Guide Book of United States Coins* (the "Red Book") by R.S. Yeoman, edited by Kenneth Bressett. The Red Book is a standard reference in the field of U.S. coinage, and highly recommended. There are also more advanced books on the subject, many of which specialize on a particular issue or topic; see the bibliography for specific titles.

COLLECTING UNITED STATES COINS

For author Jeff Garrett, the long journey of numismatic discovery began one day in the late 1960s when he received a Whitman coin album for Lincoln cents minted from 1941 through 1971. What started as mild interest soon became an obsession. Each week after receiving his weekly pay for mowing lawns or raking leaves, he would immediately rush to a bank for penny rolls to search for coins needed to fill his Lincoln cent album. After the first summer, the album was nearly filled. He soon discovered that San Francisco cents were hard to find in Florida, where he lived at the time. He also began to start buying books to read about coins. Not long after that, he made his first actual purchase of a coin—the very hard-to-find 1941-S cent—which he ordered by mail from the Littleton Coin Company. He still has this treasure, and for him it ranks as one of the greatest U.S. coins. He soon became very involved in local coin clubs and a regular at the local coin shop. This led to weekend jobs working at small coin shows, and soon after high school his numismatic career began full time. The passion of collecting still excites him today as much as when finding that last Lincoln cent was his main goal in life. Hopefully the stories you read in this book will excite and inspire you to more fully enjoy the hobby of numismatics.

How to Get Started

One of the most exciting aspects of numismatics is the tremendous variety of collecting themes available to today's numismatists. The following list illustrates some of the more popular approaches to coin collecting.

Collecting by type—A type collection consists of one example of each major change in the design or metal used. For example, a type collection of nickels would include the Shield nickel (1866–1883), the Liberty Head nickel (1883–1913), the Buffalo nickel (1913–1938), and the Jefferson nickels (1938– present). Collectors may choose to specialize further with variations of certain types as well. This would include two types of Shield nickels, the With Rays (1866–1867) and the No Rays (1867–1883). Some collectors have been known to further concentrate on type coins from the first year of issue. The most famous set of these was assembled by retired congressman Jimmy Hayes of Louisiana. His collection set the standard for this style of collecting. Type coins are also an ideal sort of diversification, due to the wide variety of designs and long time span represented by the collection. *United States Coinage: A Study by Type*, also by the authors, is an excellent road map to this style of collecting.

Collecting by series—With a focus on one design type, the goal is to assemble one example of each date and mintmark for the series. As an example, a Morgan dollar collection would

include one coin from each year (1878–1921) and from each of the five mints that struck the coins (Philadelphia, San Francisco, Carson City, New Orleans, and Denver). This sort of collecting style can be modified to fit one's budget. A circulated set of Morgan dollars is well within reach of most serious numismatists, for example, whereas a Mint State collection requires a serious investment, and a gem set would cost millions. In recent years, it has become very fashionable to assemble sets that would rank high on the registry lists assembled by PCGS and NGC. The competition for such coins can sometimes defy logic. If you are around coins long enough, you will probably witness the fever of a passionate collector. The "coin bug" is hard to shake!

Collecting commemoratives—Commemoratives were struck to mark special anniversaries or occasions. The "classic" series of commemorative coins was struck from 1892 to 1954. Many modern issues have been produced in recent years as well. The U.S. Mint continues to strike coins yearly to honor persons or events from the past. A collection of every coin struck since 1982 (when modern commemoratives were first issued) would require thousands of dollars—and lots of storage space.

Commemorative coins have been issued from 1892 to 1954 and 1982 to the present. Strictly speaking, the highest-ranking commemorative coin on the 100 Greatest U.S. Coins list is the 1915-S Panama-Pacific Exposition $50 gold piece (No. 21, octagonal version pictured).

A collector looking to complete his or her nickel type set would be looking for at least one example of each design (from left to right): the Shield nickel, the Liberty Head nickel, the Buffalo (or Indian Head) nickel, and the Jefferson nickel. (shown enlarged)

Collecting colonial coinage—These were usually copper pieces struck during the 17th and 18th centuries, which served as circulating coins in the years prior to the United States' independence. Before the first U.S. Mint began operation in 1793, coins were issued by individual states, private coiners, and foreign mints. Two designs are attributed to Benjamin Franklin.

Collecting coins on the 100 Greatest U.S. Coins list—Now, this can get expensive! We are continually amazed at the number of individuals who tell us they are trying to purchase every coin in 100 Greatest U.S. Coins that they can afford. For some, this may mean only two or three coins. We have actually known cases of collectors having assembled 40 to 50 coins on the list, with an investment into the millions of dollars. This collecting strategy has proven to be a sound move in recent years, as most of the coins on the list have soared in value since the first edition of the book was published.

Our general advice: whatever collecting strategy you choose, it usually pays to purchase the best you can afford. As even the newest collector soon finds out, quality is the key to the value of most coins. There will always be a demand for the best of the best.

How to Buy Rare Coins

There are several great sources for purchasing rare coins. Each source has its advantages, but much depends on the experience of the collector and the type of material desired.

Local coin dealers—A local coin shop can be an excellent place to get started in the field of numismatics. There is usually a large assortment of books and supplies available. Coins can be examined in person and questions about the hobby answered. Try to find an experienced dealer who has the knowledge to be an adviser and mentor in your collecting pursuits. Author Jeff Garrett owes much of his success as a professional coin dealer to the operator of a small coin shop in Dunedin, Florida. Thirty years ago, this dealer, Ed French, took the time to foster a young man's interest in rare coins. Hopefully, you can also find someone who will spend the time to help you learn more about the wonderful world of numismatics.

The Internet—Over the last ten years, the amount of rare-coin business conducted on the Internet has exploded. Nearly every major rare-coin dealer and many small ones now have full-service Web sites. Auctions are conducted almost daily on many of the dealer sites, and the ability to utilize search engines has made locating many hard-to-find items much easier. It is safe to say that the Internet has had a greater impact on the demand for rare coins than any other innovation. Qualified buyers can participate in auctions and peruse online catalogs to locate coins. There is also a tremendous amount of information about rare coins that can be found on the web. Web sites like eBay have also become popular venues for purchasing coins. Caution must be utilized, however, as there is the possibility of considerable fraud at such sites. It is

usually advisable to buy rare coins only from known dealers who back their material with guarantees of authenticity.

Coin shows—It may be fun to surf the web looking for that perfect coin for your collection, but nothing beats going to a large coin show. There are literally millions of dollars' worth of rare coins at any given venue. Coin shows are held locally, regionally, and nationally almost every week in some part of the country. We travel to between 25 and 30 shows each year to buy and sell rare coins. Many of our closest friends are fellow dealers whom we see nearly every week. Almost every sort of coin can be found at large coin shows. There are dealers who carry only Indian Head cents; there are dealers with nothing but Morgan dollars. Ancient and world coins are also well represented at most coin shows. The largest show each year is the annual summer convention of the American Numismatic Association, a federally chartered organization that has been serving collectors for more than 100 years. The show is held in large metropolitan areas around the country. Check the ANA's Web site (www.money.org) for future show dates and locations.

Rare coin auctions—When very large collections are sold, the owners or their heirs typically call on the larger numismatic auction firms. Auction firms accept consignments and sell them at public auctions or mail-bid sales. Many of the rarest and most expensive coins are sold in this manner. These sales provide an excellent opportunity to purchase hard-to-find numismatic items. Most large firms also publish beautiful auction catalogs, which in time become collectibles themselves. These catalogs provide excellent reference material regarding the value and history of many rare coins.

Coin clubs—There is no better way to fully enjoy the hobby of numismatics than to join a coin club. If you are lucky enough to have a coin club in your area, you should definitely join. Most clubs meet monthly and feature a guest speaker and a live auction. Many of the clubs have a good mix of beginning

Coin shows are fantastic opportunities for collectors to meet fellow numismatists, as well as buy, sell, and trade coins.

and advanced collectors. Nearly all serious numismatists enjoy sharing their passion with fellow enthusiasts. We both benefited greatly from attending local coin club meetings when we were younger. The mentoring made a tremendous difference in our lives. If you have young children, most clubs make an effort to serve their needs as well. Coin collecting is a fantastic hobby for young people, and we guarantee that someday their coins will be worth more than their video games! Another option is to join the American Numismatic Association or the American Numismatic Society. There are also specialty clubs for collectors of every kind.

Grading Rare Coins

Grading is the attempt to describe the state of preservation of a rare coin. Most collectors prefer the finest coins they can afford, so determining grades for rare coins is crucial. Today, rare coins are graded on a scale from 1 (worn nearly smooth) to 70 (flawless). Price differences between grades can sometimes be huge. In an attempt to ensure an expert and unbiased opinion of a coin's grade, several independent grading services began operations in the mid-1980s. The two largest services are the Numismatic Guaranty Corporation of America (NGC) and Professional Coin Grading Service (PCGS). Most of the very valuable coins sold at auction or by private treaty have been graded by PCGS or NGC.

Coin grading is often described as an art. Even the difference between a grade of MS-65 and MS-66 can be very subtle. Yet the price difference can be tens of thousands of dollars. It is highly recommended that collectors study the series they collect to gain at least a basic understanding of the variations in grade. Although a coin might be certified, it is still best to know that the coin you have purchased is not in the low end of the grade. The advice of an expert is the best route for most individuals. There are also many books on the subject of coin grading, and the ANA conducts seminars around the country on coin grading. These can be very informative for both beginners and advanced collectors.

Coin-grading services like NGC and PCGS encapsulate or "slab" the coins they evaluate, as shown here.

How Value Is Determined

Most beginners are shocked to find out that age has little to do with the value of a rare coin. Coins from ancient Rome can be purchased for less than $10 in poor condition. On the other hand, a Lincoln cent minted in the last ten years could be worth thousands in perfect condition. Factors that contribute to the value of a coin include beauty of design, historical importance, rarity, bullion value, condition, and demand.

Rarity—Rarity can be defined as the number of coins surviving from the original number minted. Many coins that are now exceedingly rare had very large mintages. Only 13 examples of the 1933 double eagle are known, for example, yet 445,500 were struck. Many of the coins in this book share similar backgrounds in terms of mintage and survivorship. Rarity can also mean the rarity of a coin in a certain grade. There are many coins that have minimal value in circulated conditions, but are extremely valuable in Gem Mint State. An 1894-O Morgan dollar is worth around $50 in Fine condition and $50,000 in Gem Mint State condition. Of course, Gem Mint State 1894-O Morgan dollars are very rare and seldom seen.

Popularity—Morgan dollars and Lincoln cents are examples of two very popular series. Thousands collect these, and examples of each are worth more than coins in series collected by very few. Author Jeff Garrett's personal favorite is U.S. gold coinage. The demand for gold coinage has always been intense. Besides the intrinsic value of the metal, gold coins seem to have an allure that copper and silver lack. Double eagles are especially popular because of their size. There are several very rare coins that would bring astronomical prices if they were of the size and popularity of a double eagle. Jeff Garrett remembers an interesting story of the unique 1870-S half dime (No. 58) from several years ago. A dealer had requested the coin be shipped to a West Coast coin show (at great expense) for customer approval. When the coin was handed to the dealer, it was simply handed back with the statement, "it's too small."

The 1870-S Liberty Seated half dime is an incredibly rare and valuable coin, but it is sometimes overlooked due to its small size. (shown enlarged)

Condition—The condition, or grade, of a coin is perhaps the most critical element when value is determined. When you combine rarity and popularity with great condition, the value of a rare coin goes through the roof. As previously mentioned, certification is usually the best option when buying an expensive coin. The values of very rare coins, even low-grade ones, can be greatly affected by condition. A well-worn but smooth-planchet copper coin is much more valuable than one that exhibits pitted surfaces. Scratches, rim dents, and discoloration can all lower the value of a rare coin considerably.

CHOOSING THE 100 GREATEST U.S. COINS

Picking the 100 Greatest U.S. Coins was no easy task. The problem is that there are too many great U.S. coins! By restricting ourselves to 100 coins, we were forced to exclude some promising candidates or combine some in order to make room for others. For instance, instead of describing all four date and design combinations of the $4 gold Stellas separately, we chose to group them together. With this fourth edition of the book, one coin has been dropped from the list to make room for another. The unique 1851 Liberty Seated silver dollar struck over a New Orleans silver dollar fell from favor, probably due to its unusual origin. Making the list for the first time is the 1974 aluminum Lincoln cent. This coin has been in the news lately, and is surrounded by legal issues similar to those of the 1933 double eagle.

We also excluded any non-official U.S. coins. This left out most colonial coins, all of the Confederate coins, and virtually all of the territorial gold coins. Many major varieties made it onto the list, but obscure varieties did not. But, even with these necessary exclusions, we believe the list we developed will satisfy the majority of collectors.

So, how did we choose the greatest U.S. coins?

In this case, the method was simple—we let someone else decide! We asked the members of the Professional Numismatists Guild (PNG), all leaders in the numismatic community, to vote on a list of the 100 Greatest U.S. Coins that we developed. We also asked them to add any coins that they felt should have been included on the list. Most respondents ranked at least ten coins, but some ranked all 100! To choose the Top 10 coins, votes were weighted (a No. 1 vote was worth 10 points, a No. 2 vote was worth 9 points, and so on). The votes and their weighted scores were then tabulated. This year saw the 1804 Draped Bust silver dollar rise to the No. 1 spot. To be sure, the voting was very close, and the next edition may see another major rarity leap to the top of the list.

The 100 Greatest U.S. Coins are presented in the following pages in rank order from the first coin to the 100th. Whether you agree with the rankings or not, we hope you'll enjoy learning about these special coins. They are truly the United States' greatest coins.

1804 DRAPED BUST SILVER DOLLAR

The text above the clouds varied in position from the first reverse (left, that of the Class I variety) and the second (right, that of the Class II and III varieties).

For many years, the 1804 silver dollar was the most valuable U.S. coin. It was knocked from that perch in 2002, when a 1933 double eagle sold for $7,590,020. A 1794 silver dollar later sold for more than $10 million. Now, the finest example of the 1804 silver dollar—the PCGS PF-68 Watters-Childs example—may regain the top auction record for a U.S. coin when it is auctioned in the next year or two.

Of course, regardless of its value, the 1804 silver dollar is once again No. 1 on the list of 100 Greatest U.S. Coins. This coin has received more press and publicity, and has had more written about it, than any other coin in the world. In fact, the 1804 silver dollar is the only coin to have been the subject of not one, but two, books: Eric Newman and Kenneth Bressett's *The Fantastic 1804 Silver Dollar* and Q. David Bowers's *The Rare Silver Dollars Dated 1804 and the Exciting Adventures of Edmund Roberts*. The 1804 dollars have been on television, they've been the highlight displays at major coin conventions, and they are always the featured coins of any auction in which they appear. More importantly, they appear at the top of just about every collector's and dealer's "wish list."

The story of the 1804 silver dollar begins in 1834, during the administration of Andrew Jackson, when the State Department ordered special sets of coins for presentation to the king of Siam and the sultan of Muscat (modern-day Oman) as diplomatic gifts. The Mint interpreted this to mean one coin of each legal denomination. However, the silver dollar and gold eagle had not been made since 1804 (and the dollars reported in 1804 were actually dated 1803), so the Mint created new dies for each and struck a small number of coins for inclusion in the sets. Today, these are known as the "original" (or Class I) 1804 silver dollars. Only eight original 1804 silver dollars are currently traced.

Around 1858, a small number of 1804 silver dollars were struck using a different reverse die and lightweight planchets. One was struck over an 1857 Swiss shooting thaler (helping later researchers to unravel the mystery of the 1804 silver dollars). This batch is known as the "first restrike" (or Class II) 1804 silver dollars. Because their edges were plain, they created an instant scandal when collectors first saw them, forcing their immediate recall and destruction. Only the overstrike on the 1857 Swiss coin has survived to represent the Class II variety; it now resides in the National Numismatic Collection at the Smithsonian Institution.

Having learned from their mistakes, the "minters" began using planchets of roughly the proper weight and adding the appropriate lettering to the edges of the coins. These coins met with more success and today six of these 1804 "second restrike" (or Class III) silver dollars are known.

All 1804 silver dollars share a common obverse die. The reverse die of the Class I 1804 silver dollars is different from that used on the Class II and Class III 1804 silver dollars. Only the Smithsonian

Institution possesses examples of all three classes! For years it has been written (and often repeated) that three 1804 dollars in the National Numismatic Collection were cleaned and of inferior quality. That is simply not the case. All three coins would grade at least Choice Proof (PF-63), with the finest example being at the Gem Proof level (PF-65). The surfaces are decidedly not cleaned, and it is not certain how this rumor began. All three coins are featured in the Smithsonian's rare coin exhibit at the Museum of American History. We encourage all to view these amazing coins in person.

In recent years, just a few 1804 dollars have crossed the auction block, the most recent being the Hawn/Queller PCGS PF-62 example, which sold for $3,877,500 in 2013. As mentioned above, the Watters-Childs PCGS PF-68 example is scheduled for sale in the next couple of years. It is perhaps the ultimate trophy coin, combining rarity and quality. 1804 silver dollars are usually held by collectors for the long term, and the ones that are in private hands and institutional collections will likely remain so.

STANDARDS · Weight: Varies from 25.40 to 26.96 grams. **Composition:** 89% silver, 11% copper. **Diameter:** Varies from 39 to 40 mm. **Edge:** Plain or lettered HUNDRED CENTS ONE DOLLAR OR UNIT. **RARITY ·** Extremely rare. Only 15 1804 silver dollars are known, including originals (eight of Class I) and restrikes (one of Class II and six of Class III). The finest example known is the amazing PF-68 Watters-Childs example that set a (then) record price of $4.14 million when it sold at auction in 1999. That example is scheduled to be sold again in the next year or two and could set a new price record for a U.S. coin. **CERTIFIED POPULATION ·** 16

Designed by Robert Scot. The obverse of each coin features a draped bust of Liberty with some of her hair tied back in a bow. LIBERTY appears above, the date below, and the stars are divided up on the sides (seven on the left, six on the right). The reverse of each coin features a heraldic eagle with outstretched wings (similar to that seen on the Great Seal of the United States). In its beak, the eagle holds a scroll with the words E PLURIBUS UNUM. In its left talon, the eagle grasps an olive branch; in its right talon, it holds a bunch of arrows. Clouds and 13 stars appear above the eagle. The outer legend reads: UNITED STATES OF AMERICA. No denomination appears anywhere on the coin.

HISTORICAL VALUES					
Choice Proof					
1960: $30,000	1980: $250,000	1st ed./2003: $3,000,000	2nd ed./2005: $3,750,000	3rd ed./2008: $5,500,000	4th edition: $6,000,000

Shown enlarged from actual size of 39 to 40 mm.

1913 LIBERTY HEAD NICKEL

Twenty years ago, if you asked any collector or dealer to name the three greatest U.S. coins, the response would most likely have been the following: the 1804 silver dollar, the 1894-S dime, and the 1913 Liberty Head nickel. Today the 1913 Liberty Head nickel ranks second on the list of 100 Greatest U.S. Coins. The coin has fallen from the top spot (which it held in the third edition of this book) partly due to the large number of other great coins entering the marketplace. While the dynamics and rankings of the greatest U.S. coins will probably continue to change, the 1913 Liberty Head nickel will no doubt remain near the top.

The 1913 Liberty Head nickel is a coin that simply should not exist. The Liberty Head nickel series ended in December 1912, replaced in 1913 by the newly designed Buffalo nickel. In fact, no 1913 Liberty Head nickels were known or even contemplated until 1919, when Samuel Brown teased the collecting community by advertising to pay $500 for any example. Apparently, this was just a ruse to legitimize coins that he already owned, for in August of 1920, Brown exhibited at least one of them at the annual convention of the American Numismatic Association. Brown eventually owned five 1913 Liberty Head nickels, reportedly the entire mintage.

How did Brown obtain the coins? It may have helped that he was the clerk of the Mint from 1912 to 1913, at which time he and some cohorts may have made the coins using Mint equipment.

The set of five 1913 Liberty Head nickels changed hands several times until the early 1940s, when the set was broken up and the coins were sold to individual buyers. Since then, the coins have taken widely divergent paths.

One went to King Farouk of Egypt, whose collection was sold after he was deposed in 1954. His 1913 Liberty Head nickel was withdrawn from the sale and sold privately, ending up in the collection of the Norweb family, who ultimately donated the coin to the Smithsonian Institution. A second example was sold to Louis Eliasberg (who formed the only complete collection of U.S. coins ever assembled). This coin is perhaps the finest of the five examples and sold in 2007 for $5 million in a private transaction.

The third example, a choice Proof, has been viewed and owned by more people than any other. In 1972, this 1913 Liberty Head nickel became the first U.S. coin to break the $100,000 barrier. It later appeared in an episode of the TV program *Hawaii Five-O* as the object of a crook's desire.

The fourth example is a highlight of the American Numismatic Association's collection, having been donated some years ago by Aubrey and Adeline Bebee. The condition of this piece is lower than that of the other 1913 Liberty Head nickels because of the curious habits of a previous owner, James McDermott, who carried it as a pocket piece for bragging rights and betting purposes.

Until recent years, the whereabouts of the fifth example were a mystery. Rumors circulated that the coin had been lost on March 9, 1962, in the fatal automobile accident of the last recorded owner, George O. Walton (read more about Walton in the "Great Collectors of the Past" appendix). In 2003, the numismatic firm of Bowers and Merena Galleries announced a $10,000 reward for the missing fifth 1913 Liberty Head nickel. Thousands of emails and letters poured into the firm from people who were positive they owned the missing coin. In an unusual twist of fate, the coin was ultimately discovered in the possession of the heirs of the Walton estate, who had kept the nickel for decades (still in Walton's custom-made display holder) under the false impression that it might not be genuine! The heirs brought the coin to the August 2003 convention of the American Numismatic Association in Baltimore, Maryland, where the nickel was examined by a panel of experts including author Jeff Garrett. The coin was declared genuine and, with much fanfare, reunited with the other four. The five 1913 Liberty Head nickels, together once again for the first time since the early 1940s, were placed on display and viewed and enjoyed by thousands of collectors. Thus, the mystery of the location of the fifth example was solved.

> **WANTED**
> **1913 LIBERTY HEAD NICKEL**
> In Proof condition, if possible. Will pay $500 cash for one.
> **SAMUEL W. BROWN,**
> North Tonawanda, N. Y.

This advertisement appeared in the December 1919 issue of the *Numismatist*. In his next advertisement, Brown increased his offer to $600—then a hefty sum.

STANDARDS • **Weight:** 5 grams. **Composition:** 75% copper, 25% nickel. **Diameter:** 21.2 mm. **Edge:** Plain. **RARITY** • Five known, all accounted for. The finest example is the PF-66 Eliasberg example discussed in the text. The Walton example, a PCGS PF-63, sold for $3,172,500 in 2013. **CERTIFIED POPULATION** • 5

Designed by Charles Barber. The obverse of the coin features a head of Liberty with her hair pulled up in a bun, wearing a coronet with the word LIBERTY inscribed and a wreath. The date appears below the head, and 13 stars surround. On the reverse of the coin, a large V (the Roman numeral for "5") figures prominently in the center, surrounded by a wreath. A small E PLURIBUS UNUM ("out of many, one") appears in an arc above the V, and a larger UNITED STATES OF AMERICA appears near the outer edge. The word CENTS appears beneath the wreath.

HISTORICAL VALUES
Choice Proof

1960: $50,000	1980: $250,000	1st ed./2003: $2,000,000	2nd ed./2005: $3,250,000	3rd ed./2008: $4,000,000	4th edition: $6,000,000

Shown enlarged from actual size of 21.2 mm.

MCMVII (1907) ULTRA HIGH RELIEF SAINT-GAUDENS DOUBLE EAGLE

President Theodore Roosevelt was a great admirer of the famous sculptor Augustus Saint-Gaudens. The two corresponded occasionally after meeting in 1901 at the Pan-American Exposition. First stating his views in 1904, Roosevelt believed that the coinage in circulation at the time was very unattractive and without artistic merit. He wanted coins created that would reflect the beauty and relief of ancient Greek coinage. He became excited about the possibility of changing the designs on all U.S. coins. Naturally, he turned to Augustus Saint-Gaudens, who was commissioned to redesign all denominations from the cent to the double eagle.

It was Saint-Gaudens's personal preference that an Indian Head obverse design be used for the double eagle. One of the greatest patterns of this series bears that design. The president was quite insistent, however, that the standing figure of Liberty with the flying eagle reverse be used. Saint-Gaudens used the goddess he had created for the 1903 Sherman Victory monument as the motif—Liberty faces forward, holding an olive branch in one hand. In emulation of Greek coins, the design was rendered in very high relief, giving an almost sculpted appearance. As a classical touch, the 1907 date was expressed in Roman numerals, as MCMVII. The Indian Head design was not discarded, but instead was used for the eagle.

The MCMVII (1907) Ultra High Relief double eagle is an experimental issue. After Augustus Saint-Gaudens became ill, his assistant, Henry Hering, executed the plaster model for his design of the new standing Liberty (now referred to as the "Saint-Gaudens" type) double eagle. After seeing the proposed design, Charles Barber, the chief engraver of the Mint at the time, strongly argued that it would be impractical to strike such a coin because each one required multiple blows from the coin press. Hering knew the relief was too high, but wanted examples struck to test the design. In February of 1907, Hering visited the Mint to check on the striking of the new coin. Hering stated: "A circular disc of gold was placed in the die and by hydraulic pressure of 172 tons, I think it was; we had our first stamping, and the impression showed a little more than half of the modeling. I had them make a cast of this for my guidance. The coin was again placed in the die for another striking and again it showed a little more of the modeling, and so it went, on and on, until the ninth strike, when the coin showed up in every detail." The resulting treasure from this experiment in striking is one of the most coveted coins in numismatics.

The son of a French cobbler, Augustus Saint-Gaudens would become the United States' foremost sculptor-artist of the late 19th and early 20th centuries.

The MCMVII (1907) Ultra High Relief (or Extremely High Relief) double eagle is a magnificent example of the minting craft. It takes the United States' most beautiful coin to a new level. Many coins are desirable for their great rarity, but the MCMVII (1907) Ultra High Relief commands a small fortune because it is literally a work of art. Perhaps no other U.S. coin, or world coin for that matter, has the visual appeal of the Ultra High Relief. It is truly sad that this gorgeous coin is so expensive and can only be possessed by a very few lucky collectors.

STANDARDS · **Weight:** 33.436 grams. **Composition:** 90% gold, 10% copper. **Net weight:** .96750 oz. pure gold. **Diameter:** 34 mm. **Edge:** Lettered E PLURIBUS UNUM with words divided by stars. One example is known with a plain edge. **RARITY** · There are 16 to 18 examples known to exist. One of the finest known pieces, a PCGS-graded PF-69, sold at auction for $2,990,000 in late 2005. **CERTIFIED POPULATION** · 13

Designed by Augustus Saint-Gaudens. The obverse depicts a standing Liberty draped in Romanesque clothing, holding a torch and an olive branch. The reverse features an eagle in flight. Mintage for this issue is estimated at 22.

HISTORICAL VALUES					
Gem Proof					
1960: $20,000	1980: $250,000	1st ed./2003: $1,000,000	2nd ed./2005: $1,650,000	3rd ed./2008: $2,500,000	4th edition: $3,000,000

Shown enlarged from actual size of 34 mm.

1933 SAINT-GAUDENS DOUBLE EAGLE

The 1933 double eagle is one of the only coins to be a central figure in a U.S. government sting operation. In April 1933, the recently inaugurated president Franklin D. Roosevelt issued Executive Order 6102, instructing all U.S. citizens to surrender their gold. Banks were prohibited from paying out gold coins or Gold Certificates. From March 15 until May 19 of 1933, the U.S. government struck a total of 445,000 double eagles. With the exception of two coins sent to the Smithsonian in 1934, it was thought that the remaining mintage of 1933 double eagles was melted in 1937. It is now known that nearly two dozen coins that had been set aside for assay purposes somehow escaped the Mint. To this day, the U.S. government claims that these coins were stolen and illegal to own. It is believed that the first 1933 double eagle was sold privately in 1937 to James G. Macallister for $500. Over the next few years, nearly a dozen examples entered the marketplace. B. Max Mehl sold a 1933 double eagle to King Farouk of Egypt in February of 1944. In March of that same year, the collection of Colonel James W. Flanagan, which included another example, was offered at public auction by Stack's. After having been alerted to the impending sale, Treasury agents confiscated the Flanagan specimen. No compensation was made, and it is believed that the coin was melted. Several others were also confiscated, and they are presumed melted. One collector, L.G. Barnard, fought the confiscation in court and lost. Private ownership of 1933 double eagles was officially deemed illegal.

In 1954, the ruling military junta in Egypt sold the King Farouk collection after the monarch had been overthrown. Farouk's 1933 double eagle was included. At the request of the U.S. government, the Egyptian government withdrew the coin from the sale. The double eagle then dropped from sight for nearly 50 years. In 1996, a coin billed as the Farouk specimen was secretly sold by a London dealer in a New York City hotel room for around $1 million. The buyers, however, turned out to be U.S. government agents, and the coin was confiscated and the sellers were arrested. A legal battle ensued. Criminal charges were dropped, and the ownership of the coin was fought for several years in court. The sellers were able to demonstrate that the U.S. government had issued export papers for the Farouk example. On January 25, 2001, just days before jury selection was to begin, both parties settled the case by agreeing to sell the coin and split the proceeds. The most interesting stipulation was that the alleged Farouk example would be the only 1933 double eagle considered legal to own. The U.S. government would officially monetize and issue this single 1933 double eagle. The coin realized an astonishing $7.5 million, a new record for any numismatic item. The buyer has yet to be identified.

Many may ask: "Why would someone pay more than $7 million for a coin?" The most obvious answer is because they can! It must be remembered that in the same room in which the 1933 double eagle sold, paintings have been sold for close to $100 million. Also, the coin's previous "forbidden fruit" status gives it incredible desirability.

The final chapter of this fascinating coin has not yet been written, however. In 2005, representatives of the estate of Israel Switt (an individual identified by several researchers as being involved in the coins' leaving the Mint in the 1930s) notified the U.S. government that they possessed 10 examples of the legendary rarity. The coins were sent to the U.S. Mint for authentication and were promptly confiscated. A long and protracted legal battle took place. The U.S. government was the victor, and for now, the 10 examples are somewhere in vaults of the U.S. Mint, perhaps Fort Knox. The Farouk coin remains the only example of this famed coin that is legal to own. The value of 1933 double eagles will remain uncertain until the U.S. government decides the fate of the coins confiscated from the Switt family.

King Farouk I, pictured here with his first wife, Queen Farida, and their first daughter, Princess Farial, spent lavishly on his coin collection, which included a 1933 double eagle.

STANDARDS · **Weight:** 33.436 grams. **Composition** 90% gold, 10% copper. **Net weight:** .96750 oz. of pure gold. **Diameter:** 34 mm. **Edge:** Lettered includes E PLURIBUS UNUM with the words divided by stars. **RARITY** · Officially 13 examples are known to exist: two in the Smithsonian's National Numismatic Collection, the Farouk specimen referenced in the text, and 10 from the estate of Israel Switt. More are rumored. **CERTIFIED POPULATION** · 0

Designed by Augustus Saint-Gaudens. The obverse depicts a standing Liberty draped in Romanesque clothing and holding a torch. The reverse features an eagle in flight. Mintage for this issue was 445,500, but nearly all examples were melted.

HISTORICAL VALUES
Choice Uncirculated

1960: $25,000	1980: $250,000	1st ed./2003: $7,500,000	2nd ed./2005: $8,500,000	3rd ed./2008: $5,000,000	4th edition: $7,500,000

Shown enlarged from actual size of 34 mm.

1849 LIBERTY HEAD DOUBLE EAGLE

Although technically a pattern or experimental coin, the 1849 double eagle is nevertheless one of the great rarities of U.S. coinage. Following the discovery of gold in California in 1848, a tremendous flow of the yellow metal made its way to the East Coast. On March 3, 1849, federal legislation to create gold dollars and double eagles was enacted. The production of double eagles would convert the bullion into coins with the least effort.

Chief Engraver James B. Longacre engraved the dies for the new coinage and supervised an attempt to strike the new denomination. In a letter dated December 24, 1849, from chief coiner Franklin Peale to Mint director Robert M. Patterson, Peale wrote: "It is with extreme regret and after the most earnest endeavors to overcome the difficulty that I am compelled to inform you that the impression upon the new die, for the double eagle, cannot be brought up by the usual coining processes." The relief of the portrait was too high, and the coins could not be struck properly for mass production. These delays in production resulted in just a handful of coins being struck late in 1849. It has not been uncommon in the history of U.S. coinage for the first year of issue to be problematic. Several interesting coins have been redesigned because the relief was too high. Although aesthetically attractive, actual production of high-relief coins was very difficult. The 1907 Saint-Gaudens High Relief double eagle is probably the most famous example. Others include the 1921 Peace dollar and the 1849 gold dollar.

All but two 1849 double eagles were melted. One was sent to secretary of the Treasury W.M. Meredith and another to the Mint Cabinet in Philadelphia. The Meredith coin may have gone to the collection of Steven Nagy in Philadelphia, but it is unknown to numismatists today. The Mint Cabinet example has been transferred to the Smithsonian Institution and is one of the most popular attractions of the National Numismatic Collection, on display in the rare coin exhibit at the Smithsonian's Museum of American History. There, the coin is the centerpiece of the Legendary Coins case, and is considered by many to be the "ruby slippers" of numismatics.

All this being said, the missing Meredith coin could appear one day. Most experts agree that the 1849 double eagle is at least as desirable as the 1933 double eagle, if not more so. The two make incredible bookends to an extremely popular series and denomination. It is reported that in 1909 J.P. Morgan offered $35,000 for the coin, a tremendous amount for the era. It can only be speculated what an example would bring if offered for sale. It is certain the eight-figure mark would be broken, and $25 million is not out of the question.

James B. Longacre's sketch of the design for the double eagle reverse. A Pennsylvania native and noted portraitist, Longacre succeeded to the position of chief Mint engraver upon the death of Christian Gobrecht in 1844.

STANDARDS · Weight: 33.436 grams. **Composition:** 90% gold, 10% copper. **Net weight:** .96750 oz. pure gold. **Diameter:** 34 mm. **Edge:** Reeded. **RARITY ·** Only one example is known to exist. That specimen now resides in the National Numismatic Collection at the Smithsonian Institution. **CERTIFIED POPULATION ·** 0

Designed by James B. Longacre. The obverse features a portrait of Liberty facing left, wearing a coronet, and surrounded by 13 stars. The reverse features an outspread eagle and shield design.

HISTORICAL VALUES
Choice Proof

1960: $100,000	1980: $1,000,000	1st ed./2003: $7,500,000	2nd ed./2005: $10,000,000	3rd ed./2008: $20,000,000	4th edition: $25,000,000

Shown enlarged from actual size of 34 mm.

MCMVII (1907) INDIAN HEAD DOUBLE EAGLE PATTERN

The 1907 Indian Head double eagle is a pattern or experimental issue. It is one of America's most stunning and desirable coins. President Theodore Roosevelt was personally involved in creating this fascinating issue. Roosevelt believed that the nation's coinage was unattractive and without artistic merit. Years earlier, while vice president, Roosevelt had become acquainted with the famous sculptor Augustus Saint-Gaudens, whose works include *Diana*, sculpted in 1892 for the original Madison Square Garden; the Sherman Victory monument in New York City; *Hiawatha* for Saratoga, New York; and many others. It is not certain when Roosevelt first decided to commission Saint-Gaudens to create a new coinage, but by December 27, 1904, he wrote to secretary of the Treasury Leslie Mortier Shaw: "I think our coinage is artistically of atrocious hideousness. Would it be possible, without asking permission of Congress, to employ a man like Saint-Gaudens to give us a coinage that would have some beauty?"

The president was enamored with the beauty and high relief of ancient Greek coinage. At one time, Roosevelt wanted to change the designs of the entire U.S. coinage. Because of the difficulty of adapting modern minting techniques to the high-relief effects that Roosevelt desired, Saint-Gaudens concentrated his efforts on the eagle and double eagle issues.

By means of extensive personal correspondence with the artist at his studio in Cornish, New Hampshire, Roosevelt contributed greatly to the design of this and several issues of the period. He wanted to include the use of an American Indian in full headdress. Saint-Gaudens wrote to Roosevelt in 1907: "I like so much the head with the head-dress, and by the way, I am very glad you suggested doing the head in that manner." Although Saint-Gaudens preferred the Indian design for the double eagle, the standing Liberty (now known as "Saint-Gaudens") theme was chosen for that denomination. The Indian Head design is similar to the design adopted for the regular-issue eagle. In his last letter to the president, Saint-Gaudens wrote: "The majority of the people that I show the work to evidently prefer with you the figure of Liberty to the head of Liberty and that I shall not consider any further on the twenty-dollar gold coin." At the request of the artist, however, one example was struck for comparison.

The pedigree of this extraordinary coin began with Charles Barber, the chief engraver of the U.S. Mint. Waldo Newcomer purchased the coin directly from his estate. The coin was then sold to the prominent collector F.C.C. Boyd. Boyd's wife sold the coin for a reported $1,500 to Abe Kosoff and Abner Kreisberg around 1945. The coin was then sold to King Farouk of Egypt for slightly less than $10,000. After King Farouk was overthrown, his collection of rare coins was auctioned in 1954. The coin sold for approximately $3,444, again to Abe Kosoff, who placed the coin with Roy E.

President Theodore Roosevelt's desire to bring artistic beauty to American coins led to the creation of the magnificent Saint-Gaudens designs.

("Ted") Naftzger Jr. In 1956 Dr. J.E. Wilkison obtained the coin for $10,000. It was sold in 1973 to Paramount International Coin Corporation as part of the Wilkison Gold Pattern Collection. The Wilkison Gold Pattern Collection was then traded to A-Mark Financial. It was then sold by private treaty to Maryland dealer Julian Leidman in 1979 for $500,000. Jack Hancock and Bob Harwell purchased the coin in the 1981 American Numismatic Association auction sale for $475,000. Several years later, it was sold to a major Northeastern collector of Saint-Gaudens coinage and is today the cornerstone of that collection. The coin has not been shown publicly for nearly three decades. This probably explains why the coin is not ranked much higher on the list of 100 Greatest U.S. Coins. It is author Jeff Garrett's personal favorite U.S. coin, and would rank No. 1 if he was the only one voting.

STANDARDS · Weight: 33.436 grams. **Composition:** 90% gold, 10% copper. **Diameter:** 34 mm. **Edge:** Lettered E PLURIBUS UNUM with words divided by stars. **RARITY ·** Only one example was struck. The coin is a gem and currently resides in a prominent Northeastern collection. If this coin were offered for sale it would probably break the price record for a U.S. coin. **CERTIFIED POPULATION ·** 0

Designed by Augustus Saint-Gaudens. The obverse features Liberty's head facing left, wearing a feathered Indian headdress, surrounded by 13 stars. Below the bust, in large letters, is the word LIBERTY. The reverse features a flying eagle above a rising sun with the date in Roman numerals.

HISTORICAL VALUES					
		Gem Proof			
1960: $25,000	**1980:** $500,000	**1st ed./2003:** $7,500,000	**2nd ed./2005:** $10,000,000	**3rd ed./2008:** $12,500,000	**4th edition:** $20,000,000

Shown enlarged from actual size of 34 mm.

1894-S BARBER DIME

The 1894-S dime is one of the most famous U.S. rarities. While several coins are rarer or more valuable than the 1894-S dime, few come with the wonderful stories and intrigue that surround this coin.

The general consensus is that 24 1894-S dimes were struck. Early explanations of the mintage figure claimed that the 24 coins were made to round out an accounting entry. However, the figure needed was $.40, not $2.40, and the fact that most surviving 1894-S dimes are prooflike in appearance tends to refute that theory—such special coins would never have been necessary to accomplish such a mundane task. In recent years, there has been a debate whether the known coins are indeed merely prooflike (with mirror surfaces, but not struck from Proof dies) or actual Proofs. The highest-grade coins known for the issue appear to be Proofs, in our opinion. It should also be mentioned that it is only about this time that collecting coins by mintmark became fashionable.

Later research revealed that the Mint superintendent at San Francisco in 1894, John Daggett, had the coins struck at the special request of banker friends. Of the 24 coins, three went to his young daughter, Hallie, whom he instructed to preserve them carefully until she was older, at which time the coins would be worth a lot of money. Being a typical child, Hallie immediately used one of the 1894-S dimes to purchase ice cream (thankfully, the coin was later recovered from circulation). However, Hallie clung to the other two, and 60 years later, in 1954, she sold her remaining pair to a California dealer.

No other Barber coin (dime, quarter, or half dollar) comes even remotely close to the rarity of the 1894-S dime. Of the original 24 1894-S dimes, only nine have been positively traced. Two were pulled from circulation (one of them now known appropriately as the "Ice Cream Specimen"), while the others are Proof or prooflike coins in varying degrees of preservation, ranging from impaired to gem. This raises the tantalizing question, "Where are the remaining 1894-S dimes?" One would think that with all the publicity surrounding this coin, not to mention the ever-increasing value of this rarity, that other examples would have surfaced. However, such has not been the case. The remainder of the coins struck were probably lost or remelted at some point. The discovery of a new example would be truly exciting news.

For decades, the 1894-S dime has been included along with the 1913 Liberty Head nickel and the 1804 silver dollar in a triumvirate of the United States' most desirable coins. The 1894-S dime was one of the first coins to cross the $100,000 price barrier, and today the finest examples are approaching the $2 million mark.

John Daggett was right: the 1894-S dime has become a very valuable coin!

Charles Barber's designs for the dime and other silver coins debuted in 1892. His depiction of Liberty reveals the influence of French medalists such as Jean-Baptiste Daniel-Dupuis, whose work is shown here.

STANDARDS · Weight: 2.462 grams. **Composition:** 90% silver, 10% copper. **Diameter:** 17.9 mm. **Edge:** Reeded. **RARITY** · Only 24 struck. Of the nine known examples, two are Gem Proofs. **CERTIFIED POPULATION** · 9

Designed by Charles Barber. The obverse shows a head of Liberty wearing a liberty cap, a wreath of laurel tied behind her head, and a band with the word LIBERTY inscribed. The date appears below the head, and the words UNITED STATES OF AMERICA form the outer legend. The reverse shows a wreath of American grains and produce surrounding the words ONE DIME. The mintmark appears below the wreath.

HISTORICAL VALUES
Choice Proof

1960: $15,000	1980: $100,000	1st ed./2003: $750,000	2nd ed./2005: $850,000	3rd ed./2008: $1,250,000	4th edition: $2,000,000

Shown enlarged from actual size of 17.9 mm.

1885 PROOF TRADE DOLLAR

Trade dollars were an interesting run of silver dollars spanning the gap between the Liberty Seated design, which ended in 1873, and the Morgan dollar design, which began in 1878. However, the trade dollars were not made for U.S. consumption; they were made specifically for trade in the Orient. In fact, trade dollars were legal tender in the United States only for a short period and even then, only in amounts up to $5! After their legal-tender status was revoked, they traded at a discount in the United States even though they were heavier than the earlier-minted Liberty Seated dollars and the soon-to-follow Morgan dollar.

With the introduction of the Morgan dollar in 1878, Congress discontinued the trade dollar for political reasons, although it had been a stellar success for its intended purpose—to facilitate commerce with China. After 1878, trade dollars continued to be minted in limited quantities for numismatic purposes. The general thought was that 1883 was the last year of the trade dollar Proofs. However, in 1907 and 1908, a small number of Proof 1884 (No. 66) and 1885 trade dollars came on the market, shocking the numismatic world because none of either date had previously been brought to the notice of collectors.

The source of both the 1884 and 1885 trade dollars was William Idler, a coin dealer directly involved with numerous U.S. rarities of dubious origin, including the 1836 "second restrike" half cent; the Proof restrikes of the 1801, 1802, and 1803 silver dollars; the Class III 1804 silver dollar; and others. Idler has been accused of being a fence for Mint employees who needed an outlet for their creations. Even his son-in-law, Captain John Haseltine (also a prominent coin dealer), admitted that Idler was very secretive about his coin collection for fear that some of his coins were subject to seizure. Whereas ten 1884 Proof trade dollars were struck and are all accounted for today, only five 1885 trade dollars are known, a number that has not changed since their first appearance in 1908. Because no records exist of their having been made in 1885 and because of the unusual way in which they entered the market, most numismatic experts believe that they were clandestine pieces made in the Mint. However, this has never diminished their desirability, their rarity, or their value. In fact, the mystery surrounding them has made them even more attractive.

All of the 1885 trade dollars were issued only as Proofs, a practice begun with the 1879 Philadelphia Mint trade dollars. Unlike the 1884 trade dollars (a few of which are also known in copper), no non-silver 1885 trade dollars are known. Four of the 1885 trade dollars remain in relatively undisturbed condition; the fifth, called "badly cleaned" in the past, was still worth $110,000 in 1980! Today, the 1885 trade dollar is one of the few U.S. coins to have broken the million-dollar barrier, with the finest known example having sold for $3.5 million in recent years.

William Barber and his colleagues made several patterns for the trade dollar. In this one, Liberty brandishes a liberty cap on a staff and wears a feathered headdress.

Despite their cloudy beginnings, the 1885 trade dollars are now readily accepted by the numismatic community, as evidenced by their inclusion in the pantheon of U.S. numismatics, the Top 10 of the 100 Greatest U.S. Coins list.

STANDARDS · Weight: 27.216 grams. **Composition:** 90% silver, 10% copper. **Diameter:** 38.1 mm. **Edge:** Reeded. **RARITY ·** Extremely rare. Only five examples were struck, all Proofs. **CERTIFIED POPULATION ·** 5

Designed by William Barber. The obverse shows Liberty in a flowing gown facing left and sitting on a bale of cotton and American produce. Her right arm is extended and holds an olive branch. In her left hand, she holds a banner with the word LIBERTY. A small scroll below the bale (just above the date) bears the motto IN GOD WE TRUST. Liberty is surrounded by 13 stars. The reverse shows a plain eagle with outstretched wings, an olive branch in its left talon, and a bunch of arrows in its right. The words UNITED STATES OF AMERICA and a scroll bearing the motto E PLURIBUS UNUM appear above the eagle. The weight and fineness (420 GRAINS. 900 FINE) and the denomination (TRADE DOLLAR) appear beneath the eagle.

HISTORICAL VALUES
Choice Proof

1960: $15,000	1980: $100,000	1st ed./2003: $1,000,000	2nd ed./2005: $1,250,000	3rd ed./2008: $2,250,000	4th edition: $3,000,000

Shown enlarged from actual size of 38.1 mm.

1794 FLOWING HAIR SILVER DOLLAR

The 1794 silver dollar was the first coin of this denomination ever issued by the United States. Ever since numismatics became popular, beginning in the 1850s, the 1794 silver dollar has been recognized as a great rarity. One collector, Jack Collins, spent more than 30 years tracking all of the known examples, uncovering only 100 demonstrably different ones. In the past few years, a handful of new examples have come to light, bringing the total of known examples to somewhere between 125 and 150.

The story of the silver dollar began around 1792, when the U.S. government deliberated its first coinage system. After careful consideration, the silver dollar and the gold eagle were made the pillars of the new system, with all other denominations being either fractions or multiples of these two.

Unfortunately, large amounts of silver were simply not available at the time, and the Mint had no funds with which to purchase any. Instead, the Mint relied on depositors who were willing to bring raw silver or foreign silver coins to the Mint for conversion into U.S. silver coins. This meant that each batch of silver had to be processed individually, sometimes more than once. From melting, to refining, to rolling out the ingots into sheets of silver, to punching out the blanks, to the actual coining, each batch was kept separate from all others. Eventually, the depositor would receive a parcel of U.S. coins in an amount equal to the value of the silver that he or she had contributed.

Of the 1794 silver dollars coined on October 15 of that year, 242 out of the total 2,000 minted were rejected as being too poorly struck and having insufficient details. In 1794, the largest coin press at the Mint was the one used to make cents and half dollars. This proved to be inadequate for striking coins as large as the silver dollar. In fact, virtually all of the 1,758 coins that survived the quality inspection are still surprisingly weak, a combination of the press capability and the fact that the faces of the dies were not parallel. Thus, finding a well-struck 1794 silver dollar is extremely difficult. Many 1794 silver dollars have also been repaired over the years, and caution should be exercised when considering the purchase of this issue.

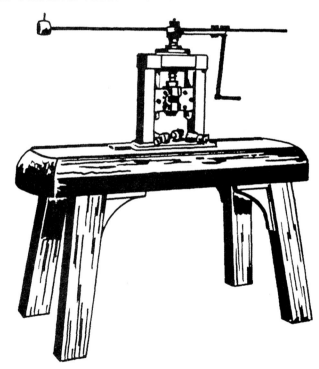

A small screw press like this one was used to produce the Mint's first copper and small silver pieces, but it proved inadequate to mint the dollar coin effectively. The Mint ordered new, larger presses to solve the problem.

STANDARDS · Weight: 26.96 grams. **Composition:** 89% silver, 11% copper. **Diameter:** Varies from 39 to 40 mm. **Edge:** Lettered HUNDRED CENTS ONE DOLLAR OR UNIT. **RARITY ·** Very rare. Only 1,758 silver dollars were struck in 1794, of which an estimated 130 examples survive. The finest example known is the Gem Uncirculated example illustrated here. The coin has fully mirrored surfaces, and it has been speculated that the coin was the first silver dollar struck at the U.S. Mint. This example is currently the auction record holder for a U.S. coin, having sold for $10,016,875 in January 2013. This incredible sum probably explains why the 1794 silver dollar now ranks in the Top Ten of the 100 Greatest U.S. Coins. **CERTIFIED POPULATION ·** 128

Designed by Robert Scot. The obverse shows a head of Liberty facing right, the word LIBERTY above, the date below, eight stars on the left side, and seven stars on the right. The reverse features a plain eagle with outstretched wings within a wreath of palm and olive branches. The outer legend reads UNITED STATES OF AMERICA.

HISTORICAL VALUES
Extremely Fine

1960: $6,500	1980: $25,000	1st ed./2003: $125,000	2nd ed./2005: $150,000	3rd ed./2008: $250,000	4th edition: $275,000

Shown enlarged from actual size of 39 to 40 mm.

1776 CONTINENTAL DOLLAR

In 1776, U.S. patriotism reached a fever pitch. The Revolutionary War was already well under way, and the United States' representatives felt confident enough to declare independence from Great Britain on July 4. To celebrate their newly found independence and to show the world that they were part of a sovereign nation capable of producing its own money, the Continental Congress initiated a plan to produce the first U.S. coins.

Elisha Gallaudet, a New Jersey engraver, was asked to prepare dies for a new coin, presumably a silver dollar to replace the depreciating $1 Continental Currency notes. Gallaudet recycled some of his own designs from paper money he had engraved earlier in the year, adding suggestions from the likes of Benjamin Franklin and David Rittenhouse (later the first director of the U.S. Mint).

A number of patterns were struck in a variety of metals: brass, tin, copper, and silver. Quantities of circulating coins were made in a pewter-like alloy, with little intrinsic value but still more "solid" than paper. The United States was unable to secure a loan of silver from the French; thus, there was no way to make the coins in that metal—if, indeed, it had been desired to do so. While the political dream of U.S. independence eventually became a reality, the economic dream of a U.S. coin faded into the background. Today, the only remnants of this dream are specimens of the 1776 Continental dollar that have survived the past 238 years, mostly in pewter, but a few in other metals.

The 1776 Continental dollar has become one of the most popular coins of the colonial era. This can be attributed to several factors. A case can be made that since many examples are found well-worn, the issue is probably the first actual circulating U.S. dollar coin. The magical date of 1776 and its ties to Benjamin Franklin also make the 1776 Continental dollar one of the most desirable coins on the 100 Greatest U.S. Coins list.

STANDARDS · Weights and Composition: Presumed to match those of the Spanish 8-reales coins ("piece of eight") then in circulation. **Diameter:** 40 mm. **RARITY** · A few silver examples are known, fewer than 10 in brass, and probably 1,000 to 2,000 in pewter. **CERTIFIED POPULATION** · 331

Designed by Elisha Gallaudet. The obverse features a sundial basking in the rays of a blazing sun with a round face. Beneath the sundial are the words MIND YOUR BUSINESS (not an admonition to keep your nose out of other people's business, but to focus your attention on your own affairs). FUGIO, referring to the fleeting nature of time, appears beneath the sun. Finally, CONTINENTAL CURRENCY appears in the outer circle, as does the date 1776. The reverse features joined links bearing the names of the 13 colonies surrounding AMERICAN CONGRESS and WE ARE ONE. Mintage unknown.

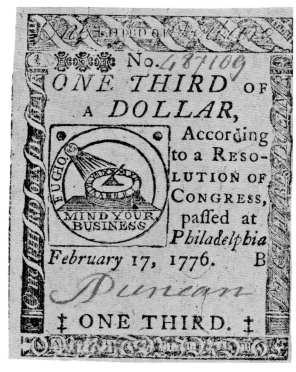

When designing the Continental dollar coin, engraver Elisha Gallaudet reused some of the motifs he had employed on paper notes like this one.

HISTORICAL VALUES
Uncirculated

1960: $300	1980: $10,000	1st ed./2003: $35,000	2nd ed./2005: $60,000	3rd ed./2008: $75,000	4th edition: $100,000

Shown enlarged from actual size of 40 mm.

1943 BRONZE LINCOLN CENT

STANDARDS · **Weight:** 3.11 grams. **Composition:** 95% copper, 5% tin and zinc. **Diameter:** 19 mm. **Edge:** Plain. **RARITY** · Extremely rare. Approximately a dozen 1943 bronze cents are known, with examples seen from all three Mints. All known examples but one were pulled from circulation, although at least two of those have been certified at the Mint State level. Choice examples of this date are currently valued at nearly $500,000. **CERTIFIED POPULATION** · 16

The U.S. Mint produced more than 1 billion "Steelies" in 1943, but a small number of bronze cents dated that year also escaped.

One of the greatest numismatic rarities of the 20th century is the 1943 bronze cent. The popularity of this rarity is reflected in its high ranking over the years on the list of 100 Greatest U.S. Coins.

The 1943 bronze cents were actually mistakes that caused the government considerable embarrassment. In 1943, the U.S. Mint began using steel blanks (known as "planchets") for the cents to conserve copper for use in World War II. More than a billion "Steelies," as they are known popularly, were struck by the three mints in 1943. The Philadelphia Mint alone produced more than 684 million examples. However, a handful of rare 1943 cents were discovered struck by mistake on old-style bronze blanks. Presumably, the error occurred when left-over bronze planchets were mixed with a batch of the new steel planchets and went through the usual striking methods, then escaped into circulation, evading the quality control procedures at the Mint.

Until the 1960s, the Mint's official policy was that it did not make mistakes, despite the fact that its own chief engraver once owned a 1943 bronze cent. Later, that policy was relaxed, and the Mint now acknowledges the possibility that some 1943 bronze cents could have been produced in error.

Rumors of the 1943 bronze cent's existence began almost immediately after the coins were struck. For decades, it was thought that the first one was discovered in 1947, when a fellow named Sam Lutes found one in his change. Recently, national headlines announced the rediscovery of an example that had first been found in change in 1944. At that time, authentication was difficult, and the finder's family held the coin for more than 60 years. In mid-2008 it reportedly sold for more than $100,000. Discoveries are rare, however, and today only a dozen or so 1943 bronze cents are known, yielding a discovery rate of less than one coin every four years. No doubt even this rate will diminish in the future, and the 1943 bronze cent will remain one of the great 20th-century rarities.

Many coin dealers used the 1943 bronze cent as a publicity stunt by offering huge rewards for a genuine example (their money was safe because there was little chance that they would ever have to honor their offers). In fact, many of today's collectors got their start by searching for a 1943 bronze cent in pocket change. Another result of the publicity, a negative one, is that coin dealers around the country have had to answer innumerable questions about 1943 cents, mostly from collectors who are convinced that they have genuine 1943 bronze cents. Unfortunately, many 1943 "Steelies" have been copper-plated and offered as genuine bronze cents. As an aid to novice collectors, here's a simple test to determine if your 1943 "bronze" cent is really bronze: if your coin is attracted to a magnet, it's a copper-plated "Steelie"; if not, have your coin checked out by an expert—it may be a new discovery!

Designed by Victor David Brenner. The obverse depicts a bust of Abraham Lincoln facing right, **IN GOD WE TRUST** above, **LIBERTY** to the left, and the date to the right. The reverse is plain and understated (but impressive), with ears of wheat on either side, and a big **ONE CENT** in the middle. A smaller **E PLURIBUS UNUM** appears above and **UNITED STATES OF AMERICA** appears below **CENT**.

HISTORICAL VALUES					
Extremely Fine					
1960: $5,000	**1980:** $20,000	**1st ed./2003:** $50,000	**2nd ed./2005:** $60,000	**3rd ed./2008:** $100,000	**4th edition:** $200,000

1792 HALF DISME

STANDARDS · **Weight:** 1.35 grams. **Composition:** 89% silver, 11% copper. **Diameter:** 17.5 mm. **Edge:** Diagonally reeded. **RARITY** · Of all the 1792 federal coins, the 1792 half disme is the most available today. However, "available" is a relative term when compared with unique and semi-unique pieces, so by any other standards the 1792 half disme is a rare animal indeed. Prices have soared for this popular issue in recent years. **CERTIFIED POPULATION** · 124

In 1792, as part of an attempt to develop a national coinage, Mint employees struck approximately 1,500 silver half dismes in the cellar of a saw maker named John Harper. These tiny silver coins bore the image of Liberty on one side and a flying eagle on the other. They were valued at 5¢ each (or half of a dime).

Collectors sometimes have trouble pronouncing the word *disme*. Is it the phonetically obvious "diz-mee," or is it the traditional way in which we pronounce *dime* today (the word into which *disme* transmogrified)? Actually, the answer is neither. *Disme* is a French word pronounced "deem." Thus, *half disme* is properly pronounced "half deem."

A couple of interesting stories surround the 1792 half disme. One story suggests that President George Washington provided his own personal silver service to be turned into half dismes, yielding enough to distribute to friends, family, government officials, and VIPs. Another is that the likeness on the coin is that of Washington's wife, Martha, who does bear a strong resemblance to the lady on the coin.

Is the 1792 half disme a pattern or a circulation strike? Generally, pattern coins are struck in extremely limited quantities (usually fewer than a dozen pieces) just to test how a design will appear in coin form. A mintage of 1,500 pieces suggests that the 1792 half disme was much more than just a pattern, but because they were struck outside the U.S. Mint, because no other half dismes or half dimes were made until 1794, and because the 1792 half dismes were not monetized through official channels (as were "real" coins later on), most numismatists consider them to be patterns. Some experts consider them quasi-official coins, and a smaller group considers them to be one of the first "real" coins made by our government. Perhaps the best test is that these did indeed circulate as coins, and in his message to Congress in December 1792, President Washington specifically stated that they had been made as regular coinage. Thus, it is only logical that most known pieces show signs of extensive wear.

Legend has it that President George Washington provided his own silverware to be melted for the first half dismes, and that the bust of Liberty featured on those coins is modeled upon the president's wife, Martha Washington.

Another way to approach the question is to point out the existence of a unique 1792 half disme struck in pure copper. Such a piece indicates that the dies were first tested on a blank of base metal, the designs and striking qualities were approved, and a production run of 1,500 half dismes began. If the copper piece were a pattern (or a die trial), how can the silver versions that followed be anything other than "real" coins?

A few examples of the 1792 half dismes are known in amazing, gem condition. Some feature prooflike surfaces, suggesting presentation piece status. Perhaps one of these exceptional coins was made as a gift to President Washington as an example of our nation's first coinage. The coin pictured once belonged to David Rittenhouse, the first director of the U.S. Mint.

Designed by an unknown artist, possibly Robert Birch. The obverse shows a bust of Liberty facing left, her curly hair falling loosely behind her. The date 1792 appears beneath the bust and the legend LIB PAR OF SCIENCE & INDUSTRY (for "Liberty, Parent of Science & Industry") encircling. The reverse features a somewhat scrawny eagle in flight with HALF DISME and a star below. The outer legend reads: UNI STATES OF AMERICA.

HISTORICAL VALUES					
Very Fine					
1960: $500	1980: $5,000	1st ed./2003: $35,000	2nd ed./2005: $50,000	3rd ed./2008: $85,000	4th edition: $85,000

1793 FLOWING HAIR, CHAIN REVERSE CENT

STANDARDS · Weight: 13.478 grams. **Composition:** Pure copper. **Diameter:** 26 mm. **Edge:** Ornamented with bars and vines. **RARITY ·** Very scarce. More than 36,000 Chain cents were produced, but many have been lost or destroyed over the years. Most survivors are well worn, but a few exist in magnificent Uncirculated condition. Until recent years, the 1793 Chain cent was fairly affordable in low-grade condition. Expect to pay at least $15,000 for an example with decent details and good surfaces. One superb example sold for $1,380,000 at auction in 2012. **CERTIFIED POPULATION ·** 825

The 1793 Chain cent, so named because of the connected links that appear on the back, is one of the simplest yet most popular and enduring designs on any U.S. coin.

Despite the promise expressed in the 1792 pattern coins, the 1793 Chain cents seem dull and flat, probably the work of an inexperienced engraver. The simple design provoked immediate criticism, not only for the quality of the engraving but also for the symbolism expressed on the coin.

Credit for the design goes to Henry Voigt, then chief coiner of the Mint, who was also responsible for the 1792 silver-center cents. Voigt must have been terribly embarrassed when the first reviews of his 1793 Chain cents appeared in several newspapers around the country. Derided for her frightened look, Voigt's Liberty did, indeed, possess flowing, unkempt hair and eyes that conveyed fear, not peace or strength. Furthermore, the back of the coin included a chain of 15 links in a never-ending circle, perceived by the public as representing the bondage and tyranny of the British masters from which the colonies had so recently freed themselves! Others viewed the chains as representing slavery, a practice common in some parts of the new American nation and reviled in others.

Apart from the aesthetics of the design, the 1793 Chain cent failed on other counts. The relief detail was so shallow that the design faded after just a short amount of time in circulation. The lack of a highly-raised border meant that the design elements had insufficient protection from wear and that the coins would not stack properly. These considerations led to a design change in mid-1793 to the 1793 Wreath design (which suffered the same fate as the Chain cent when it was replaced with the Liberty Cap design even later in the year).

The **AMERICA** reverse variety of the Chain cent. Cornelius Vermeule has noted that the men who cut the dies for this coin represented "a host of backgrounds as diverse as those of the Revolutionary patriots themselves" *(Numismatic Art in America).*

The inexperience of the engraver can be seen on the back of some 1793 Chain cents, as some varieties have AMERICA abbreviated as AMERI., because the engraver failed to leave enough room on the coin to spell out the word completely!

Designs attributed to Henry Voigt. The obverse shows a head of Liberty facing right, **LIBERTY** above, and the date below. The reverse features a chain of 15 links encircling the words **ONE CENT** and the fraction 1/100. The legend **UNITED STATES OF AMERICA** appears in a circle near the edge (sometimes with **AMERICA** abbreviated as mentioned above).

HISTORICAL VALUES
Extremely Fine

1960: $750	1980: $10,000	1st ed./2003: $25,000	2nd ed./2005: $40,000	3rd ed./2008: $75,000	4th edition: $100,000

MCMVII (1907) ULTRA HIGH RELIEF SAINT-GAUDENS DOUBLE EAGLE PIEDFORT
DIAMETER OF AN EAGLE

STANDARDS · **Weight:** 33.436 grams. **Composition:** 90% gold, 10% copper. **Diameter:** 27 mm. **Edge:** Lettering E PLURIBUS UNUM with words divided by stars. **RARITY** · Only two examples are known to survive, both in the Smithsonian Institution. Although this incredible rarity has seldom been displayed by the Smithsonian, it is currently on display as part of the National Numismatics Collection exhibit at the Museum of American History. We highly recommend seeing these coins in person. **CERTIFIED POPULATION** · 0

The year 1907 saw a great deal of experimentation at the U.S. Mint. As mentioned, President Roosevelt was insistent that sculptor Augustus Saint-Gaudens redesign the U.S. coinage. One of the experimental issues produced was a double eagle of the MCMVII (1907) design struck on a normal weight planchet, but with the diameter of an eagle. The resulting coin was a piedfort, meaning much thicker than normal. This Ultra High Relief double eagle was almost double the thickness of a standard double eagle and was smaller than the regular High Relief double eagle (note the picture of the obverses here). Moreover, each coin required nine strikings from a 172-ton hydraulic press.

In addition to the excessive strikings, there was also a legal issue. It was and is illegal to mint coins of two denominations using same-diameter planchets. Mint authorities were well aware of this problem. The coin may have been made purely as a novelty. In a letter to Mint director Frank A. Leach dated January 8, 1908, the Mint Collection curator, T.L. Comparette, stated that "It is an entirely illegal 'coin' and for that reason should not I believe be put into a collection of historical coins, yet it was produced by the government and for that reason the few specimens will in years after command enormous prices, easily $3,000 each. Dealers are now offering large prices for them." Whatever the motive for the production, the 1907 Ultra High Relief double eagle piedfort struck on an eagle planchet is a captivating piece of minting history and one of the United States' most alluring coins.

Most coin collectors were unaware of this incredible issue up until recently. The only two surviving examples are housed in the Smithsonian Institution and have seldom been displayed. Even many very knowledgeable rare-coin dealers have never heard of this fantastic issue. It is hard to appreciate this enigmatic rarity without seeing it in person. The size and scale of the design are completely mesmerizing.

An early model by Saint-Gaudens for the double eagle obverse. Unlike in the finished coin, Liberty is winged and carries a shield.

One of the first times this issue became known was after the publication of a wonderful book about gold patterns that was written by David Akers in the late 1970s. Then, in 2009, the U.S. Mint recreated this alluring issue. The coins proved quite difficult to produce, given the extremely high relief of the design. The 2009 version is very popular with collectors and has risen in value substantially over the last several years. It is interesting that a coin that was so elusive and mysterious was later mass produced. Some collectors welcome the chance to own one, while others lament the reproduction of such a classic issue.

Designed by Augustus Saint-Gaudens. The obverse depicts a standing Liberty draped in Romanesque clothing holding a torch, the design taken from the Sherman Victory monument. The reverse features an eagle in flight. Mintage is reportedly 13 examples.

HISTORICAL VALUES					
Gem Proof					
1960: $20,000	1980: $250,000	1st ed./2003: $2,500,000	2nd ed./2005: $3,500,000	3rd ed./2008: $6,500,000	4th edition: $7,000,000

1861 "PAQUET REVERSE" LIBERTY HEAD DOUBLE EAGLE

STANDARDS · **Weight:** 33.436 grams. **Composition:** 90% gold, 10% copper. **Net weight:** .96750 oz. pure gold. **Diameter:** 34 mm. **Edge:** Reeded.

RARITY · Only two examples are known. One, a PCGS-graded MS-61 discovered in Paris in the 1970s, was part of the Dallas Bank Collection sold in 2001. Reportedly it sold privately in recent years for $2.5 million. The other traces its pedigree to 1865, when it was sold by W. Elliot Woodward for $37. Later part of the Norweb, Farouk, and Green collections, that specimen has been graded by NGC MS-67 and is the ultimate combination of rarity and condition. **CERTIFIED POPULATION** · 2

The normal reverse of the 1861 double eagle.

A t one time, this incredibly rare coin was considered a pattern or experimental issue. It has been shown, however, to be a regular-issue U.S. coin struck for general circulation. In 1860, Anthony Paquet, an engraver at the Philadelphia Mint, modified the reverse design for the double eagle. The new design was very similar to the standard issue, but the reverse letters were much taller and more slender in appearance. There are also several technical variations with regard to the positioning and size of the lettering. In late 1860, the Paquet Reverse became the standard design that was adopted for the regular-issue coinage of 1861 double eagles. Dies were shipped to the branch mints of New Orleans and San Francisco. Actual coinage on high-speed presses began in January of 1861 in Philadelphia, but it was feared that the wider fields and narrow rim would cause breakage of the dies, so the use of planchet dies was discontinued. However, those dies that were used for coinage experienced no problems at all, proving their withdrawal was unnecessary.

Regardless, Mint director James Ross Snowden recalled the new design and ordered the melting of the 1861 double eagles made at the Philadelphia Mint. The entire Philadelphia run was destroyed, with the exception of a few coins. Snowden also ordered production to cease in New Orleans and San Francisco. The order reached New Orleans in time to prevent any coinage. However, because the transcontinental railroad was still several years from completion and the telegraph did not extend past St. Joseph, Missouri, word to stop coinage did not reach San Francisco until 19,250 coins had been struck. Charles H. Hempstead, superintendent of the San Francisco Mint, replied to the instructions on February 9, 1861: "I was unable to prevent the striking and issuing of a large number of double eagles, coined with the new dies." No effort was made to recall the issue, and it has become a rarity as well (No. 50).

The 1861 Paquet Reverse double eagle has been a known rarity since nearly the year it was struck. Today, just two examples of the Philadelphia mintage are known of this extremely rare coin. For many years, it was not certain if this coin was a pattern or a regular-issue U.S. gold coin. Modern research has proven the legitimacy of this fabled rarity. Another stumbling block to the popularity of this great coin is the fact that only very rarely has an example traded hands. With the explosion of interest in U.S. double eagles, the 1861 Paquet Reverse double eagle is now held in the same regard as the great classics of the series.

Designed by James B. Longacre and Anthony C. Paquet. The obverse features a portrait of a coronet Liberty head facing left and is surrounded by 13 stars. The reverse features an outspread eagle and shield design. Mintage for this issue is unknown.

HISTORICAL VALUES
Uncirculated

1960: $5,000	1980: $75,000	1st ed./2003: $350,000	2nd ed./2005: $750,000	3rd ed./2008: $2,000,000	4th edition: $2,000,000

1872 AMAZONIAN GOLD PATTERN SET

STANDARDS · **Weight:** Gold dollar, 1.672 grams; quarter eagle, 4.18 grams; $3 gold coin, 5.015 grams; half eagle, 8.359 grams; eagle, 16.718 grams; double eagle, 33.436 grams. **Composition:** 90% gold, 10% copper (for all). **Diameter:** Gold dollar, 15 mm; quarter eagle, 18 mm; $3 gold coin, 20.5 mm; half eagle, 21.6 mm; eagle, 27 mm; double eagle, 34 mm. **Edge:** Reeded (for all). **RARITY** · Each coin is unique in gold. **CERTIFIED POPULATION** · 1 set, 6 coins.

The set of 1872 "Amazonian" pattern coins in gold is one of the most celebrated rarities in the entire series of U.S. coins. This spectacular set is unique in many ways: (1) it is the only set of its kind ever made, (2) it is the only set of gold patterns ever produced with a common design theme, and (3) the $3 gold piece in the set is the only pattern of this denomination ever to have been struck in gold!

In 1872, William Barber produced a relatively large number of pattern coins, including so-called "commercial dollars" (precursors of the 1873 trade dollars); "Amazonian" quarters, half dollars, and dollars with a partially nude seated Liberty; and "Amazonian" gold coin patterns that showed just the head of Liberty.

The Amazonian gold coin set included patterns for a $1 piece, quarter eagle, $3 piece, half eagle, eagle, and double eagle. Two sets were struck in aluminum, and one set was struck in gold.

The first mention of this spectacular set came in 1886, when Robert Coulton Davis included it in a list of known pattern coins. Later the set came into the possession of William Woodin, who was later a secretary of the Treasury and coauthor of the Adams-Woodin pattern reference book. Subsequently, the set was dispersed, with the gold dollar going one way and the other five coins becoming part of King Farouk's collection. When the Farouk collection sold at auction in 1954, Dr. John Wilkison purchased all of the Amazonian gold pattern coins (there offered as individual lots), paying the equivalent of $2,583 for the double eagle alone, the highest price of any coin in the sale. Eight years later, in 1962, Wilkison purchased the gold dollar, finally reuniting all of the coins in this unique set.

Dr. Wilkison was the foremost collector of gold pattern coins. Of all the coins in his remarkable collection, Wilkison considered the Amazonian set to be, by far, his favorite.

In 1973, Paramount International Coin Corporation purchased Dr. Wilkison's complete collection of gold patterns. David Akers produced a special hardcover reference book highlighting each of the patterns in the Wilkison collection. At the 1983 American Numismatic Association convention, the set sold for $418,000 at auction—this at a time when 1913 Liberty Head nickels were worth around $150,000. Eventually, the set ended up in the collection of gold Proof coins assembled by connoisseur Ed Trompeter, wherein he, too, considered the Amazonian set to be the crown jewel. Today, the gold Amazonian pattern set is one of the centerpiece items of a spectacular collection of U.S. pattern coins that traded hands in recent years for more than $25 million.

William Barber's silver Amazonian patterns, which share the same reverse as the gold set, are equally beautiful, and are avidly sought after by collectors of U.S. pattern coins. Shown at left is Judd-1205, the $1 pattern struck in silver.

Designed by William Barber. The obverse of each coin features a head of Liberty wearing a liberty cap bound by a band with the word "LIBERTY" written upon it. The head is surrounded by 13 stars; the date "1872" is below the bust. This head is an enlarged version of that used on Barber's Amazonian pattern quarters, half dollars, and silver dollars, thus the appellation was applied to the gold patterns, as well. The reverse of each coin features an eagle protecting a shield and a scroll that reads "IN GOD WE TRUST." This design is identical on all of the 1872 silver and gold Amazonian pattern coins.

HISTORICAL VALUES
Choice Proof

1960: $15,000	1980: $500,000	1st ed./2003: $3,000,000	2nd ed./2005: $3,250,000	3rd ed./2008: $5,500,000	4th edition: $6,000,000

1822 CAPPED HEAD HALF EAGLE

STANDARDS · **Weight:** 8.75 grams. **Composition:** 92% gold, 8% silver. **Diameter:** 25 mm. **Edge:** Reeded. **RARITY** · Of the three known coins, two are in the Smithsonian's National Numismatic Collection. **CERTIFIED POPULATION** · I

The 1822 half eagle is certainly one of the rarest, most famous, and most desirable of all U.S. coins. A scant three specimens are known, and two of these coins are permanently housed in the Smithsonian Institution and will never be owned privately again. Thus, the 1822 half eagle is unique in private hands, even though in 1822 the U.S. Mint at Philadelphia produced nearly 18,000 half eagles. Other dates of the same period have comparable mintages (some even lower), yet none can compare with the rarity of the 1822.

The extreme rarity of the 1822 half eagle stems from the ever-changing relationship of the price of gold relative to that of silver. In 1792, the year the U.S. Mint was established, the price of gold was approximately 15 times that of silver. At that ratio, and given their weight, a half eagle was worth five silver dollars. By the 1820s, the price of silver had dropped, due primarily to over-production in Mexican and South American mines, making gold worth 18 times that of silver. At that ratio, a half eagle became worth six silver dollars, or 20 percent more than its face value. As a result, virtually all of the earlier U.S. gold coins were pulled from circulation and melted down.

Walter Breen referenced a public assay in Paris in 1831, in which 40,000 U.S. half eagles of "recent mintage" were destroyed. Even if this were the only such melting (and it was not), the number of coins destroyed was more than twice the entire mintage of the 1822 half eagle! Thus, it is easy to see why the 1822 is such a great rarity today. Only a few examples escaped into circulation before the entire remainder of the mintage was destroyed. Many of the early half eagles suffered similar fates, but none came close to the near-extinction of the 1822.

For decades, the 1822 half eagle was the holy grail of U.S. gold coins. Lorin G. Parmelee, a fabulously wealthy Boston resident, spent years searching for an example in the late 1800s. He finally acquired a piece—only to discover that the coin was counterfeit! When Harlan P. Smith cataloged the Parmelee Collection for auction, the fake was

Despite his enormous wealth and considerable efforts, J.P. Morgan was never able to acquire an 1822 half eagle.

recognized. As coincidence would have it, Smith, himself a major collector of gold coins, had a genuine specimen, which he placed into the sale for "show" but did not allow it to sell. The renowned New York banker J.P. Morgan desperately wanted to own an 1822 half eagle, although his numerous attempts were unsuccessful. In 1908, he was outbid at auction for an 1822 half eagle, an experience that haunted him for years. In 1941, Morgan offered a shocking $35,000 to William F. Dunham for his 1822 half eagle—a price that was beyond comparison at the time—but once again, he was fruitless in his pursuit. The next time an 1822 half eagle was offered for sale (in 1982 as part of the Louis E. Eliasberg Collection), it required a winning bid of $687,500 to buy.

The same coin is slated to be sold at auction again in the next year or so. Its ranking could rise once collectors have a chance to see this great coin cross the auction block. The coin has not been sold in more than 30 years, and the next auction will probably be a "once-in-a-lifetime" opportunity for some lucky (and rich) collector. It should also be noted that in the first two editions of the *100 Greatest U.S. Coins*, the 1822 half eagle was the only regular-issue, circulation-strike coin that ranked in the Top 10.

Designed by John Reich. The obverse depicts a large portrait of Liberty, surrounded by 13 stars, with the date below. The reverse features an eagle with spread wings, holding an olive branch and arrows. Surrounding the eagle are the inscriptions UNITED STATES OF AMERICA and 5 D., with the motto E PLURIBUS UNUM above the eagle's head.

HISTORICAL VALUES
Extremely Fine

1960: $25,000	1980: $650,000	1st ed./2003: $2,500,000	2nd ed./2005: $3,500,000	3rd ed./2008: $5,000,000	4th edition: $5,000,000

1879 AND 1880
$4 GOLD "STELLAS"

STANDARDS · Weight: 7 grams (although restrikes vary in exact weight). **Composition:** 86% gold, 4% silver, and 10% copper. **Diameter:** 22 mm. **Edge:** Reeded. **RARITY ·** 1879 Flowing Hair "Stellas" are by far the most common of the four varieties, with between 300 and 400 specimens known. The other three varieties are exceedingly rare. A superb 1880 Coiled Hair "Stella" sold for $2,574,000 in 2013. **CERTIFIED POPULATION ·** 659

Beginning in the 1870s, several countries advocated the establishment of a universal coin that would correlate to several international currencies. A few efforts were made early in the decade, hence coins such as the 1874 Bickford pattern $10 gold pieces, but the most serious attempts came in 1879. That year, the United States' minister to Austria-Hungary, John A. Kasson, proposed a $4 gold coin with a metallic content stated in the metric system, making it easier for Europeans to use. Per Kasson's proposal, this new coin would approximate in value the Spanish 20-peseta, Dutch 8-florin, Austrian 8-florin, Italian 20-lire, and French 20-franc pieces, among other denominations. The purpose of the $4 gold coin was to facilitate international trade and travel for U.S. citizens—the same motivation behind the 1874 Bickford $10 gold piece and other gold patterns.

Congress became interested enough in Kasson's suggestion to order the Mint to produce a limited run of the $4 gold pieces so that Congressmen could review the coins. Soon thereafter, Chief Engraver Charles Barber prepared an obverse design that depicted a portrait of Liberty facing left with long, flowing hair. Meanwhile, George Morgan created a motif featuring a portrait with coiled hair.

The 1879 Flowing Hair Stella is the most available of the four known varieties, as this was the version produced for Congress. Although 425 pieces were supposedly struck, it is likely that as many as 725 were minted in total. One numismatic legend states that most Congressmen gave their "Stellas" to mistresses as gifts, which would explain the large number of ex-jewelry specimens known today. The other three varieties, the 1879 Coiled Hair, the 1880 Flowing Hair, and the 1880 Coiled Hair, are all significantly more rare.

The Stella has become one of the most popular U.S. coins ever produced. Wealthy collectors have created a demand that now far outstrips supply. Even circulated examples now command a six-figure price in most cases.

Designed by Charles Barber, the Flowing Hair version features a portrait of Liberty with loose, fluid hair locks. At the edge, the inscription 6 G .3 S .7 C 7 G R A M S is found, indicating the weights and standards of the coin. On the reverse, the eponymous star is located in the center, containing the words ONE STELLA 400 CENTS. Circumscribing the star are the words E PLURIBUS UNUM / DEO EST GLORIA, further encircled by UNITED STATES OF AMERICA / FOUR DOL. The Coiled Hair version, designed by George T. Morgan, is similar, with the only difference being the obverse portrait. On the Coiled Hair variety, Liberty is wearing a coronet and the hair is braided. The word LIBERTY is inscribed on the headband.

HISTORICAL VALUES					
1879 Flowing Hair, Choice Proof					
1960: $5,000	1980: $25,000	1st ed./2003: $75,000	2nd ed./2005: $100,000	3rd ed./2008: $150,000	4th edition: $175,000
1879 Coiled Hair, Choice Proof					
1960: $10,000	1980: $75,000	1st ed./2003: $250,000	2nd ed./2005: $350,000	3rd ed./2008: $450,000	4th edition: $650,000
1880 Flowing Hair, Choice Proof					
1960: $10,000	1980: $45,000	1st ed./2003: $125,000	2nd ed./2005: $150,000	3rd ed./2008: $250,000	4th edition: $300,000
1880 Coiled Hair, Choice Proof					
1960: $15,000	1980: $100,000	1st ed./2003: $350,000	2nd ed./2005: $500,000	3rd ed./2008: $750,000	4th edition: $1,000,000

1877 HALF UNION $50 GOLD COINS

TWO DESIGNS

STANDARDS · Weight: 83.591 grams. **Composition:** 90% gold, 10% copper. **Diameter:** 50.8 mm. **Edge:** Reeded. **RARITY ·** Two are known to exist, and both are in the Smithsonian Institution. They have been off the market since 1909, and it is only speculation what the market price for these awesome coins would be. It is nearly certain that one of these would bring at least $10 million if offered for sale. Some copper and gold-plated copper impressions exist and are rare. **CERTIFIED POPULATION ·** 0

These two coins are pattern issues that were produced by the Mint in 1877 to test the feasibility of a large-denomination gold coin. The original proposal for these coins came from California, which used only coins at the time because paper money was illegal under the state constitution. Gold $50 coins would have greatly facilitated banking, as indeed such coins (of different design) had done from 1851 to 1855. There was also political pressure to increase the use of gold for minting operations. However, the idea was rejected, and a regular-issue half union never materialized. Only one each of two designs of these magnificent coins was struck in gold. They are now both housed in the National Numismatic Collection at the Smithsonian Institution.

It was thought for several decades that both half unions had been melted shortly after production. However, they were among certain non-publicized coins held by the Mint Cabinet and somehow traded away in the late 19th century. In 1909, they sur-faced in the estate collection of William Idler, who had procured them from the Mint. That same year, Captain John Haseltine and Stephen Nagy sold both coins to future Treasury secretary William Woodin of New York for the then-astronomical sum of $10,000 each. The sale was widely publicized, and the U.S. government pressured Mr. Woodin to return them to the Mint Cabinet. A very favorable trade was evidently worked out to the satisfaction of both parties. Woodin should have been satisfied, for he obtained an enormous number of other U.S. pattern coins in return, many of which were unique and unknown.

Today, we do not know which pattern coins were traded for the pair of gold half unions. In 1913, Edgar H. Adams and William Woodin published a monograph on the subject of U.S. pattern coinage that became for many years the standard reference work for the subject. It is thought that Woodin's trade with the U.S. government formed the foundation of his collection and facilitated the production of the Adams-Woodin pattern book.

The half unions were on display at the Smithsonian's Museum of American History from the 1960s up until about 10 years ago, at which time they were moved to the numismatic exhibit at the Castle on the Mall. Today, they are back at the Museum of American History, in the "Legendary Rarities" case of the "Stories on Money" exhibit. We highly recommend a visit to Washington, D.C., to view these fascinating jewels of the National Numismatic Collection.

The two half unions are both on display at the Smithsonian's Museum of American History.

Designed by William Barber. The obverse of both coins features the portrait of Liberty facing left, one with a slightly larger head. The coin with the smaller head has four stars beneath LIBERTY. The reverse design is similar to that of $20 gold coins of the era (by Longacre), with an outspread eagle and shield. Mintage is just one of each type.

HISTORICAL VALUES

Type One, Choice Proof					
1960: $50,000	**1980:** $1,000,000	**1st ed./2003:** $4,500,000	**2nd ed./2005:** $7,500,000	**3rd ed./2008:** $10,000,000	**4th edition:** $12,500,000

Type Two, Choice Proof					
1960: $50,000	**1980:** $1,000,000	**1st ed./2003:** $4,500,000	**2nd ed./2005:** $7,500,000	**3rd ed./2008:** $10,000,000	**4th edition:** $12,500,000

1792 DISME

STANDARDS · **Weight:** Varies from 3.758 to 3.953 grams for the copper versions, slightly less for the silver versions. **Composition:** Pure copper or silver, respectively. **Diameter:** 23 mm. **Edge:** Reeded or plain. **RARITY** · Extremely rare. Only 3 known in silver, fewer than 20 examples are known in copper. The National Numismatic Collection contains a stunning example in copper that has retained much of the original mint red. **CERTIFIED POPULATION** · 13

The 1792 disme is part of a series of extremely rare patterns struck at the U.S. Mint, or in private facilities nearby, in anticipation of full production of coins in 1793. Fewer than 20 of the 1792 dismes are known, most made of copper and only two or three made of silver.

The designs and legends on the 1792 disme are nearly identical to those on the 1792 half disme (No. 12). The major difference between the two is the style of Liberty's portrait. Interestingly enough, the head on the 1792 disme is very similar to that on the 1793 half cent, perhaps indicating that the same artist had his hand in all three of these coins. Unfortunately, this design was never used for a regular-issue disme (or, as the denomination came to be known, dime). In fact, no dimes were made until 1796, by which time a new engraver had been hired to create a completely different design. Thus, most collectors have never seen an example of the 1792 disme other than as a picture in a reference book.

Most known examples have diagonally reeded edges, although at least two examples are known with a plain edge. The purpose of edge reeding was to prevent clipping (shaving or cutting on the edges to remove small amounts of silver), which, done enough times on enough coins, could add up to a significant amount of value.

Collecting early U.S. coinage is once again becoming very popular, as it is now realized that many of these fascinating issues are closely related to the creation of this great nation. In fact, many of our founding fathers were personally involved with the production of these coins. Many members of the House of Representatives wanted the portrait of President Washington on the obverse of the coinage. Washington is believed to have felt this was too closely tied to monarchical practice and disapproved of the idea.

President Washington did not wish for his visage to appear on American money, feeling that this would be too similar to the practice of the monarchy from which the United States had just won her freedom.

The bust of Liberty featured on the 1793 half cent bears a striking resemblance to the bust used on the 1792 disme.

Designs attributed to a variety of artists, including Adam Eckfeldt and Robert Birch. The obverse of the coin shows a head of Liberty facing left, her hair flowing wildly behind her. The date appears beneath the bust. The encircling legend reads: LIBERTY PARENT OF SCIENCE & INDUS (the INDUS stands for "Industry"). The same legend is found on other 1792 pattern coins, including the Birch cent, the silver-center cent, and the half disme. The reverse shows the word DISME below an eagle in flight. UNITED STATES OF AMERICA makes up the outer legend.

HISTORICAL VALUES					
Extremely Fine					
1960: $1,000	1980: $17,500	1st ed./2003: $75,000	2nd ed./2005: $150,000	3rd ed./2008: $250,000	4th edition: $300,000

1915-S PANAMA-PACIFIC EXPOSITION $50 GOLD PIECES
Octagonal and Round

STANDARDS • **Weight:** 83.591 grams. **Composition:** 90% gold, 10% copper. **Diameter:** 44 mm. **Edge:** Reeded. **RARITY** • Survival of the original net mintage is high, perhaps 80 to 90 percent. Many specimens of this issue were kept as pocket pieces, and circulated examples are sometimes encountered. Average Uncirculated (MS-62 to MS-63) coins can be purchased for around $50,000. Gem examples are quite rare and trade for nearly $120,000 each **CERTIFIED POPULATION** • 1,717

The 1915-S Panama-Pacific $50 gold coins were designed to commemorate the opening of the Panama Canal. Weighing in at nearly 2.5 ounces of gold each, these magnificent coins, also known as "slugs," are very popular with collectors.

Their size alone is a compelling reason to admire them. The Panama-Pacific "fifties" are also very scarce. Although 1,509 octagonal and 1,510 round examples were originally struck, unsold pieces were melted. The round issue has a surviving mintage of only 483 pieces, the lowest of any commemorative ever produced. Octagonal examples have a slightly higher net distribution figure of 645 coins. The octagonal and round issues were sold individually during the 1915 Panama-Pacific Exposition for $100 each. According to the Exposition price list, this entitled the buyer to the commemorative half dollar, gold dollar, and quarter eagle at no additional cost. A framed or leather-cased set of all five coins cost $200. A complete double set, including 10 coins mounted in a copper frame (to display both the obverse and reverse), could be had for $400. The seller was Farran Zerbe, professional numismatist and entrepreneur, who held the franchise. These fabulous sets have traded hands for hundreds of thousands of dollars. Mint superintendent T.W.H. Shanahan produced the first specimens of each denomination in a special ceremony. This set was housed in a special gold presentation case made by Shreve and Co.

At one time, a complete set of Panama-Pacific coins in the original frame or box was one of the most desirable items in U.S. numismatics. Boxed sets regularly traded for more than $100,000. The small boxes alone were worth more than $5,000 each. The copper frames traded for in excess of $20,000. However, the advent of coin certification changed the demand for original boxed sets. Today, most sets have been broken up with the coins individually graded by a major certification service. The original boxes without the coins are occasionally offered at auction and seldom bring more than $2,000.

The Palace of Fine Arts is the only remaining original building on the 635-acre fairgrounds of the 1915 Panama-Pacific Exposition in San Francisco, California.

Designed by Robert Aitken. The obverse features the head of Minerva, the goddess of wisdom, skill, and agriculture. The date 1915 is presented as Roman numerals MCMXV. On the reverse is an owl seated on the branch of a long-leafed pine tree with very large cones. Eight dolphins at the border encircle each side of the octagonal issue. Net distribution figures for the issue are 645 octagonals and 483 rounds.

HISTORICAL VALUES

Octagonal, Choice Uncirculated					
1960: $2,500	1980: $15,000	1st ed./2003: $35,000	2nd ed./2005: $50,000	3rd ed./2008: $75,000	4th edition: $80,000

Round, Choice Uncirculated					
1960: $3,500	1980: $20,000	1st ed./2003: $45,000	2nd ed./2005: $65,000	3rd ed./2008: $75,000	4th edition: $80,000

1870-S INDIAN PRINCESS HEAD $3 GOLD PIECE

STANDARDS · **Weight:** 5.015 grams. **Composition:** 90% gold, 10% copper. **Diameter:** 20.6 mm. **Edge:** Reeded. **RARITY** · Only one 1870-S $3 gold piece is known, thus determining this incredible rarity's value is difficult. Although the exact amount may be debatable, numismatists would agree that if the Bass coin ever sold again, it would sell for millions. **CERTIFIED POPULATION** · 0

Although this book describes many prohibitively rare coins, very few coins can claim the status of being unique. Even in the field of U.S. gold coinage—an arena laden with extreme rarities—only a handful of select rarities are truly unique. One of these is the 1870-S $3 gold piece, a coin whose history remains somewhat uncertain, even after extensive research.

From its inception, dies for each of the branch mints were prepared at the main mint in Philadelphia, where mintmarks were added before the dies were shipped out. However, due to an oversight, the two dies for the 1870 $3 gold pieces were sent to the San Francisco Mint without mintmarks. This unusual error put the superintendent of the San Francisco Mint, General O.H. LaGrange, in a difficult situation. He needed an example of an 1870-S $3 gold piece for placement in the cornerstone of the new San Francisco Mint, then under construction. However, LaGrange was ordered to return the dies without mintmarks to Philadelphia, so that the proper mintmark could be added. To solve the predicament, LaGrange took the unusual step of directing the coiner, J.B. Harmstead, to engrave a small "S" into the bottom of the reverse, thus allowing the production of a legal coin (in a sense, at least) for the ceremonial laying of the cornerstone.

Subsequently, LaGrange returned the two dies to the Philadelphia Mint, with a note explaining the hand-engraved mintmark and its purpose.

However, Harmstead seems to have struck not one, but two 1870-S $3 gold pieces. In March 1911, a second piece appeared on the market, coming from the collection of William H. Woodin (later a secretary of the Treasury and coauthor of the first book on U.S. patterns). A small slip of paper accompanied the Woodin coin: "This is a duplicate of the coin struck for the Cornerstone of the San Francisco Mint and the only one in existence. J.B. Harm-

stead." Previous owners had used the coin as a jewelry piece, adding a suspension loop to the top edge. By 1911, the loop had already been removed and the coin sold for an astounding $11,500, despite the flaws. The coin eventually ended up in the collection of Louis Eliasberg, the owner of the only complete collection of U.S. coins ever assembled. In 1982, Eliasberg's 1870-S $3 gold piece sold for $687,500, the second-highest price ever achieved for a U.S. coin until that time. It is now on display at the American Numismatic Association's Money Museum in Colorado Springs, Colorado, as part of the Harry W. Bass Jr. Reference Collection. Although many Bass coins were sold at auction, the 1870-S $3 piece was retained as the prize of the collection, along with a full collection of $3 gold coins of other dates and mints, an incredible cabinet of U.S. gold coins of all denominations from 1795 to 1834, and a selection of currency and pattern coins.

Now that the 1870-S $3 coin is housed in a museum, no other complete sets of $3 gold coins may be completed. Several other coins in the U.S. gold series are similarly out of reach. The 1849 double eagle, housed in the Smithsonian's National Numismatic Collection, is another example.

Designed by James B. Longacre. The obverse features a head of Liberty wearing a feathered headdress. The word LIBERTY is inscribed on the headband. The legend UNITED STATES OF AMERICA is engraved at the perimeter. The reverse depicts the denomination 3 DOLLARS, and the date is encircled by a wreath of corn and grain.

HISTORICAL VALUES
Very Fine

1960: $25,000	1980: $650,000	1st ed./2003: $2,500,000	2nd ed./2005: $3,000,000	3rd ed./2008: $5,000,000	4th edition: $5,000,000

1909-S V.D.B. LINCOLN CENT

STANDARDS · Weight: 3.11 grams. **Composition:** 95% copper, 5% tin and zinc. **Diameter:** 19 mm. **Edge:** Plain. **RARITY ·** Scarce. Although the mintage of 484,000 is high compared to the other rarities in this book, the surviving 1909-S V.D.B. cents are all well distributed among collectors, and sometimes a bit of a hunt is required to find nice examples. **CERTIFIED POPULATION ·** 22,767

The 1909-S V.D.B. cent has long been considered one of the key dates in the series, filling the dreams of collectors young and old. While the mintage of 484,000 may seem high compared to many other U.S. rarities, one must understand that there are millions of people who collect Lincoln cents. There are simply not enough 1909-S V.D.B. cents to satisfy all of the collector demand, making this coin a perennial favorite and earning it a place on our list of 100 Greatest U.S. Coins. Of the coins listed thus far, this is the first that is generally available today on a widespread basis. The 1909-S V.D.B. cent has seen added popularity with the 100th anniversary of issue and redesign of the Lincoln cent in 2009.

In 1905, President Theodore Roosevelt commissioned the famous U.S. sculptor and artist Augustus Saint-Gaudens to prepare designs for all denominations, including the cent. Initially, Saint-Gaudens's design for the obverse featured a flying eagle motif similar to James Barton Longacre's designs on the small cents from 1856 to 1858. This design was abandoned in favor of a head of Victory in profile wearing an Indian headdress, but Saint-Gaudens and Roosevelt liked this design so much that they used it for the 1907 eagle instead. Unfortunately, Saint-Gaudens died of cancer before making any more progress on the cent design, so it was not until 1909 that Victor David Brenner created the famous bust of Abraham Lincoln with which we are all so familiar today.

Brenner's design broke new ground by placing the image of an actual person on a coin made for circulation. In what some naive observers considered a break with numismatic tradition, Brenner placed his initials near the bottom of the back of the coin. Despite their small size, the letters V.D.B. were obvious enough that they created uproar with the public and Mint officials, who immediately demanded their removal. The offending initials were expunged later in 1909, resulting in the creation of four 1909 Lincoln cent varieties for collectors to acquire: 1909 with and without V.D.B.

Sculptor Victor David Brenner's iconic Lincoln cent design debuted in 1909, but was quickly modified that same year to remove the artist's initials from the reverse.

and 1909-S with and without V.D.B. Of the four varieties, the 1909-S V.D.B. is by far the rarest. Low-grade examples of the date can be found without difficulty, but authentication is a must. The 1909-S V.D.B. cent is probably one of the most counterfeited issues in the U.S. series. High-grade examples are relatively available, with the value closely tied to the amount of original mint red still adhering to the surface. Red, superb MS-67 examples have traded for more than $100,000.

Designed by Victor David Brenner. The obverse depicts a bust of Abraham Lincoln facing right, **IN GOD WE TRUST** above, **LIBERTY** to the left, and the date to the right. The reverse is plain and understated (but impressive), with stylized ears of wheat on either side and a big **ONE CENT** in the middle. A smaller **E PLURIBUS UNUM** appears above the denomination, and **UNITED STATES OF AMERICA** appears below.

HISTORICAL VALUES
Choice Uncirculated

1960: $150	1980: $750	1st ed./2003: $1,500	2nd ed./2005: $2,500	3rd ed./2008: $2,750	4th edition: $2,750

1794 "STARRED REVERSE" LIBERTY CAP LARGE CENT

STANDARDS · **Weight:** 208 grains. **Composition:** Pure copper. **Diameter:** 28 mm. **Edge:** Lettered, ONE HUNDRED FOR A DOLLAR.

RARITY · Rare. Today, fewer than 100 "Starred Reverse" cents are known. The finest is a PCGS AU-50 that sold for $632,500 in the sale of the Walter J. Husak collection. **CERTIFIED POPULATION** · 36

One of the more curious U.S. coins (and a classic rarity) is the 1794 "Starred Reverse" cent, technically known as Sheldon-48, from Dr. William H. Sheldon's *Penny Whimsy*, a book describing all of the large cent varieties from 1793 to 1814. A close look at the back of this fascinating coin reveals tiny stars hidden in the tooth-like border decorations.

Apparently, the engraver of the "Starred Reverse" cent started the die for the back of the coin by stamping a ring of 94 stars near the outer edge. Such a border is unheard of on any U.S. coin issued for circulation, but a precedent exists in the pattern quarter dollar of 1792 (No. 72), which shows a border of 87 tiny stars. In fact, it was once believed that the die for the "Starred Reverse" cent was a leftover die from the 1792 pattern quarter, until someone actually counted the stars!

Raised borders are placed on coins to aid in their stacking and to prevent wear to the field or lower surface of the coin. Without borders, the high points of coins rock against each other, resulting in a precarious stack that falls over easily. A look at the very first U.S. large cents shows the evolution of the borders from plain, raised lips on the 1793 Chain cents, to raised rings of beads on the 1793 Wreath cents, to the heavy denticles on the 1794 cents—all the result of the search for a "perfect" raised border.

Perhaps because the ring of stars was considered unsatisfactory as a border, the engraver completed the die by adding denticles (the tooth-like projections pointing in from the outer edge), some of which hid or obliterated the underlying stars. Most of the surviving examples of the 1794 "Starred Reverse" cent show much wear and/or corrosion, but a collector only needs to see a single star to make a positive attribution of this rarity. As one might expect, the more stars that are visible, the more valuable the coin. Many are also known with porous surfaces, and these result in a substantial discount in value. Although many large-cent specialists prefer coins that have not been certified, the high cost of this issue makes certification highly recommended.

The 1794 "Starred Reverse" large cent is a great coin but was undiscovered or unappreciated for more than 85 years. The legendary dealer Henry Chapman is credited with the discovery of this important variety in the 1870s. The discovered coin was sold by the Chapman brothers in an 1880 auction for the modest sum of $4.25.

While a collector only needs to identify a single star to confirm that his or her Liberty Cap cent is of the "Starred Reverse" variety, more visible stars means a more valuable coin.

Designed by Robert Scot. The obverse features a bust of Liberty facing right, her hair flowing loosely behind her head. A liberty cap and supporting pole appear behind her head. LIBERTY appears above the bust, the date below. The reverse shows the words ONE CENT within a plain wreath, the fraction "1/100" below, and UNITED STATES OF AMERICA surrounding.

HISTORICAL VALUES					
Very Fine					
1960: $1,500	1980: $10,000	1st ed./2003: $75,000	2nd ed./2005: $85,000	3rd ed./2008: $125,000	4th edition: $150,000

1792 BIRCH CENT

STANDARDS • **Weight:** 14.29 grams. **Composition:** Pure copper. **Diameter:** 33 mm. **Edge:** Plain or lettered. **RARITY** • Extremely rare. There are only 12 or 13 examples thought to exist of the four known varieties of the 1792 Birch cent. **CERTIFIED POPULATION** • 4

The three pattern cents made in 1792 included the Birch cent, the silver-center cent (left), and a fusible alloy cent (below) that used the same design as the silver-center variety.

I n 1792, the United States prepared to open its first official mint. Land was purchased, buildings were torn down and erected, machinery was ordered, and a variety of artists began preparing dies for coins.

One such artist, Robert Birch, engraved dies for a large one-cent piece to be made of pure copper. The earliest versions of Birch's cent, known today by a unique piece in white metal, showed Liberty with a much smaller hairdo of curlier hair. Also, on the original version, the back of the coin bore the legend G.W. PT. (for "George Washington—President") in place of the 1/100 fraction, and a smaller ribbon bow. Birch probably changed the design because Washington objected to having his image (or any reference to him) placed on a coin. Birch's final version, as illustrated here, is one of the most popular of all U.S. pattern coins.

According to Mint records, a small purchase of copper was made on September 11, 1792, enough to make between 100 and 200 Birch cents. This is consistent with the present rarity of this piece, which now numbers in the vicinity of a mere handful of examples. Versions are known with edges that are plain or lettered with TO BE ESTEEMED BE USEFUL. The obverse of the Birch cent bears a strong resemblance to the design on the 1792 half disme, suggesting that Birch may have had a hand in that design as well.

Of the three types of 1792 pattern cents (silver center cent, fusible alloy cent, and the Birch cent), the Birch cent matches most closely the standards set forth in the Coinage Act of 1792. Thus, a strong argument can be made that this is the first official U.S. cent; they were struck at the U.S. Mint by Mint employees, on Mint equipment, and made according to official government standards well in advance of the cents of 1793.

Collecting early U.S. coinage is again very popular, as it is now realized that many of these fascinating issues are closely related to the creation of this great nation. Many of our founding fathers were personally involved with the production of these coins. The demand for any early U.S. coin should only increase in years to come.

Collectors should be aware that deceptive electrotype copies exist of the Birch cent. Electrotypes (as they are known in the trade) are high-quality copies made one at a time in a painstaking process that requires the use of a genuine coin. An electrotype consists of two thin copper shells joined together and filled with a lead core. Electrotypes make a dull thud when tapped with a pencil (genuine coins give off a high-pitched ringing sound), and the edge will show a seam where the obverse and reverse shells were joined together. Because of their high quality, electrotypes have a following all their own, but their value is a mere fraction of that of a real coin.

Designed by Robert Birch. The obverse features a bust of Liberty facing right, with her hair flowing behind her. The date 1792 appears below the bust. The encircling legend reads: LIBERTY PARENT OF SCIENCE & INDUSTRY. The reverse features the denomination ONE CENT within a wreath, with the fraction 1/100 just below the ribbon bow. The outer legend reads: UNITED STATES OF AMERICA.

HISTORICAL VALUES					
Very Fine					
1960: $1,500	1980: $35,000	1st ed./2003: $200,000	2nd ed./2005: $240,000	3rd ed./2008: $350,000	4th edition: $500,000

MCMVII (1907) HIGH RELIEF SAINT-GAUDENS DOUBLE EAGLE

STANDARDS · Weight: 33.436 grams. **Composition:** 90% gold, 10% copper. **Net weight:** .96750 oz. pure gold. **Diameter:** 34 mm. **Edge:** Lettered E PLURIBUS UNUM, with the words divided by stars. **RARITY ·** Perhaps 4,000 to 5,000 survive in all grades. Although only 11,500 were struck, many were saved because of the coin's beauty. Most examples seen today are in Mint State, some of which are amazing gems. Well-worn pocket pieces are also seen. Due to the issue's popularity, these coins are expensive compared to their relative rarity. **CERTIFIED POPULATION ·** 8,490

The MCMVII (1907) High Relief double eagle is a masterpiece of the U.S. gold series. The coin has a distinct, sculpted appearance. Nearly all collectors consider it one of the most beautiful coins ever produced. This coin is the circulation version of the MCMVII (1907) Ultra High Relief. Theodore Roosevelt considered the coin designs at the time to be unattractive and without artistic merit, and personally requested that Augustus Saint-Gaudens (a prominent U.S. sculptor of the era) design new eagles and double eagles. After Saint-Gaudens's death in 1907, Mint engraver Charles Barber was ordered to begin striking the High Relief double eagles. President Roosevelt even exclaimed, "Begin the new issue even if it takes you all day to strike one piece."

Although the high-relief design was fabulous from an artistic standpoint, it was impractical for commercial uses. Bankers complained that the coins would not stack properly, and the high-relief design required at least three to five blows from the minting press. The Roman numerals were also too confusing for the U.S. public. Later in 1907, the relief was dramatically lowered and the Roman numerals replaced with Arabic numerals.

There are two distinct varieties of the 1907 High Relief issues: the Wire Rim and Flat Rim. These varieties were not created on purpose, but were the result of different collars used in the minting process. Loose collars resulted in extra metal being forced between the collar and the dies, resulting in a thin wire rim. On some coins, the wire rim is seen on only one side. The Flat Rim coins are considered to be slightly scarcer, but the Wire Rim and Flat Rim varieties are valued about equally in today's markets.

The 1907 High Relief double eagle is one of the most popular and desirable coins ever produced by the U.S. Mint. The High Relief is not an extremely rare coin, but it has for decades been one of the most sought-after U.S. gold coins. The beauty of the sculptural design elevates the issue to the level of fine art. If most collectors could own only one coin, this would probably be the one. The 1907 High Relief is also known in the so-called Proof format. These appear to be special issues with a swirling matte finish, unlike the traditional Matte Proofs, which were struck from 1908 to 1915. At least a hundred are known of this interesting issue.

President Roosevelt greatly admired the 1905 inaugural medal designed for him by Saint-Gaudens. Although the medal was executed by the latter's pupil Adolph Weinman, the distinctive Saint-Gaudens style is unmistakable.

Designed by Augustus Saint-Gaudens. The obverse depicts a standing Liberty draped in Romanesque clothing holding a torch. The reverse features an eagle in flight. Mintage for this issue is 11,500.

HISTORICAL VALUES					
Choice Uncirculated					
1960: $500	1980: $7,500	1st ed./2003: $15,000	2nd ed./2005: $20,000	3rd ed./2008: $25,000	4th edition: $25,000

1870-S LIBERTY SEATED SILVER DOLLAR

STANDARDS · **Weight:** 26.73 grams. **Composition:** 90% silver, 10% copper. **Diameter:** 38 mm. **Edge:** Reeded. **RARITY** · Extremely rare. The estimated population for this date is a mere 12 coins. Most are well circulated and/or accompanied by a problem of one sort or another (test cut, corrosion, cleaning, repaired initials). The finest 1870-S silver dollar is a Mint State example that sold at auction in May 2003 for more than $1 million. **CERTIFIED POPULATION** · 9

Mint records contain no evidence that any 1870-S silver dollars were struck, yet around a dozen examples are known to exist. Each year, the Philadelphia Mint prepared dies for the branch mints. Unfortunately, no records survive of shipments of silver-dollar dies to San Francisco in 1869 or 1870. However, coiner J.B. Harmstead returned two dies without mintmarks in May 1870, anticipating the proper replacements from the Philadelphia Mint. The 1870-S silver dollars were all struck from the same pair of dies, but the mintmark is different from that on any San Francisco Mint dollars of the period. Harmstead may have received some 1870-dated obverse dies. However, without any mintmarked reverses, he may have added his own, thus accounting for the difference in the appearance of the mintmark on the 1870-S silver dollars.

The 1870-S Seated dollar was actually unknown to the numismatic community until one was displayed at an American Numismatic Society exhibit in 1914 by H.O. Granberg, a railroad and banking magnate of the day. For several years, the coin was thought to be unique. Others eventually surfaced, and today the 1870-S silver dollar is one of the most coveted U.S. silver coins.

The origin of the 1870-S silver dollar is closely linked to the building of the San Francisco Mint and the laying of the cornerstone on May 25, 1870. Coins of all denominations struck at the time were prepared for placement in the cornerstone of the new mint in San Francisco. Presumably, one of these still remains in that location. Others were probably struck as mementos, as several of the known coins are well-worn and ill preserved. If the corner-

Portraitist Thomas Sully (1783–1872) produced this sketch, on which Gobrecht based his obverse design for the dollar.

stone of the old Mint were ever found, it would be quite the numismatic discovery.

Designed by Christian Gobrecht. The obverse shows Liberty in a flowing gown, sitting on a rock. Her left hand holds a staff surmounted by a liberty cap; her right hand steadies a shield and holds a band bearing the word LIBERTY. An arc of 13 stars appears around Liberty, and the date appears at the base of the obverse, below the rock. The back shows an eagle with a shield on its chest, an olive branch in its right talon, and a bunch of arrows in its left. The words UNITED STATES OF AMERICA appear above the eagle; the abbreviation ONE DOL. appears below. A scroll with the motto IN GOD WE TRUST hovers above the eagle. The mintmark appears just below the eagle.

HISTORICAL VALUES
Extremely Fine

1960: $15,000	1980: $75,000	1st ed./2003: $200,000	2nd ed./2005: $250,000	3rd ed./2008: $750,000	4th edition: $850,000

1895 MORGAN SILVER DOLLAR

STANDARDS · Weight: 26.7 grams. **Composition:** 90% silver, 10% copper. **Diameter:** 38 mm. **Edge:** Reeded. **RARITY ·** Rare. A surprising number of circulated Proof 1895 silver dollars exist, by some estimates as many as 50 to 75. The author has seen one example that was Extremely Fine condition, but with a clean hole drilled through the top. As "common" as the circulated Proofs are, none have sold for less than $20,000 in recent years. Most examples fall in the PF-62 to PF-64 category. Gems are scarce, and superb examples are extremely rare. A couple of incredibly beautiful PF-68 examples are known. **CERTIFIED POPULATION ·** 896

The 1895 silver dollar is known as the "King of the Morgan dollars" and is usually the last coin that collectors need to complete their sets.

Mint records show that 12,000 1895 dollars were made for circulation and 880 Proofs were made for sale to collectors at a premium. If the mintage figure of 12,000 pieces were correct, the 1895 dollar would be by far the rarest of any Morgan silver dollar (the only other dates that come close are the 1893-S and 1894, both with mintages of 100,000 or more). However, the mintage figure is not correct, making the 1895 silver dollar much rarer than it appears even at first glance. Either the 12,000 figure is an accounting entry for coins of another year (likely 1894) or the 12,000 1895 silver dollars are hidden away somewhere, as no "circulation strike" has ever been seen. The several 1895 dollars that are worn are all believed to be Proofs that escaped into circulation. A true Uncirculated 1895 silver dollar would be one of the greatest finds in numismatic history.

Because of the great demand for this date, prices for 1895 silver dollars are considerably higher than for Proofs of other dates of comparable mintage. For instance, a Gem Proof 1895 dollar trades in the $65,000 to $75,000 range, while Gem Proofs of most other dates sell in the $7,000 to $8,000 range.

Such is the value of popularity!

George T. Morgan, chief engraver of the U.S. Mint from 1917 to 1925, designed many coins but is best known for his Morgan dollar.

Designed by George Morgan. The obverse features a large head of Liberty facing left, wearing a liberty cap banded with the word **LIBERTY** and a wreath of American agricultural produce. E PLURIBUS UNUM appears in an arc around Liberty's head; the date appears below. On either side of the obverse, 13 stars are divided, with seven on the left and six on the right. The reverse features a plain eagle with wings raised and outstretched, holding an olive branch and arrows in its talons. **IN GOD WE TRUST** appears above the eagle in Gothic lettering. A wreath arcs around below the eagle, and the legends **UNITED STATES OF AMERICA** and **ONE DOLLAR** appear in a circular arrangement on the outside of the coin.

HISTORICAL VALUES
Choice Proof

1960: $1,500	1980: $17,500	1st ed./2003: $25,000	2nd ed./2005: $35,000	3rd ed./2008: $55,000	4th edition: $60,000

1854-S PRESENTATION-STRIKE LIBERTY HEAD DOUBLE EAGLE

STANDARDS · **Weight:** 33.436 grams. **Composition:** 90% gold, 10% copper. **Net weight:** .96750 oz pure gold. **Diameter:** 34 mm. **Edge:** Reeded.

RARITY · Only one example is known to exist. The coin resides in the National Numismatic Collection of the Smithsonian Institution. If offered for sale, this coin would probably sell for several million dollars.

CERTIFIED POPULATION · 0

While doing numismatic research at the Smithsonian Institution, we had the privilege of personally examining the trays in the cabinet of the National Numismatic Collection. The coins from the year 1854 are fairly routine until you come to the 1854 double eagle. The coin is an 1854-S and is a deeply mirrored example. It was first noticed in 1951 by Walter Breen and Stuart Mosher (then curator of the collection and editor of *The Numismatist*). The coin is recorded as having been sent to the Mint Cabinet by Superintendent Lewis A. Birdsall. The Mint Cabinet was transferred to the Smithsonian in 1923. The coin has always been categorized as a branch-mint Proof. The surfaces of the coin are prooflike, but without the deep, orange-peel appearance that true Proofs of the era display. It is our opinion that the coin would be more accurately described as a presentation strike. The coin is probably the first coin struck for the year, being a presentation example to recognize the opening of the San Francisco Mint. It is nonetheless an extraordinary coin, and one of the most important double eagles ever struck. This coin was overlooked in the first edition of this book and will undoubtedly rise in fame and prestige in future editions. The ranking of the 1854-S Presentation-Strike double eagle will without doubt rise considerably as well.

The 1854-S double eagle is considered one of the legendary rarities in the National Numismatic Collection, which is housed in the Smithsonian Museum of American History. This outstanding rarity is featured in the rare coin exhibit along with many of the other landmark coins from the collection.

The Smithsonian's Museum of American History opened its rare coin exhibit, which features the treasures of the National Numismatic Collection such as the 1854-S Presentation-Strike Liberty Head double eagle, in 2009.

Designed by James B. Longacre. The obverse features a portrait of Liberty facing left, wearing a coronet and surrounded by 13 stars. The reverse features an outspread eagle and shield design.

HISTORICAL VALUES
Presentation Strike

1960: $25,000	1980: $250,000	1st ed./2003: —	2nd ed./2005: $2,000,000	3rd ed./2008: $4,000,000	4th edition: $5,000,000

1854-O LIBERTY HEAD DOUBLE EAGLE

STANDARDS · **Weight:** 33.436 grams. **Composition:** 90% gold, 10% copper. **Net weight:** .96750 oz. pure gold. **Diameter:** 34 mm. **Edge:** Reeded. **RARITY** · In 1854, 3,250 double eagles were minted in New Orleans. We estimate that only 25 to 30 examples are known in all grades, and there are no known Mint State coins reported. About Uncirculated examples have recently traded for more than $500,000. **CERTIFIED POPULATION** · 31

The 1854-O double eagle is one of the great rarities of the Liberty Head series. The date boasts a tiny mintage of just 3,250 pieces. Most of the double eagles likely were immediately placed into circulation, as today there are no known Mint State examples. The average coin is moderately worn, with scattered bagmarks. Many have been harshly cleaned in the past. Genuine examples of this date exhibit raised die lines on the TY of LIBERTY. A few examples are also seen with minor die defects.

The low mintage of the 1854-O double eagle was a function of shifting priorities more than any other factor. Most of the production at the New Orleans Mint in 1854 was focused on silver coins (half dimes, dimes, quarter dollars, and half dollars) and other gold denominations (quarter eagles, $3 pieces, half eagles, and eagles). The low mintage can also be attributed to the opening of the San Francisco Mint. Gold found in California could now be struck in that state. Thus, the 1854-O double eagle is more of an accidental rarity than a deliberate one. Ironically, yesteryear's low priority at the New Orleans Mint has turned into a top priority with today's collectors.

One of the highlights of the discovery of the SS *Republic* treasure is an outstanding AU-58 example of an 1854-O double eagle. The SS *Republic* featured an example of nearly every Type I double eagle with the exception of an 1856-O, an 1861 Paquet Reverse, and an 1866-S No Motto. This treasure, as well as the coins from the SS *Central America*, have created a tremendous interest in U.S. double eagles. With the recent rise in world gold prices, the denomination will most likely see continued price advancements.

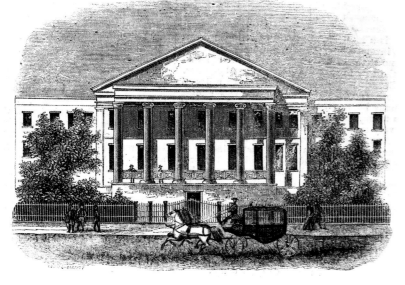

The rarity of the 1854-O double eagle arose due to shifting priorities at the New Orleans Mint (shown above), as well as the opening of the San Francisco Mint.

Designed by James B. Longacre. The obverse features a portrait of Liberty facing left, wearing a coronet, surrounded by 13 stars. The reverse features an outspread eagle and shield design. Mintage for this issue is 3,250 coins.

HISTORICAL VALUES
Extremely Fine

1960: $500	1980: $35,000	1st ed./2003: $75,000	2nd ed./2005: $125,000	3rd ed./2008: $300,000	4th edition: $350,000

1798 "SMALL EAGLE" CAPPED BUST HALF EAGLE

STANDARDS · Weight: 8.75 grams. **Composition:** 92% gold, 8% copper. **Diameter:** 25 mm. **Edge:** Reeded. **RARITY ·** Of the eight examples known, three are in museums. The most recent discovery surfaced a few years ago and was purchased by John Dannreuther of Memphis, Tennessee. More information on this coin and many others can be found in the excellent and highly recommended reference by Dannreuther and Harry W. Bass Jr., *Early U.S. Gold Coin Varieties, 1795–1834*. **CERTIFIED POPULATION · 4**

Although the Coinage Act of 1792 provided for a gold half eagle of 135 grains (8.75 grams) and other denominations, no gold coins were produced until 1795. Around May of that year, Mint director David Rittenhouse assigned engraver Robert Scot the task of producing half eagle dies. Rittenhouse left the Mint at the end of June and was replaced by Henry William DeSaussure, who ordered that gold coin production should begin. When the half eagle debuted, it featured a design known today (per terms mostly devised by Kenneth Bressett for use in *A Guide Book of United States Coins*) as Capped Bust Right, Small Eagle Reverse.

The obverse depicts Liberty facing right wearing a cap with the word LIBERTY above and the date below. The small-eagle reverse motif was apparently taken from an ancient Roman onyx cameo that depicted an eagle perched on a palm branch, its wings outstretched, holding aloft a circular wreath in his beak. The inscription UNITED STATES OF AMERICA is featured at the periphery. Strangely, there is no indication of denomination on the piece, but then again, most 18th-century merchants weighed all coins and made value decisions based on their own findings.

This design lasted until 1798. The Heraldic Reverse was also struck during this time period. Why so many designs and die combinations were used during such a short time is a mystery. It has been suggested that Mint operations were chaotic in the early years of operation. Regardless of the reason, many great rarities were created. The 1798 Small Eagle Reverse half eagle is a classic American rarity.

Author Jeff Garrett handled an example of this great rarity in the mid-1980s. The coin had been advertised in *Coin World* magazine. A gentleman called one day to inquire about the availability of the piece and to get a price quote. After hearing the price, he

hung up. A few days later, the mystery man arrived with the asking price in cash. Anonymity was requested, and the coin was sold and has not been seen since.

In addition to being the first director of the U.S. Mint, David Rittenhouse was a noted architect, inventor, and mathematician.

Designed by Robert Scot. The obverse depicts Liberty wearing a soft liberty cap and facing right. The stars are placed around the obverse rim, and the date is located at the base of the obverse. The small eagle reverse shows an outstretched eagle with wings spread, holding a circular wreath in its beak.

HISTORICAL VALUES
Extremely Fine

1960: $3,500	1980: $75,000	1st ed./2003: $250,000	2nd ed./2005: $275,000	3rd ed./2008: $400,000	4th edition: $500,000

1838 PROOF LIBERTY HEAD EAGLE

STANDARDS · **Weight:** 16.718 grams. **Composition:** 90% gold, 10% copper. **Net weight:** .48375 oz. pure gold. **Diameter:** 27 mm. **Edge:** Reeded.

RARITY · Mintage for this issue is four Proofs. Today three Proof examples of this date are known. One is in the National Numismatic Collection of the Smithsonian Institution and the remaining two are now in private collections. **CERTIFIED POPULATION** · 3

Congress originally established a relative value of silver to gold at 15 to 1. This proved inaccurate, as the true marketplace value was closer to 16 to 1. The result was that early U.S. gold coinage could be melted and sold for more than its face value in terms of silver, which is why so many early issues are rare today. In 1804, the Mint suspended production of the $10 denomination. The Coinage Act of 1834, reduced the weight of gold coins, thereby eliminating the incentive to melt gold coinage. However, for the time being, only $2.50 and $5 gold coins were minted. In July of 1838, the secretary of the Treasury ordered the resumption of production for the $10 denomination. Christian Gobrecht prepared new dies, and coinage began late that year. On December 6, 1838, four specimen "Proofs" were delivered to the secretary of the Treasury. Today, three examples of this incredibly beautiful coin still survive. One piece was placed in the Mint Cabinet and now resides in the Smithsonian Institution as part of the National Numismatic Collection. A second specimen found its way into the collection of the infamous King Farouk and was sold in the 1954 palace sale along with three other coins for only $590. That coin was purchased by John Jay Pittman, who considered it his premier U.S. Proof gold coin. When his collection was sold at auction in 1998, the 1838 Proof eagle alone realized $550,000. The third example, a Gem Proof, resides in a private collection.

The 1838 Proof eagle is one of the premier rarities of the U.S. series. Besides the low mintage, the design for the eagle was modified slightly in 1840—thus creating a scarce two-year type—and the coin is also the first issue of a very long-lived series (struck from 1838 to 1907).

Of course, the 1838 is just one of many truly rare coins of the series. Many are especially difficult to locate in the higher states of preservation, as eagles were the workhorse denomination of U.S. gold and are usually found well-worn. Therefore, high-grade examples of the very early dates of the series are seldom seen and command significant premiums.

Given that early examples of U.S. coinage in Proof are extremely rare and desirable—not to mention the 1838 is one of the greatest first-year issues created—the desirability of this issue cannot be overstated.

Designed by Christian Gobrecht. The obverse features a portrait of Liberty with her head facing left surrounded by 13 stars. The reverse has an eagle with wings spread clutching arrows and an olive branch.

HISTORICAL VALUES
Choice Proof

1960: $5,000	1980: $100,000	1st ed./2003: $500,000	2nd ed./2005: $600,000	3rd ed./2008: $1,250,000	4th edition: $1,500,000

1849-C "OPEN WREATH" LIBERTY HEAD GOLD DOLLAR

STANDARDS · **Weight:** 1.672 grams. **Composition:** 90% gold, 10% copper. **Diameter:** 13 mm. **Edge:** Finely reeded. **RARITY** · Four specimens are known. Interestingly, one of these pieces has been described in catalogs all the way from Very Fine to Mint State! The finest example is a prooflike MS-63 that only came to light a few years ago, and sold in July 2004 for $690,000, setting a record price for a gold dollar and perhaps the highest price per ounce for a single piece of gold! **CERTIFIED POPULATION** · 4

The "Close Wreath" reverse, on which the ends of the wreath are closer to the numeral.

The 1849-C "Open Wreath" gold dollar is the undisputed king of the gold dollars, if not one of the scarcest U.S. gold coins. Not only is it an extreme rarity, but it is also a coin veiled in mystery. After gold was found in the hills of North Carolina, a congressional act was passed in 1835 allowing for the establishment of a mint in Charlotte. Three years later, the Charlotte Mint opened, producing quarter eagles and half eagles exclusively. In 1849, Congress passed another act mandating that a $1 coin be struck in gold. The dies for the gold dollar were made in Philadelphia and then sent to Charlotte. Two reverse dies were prepared: one with a closed wreath and a second featuring an open wreath. Although both dies were delivered to Charlotte, the majority of the gold dollars struck were from the "Close Wreath" die. Perhaps the "Open Wreath" die was used for a short trial run.

Unlike most of the coins documented in this book, the 1849-C Open Wreath remained unknown to numismatists for decades after it was struck. The first specimen came to light in 1933, when prominent Baltimore collector Waldo Newcomer offered a specimen for sale. After it resided in another collection for about 10 years, the coin was acquired by Dallas numismatist Robert Schermerhorn. Soon after he bought the discovery piece, a second specimen surfaced. W.W. McReynolds, a jeweler who lived in Schermerhorn's neighborhood, found the new coin. A few numismatists felt the coincidence was uncanny, suspecting that McReynolds copied Schermerhorn's coin. However, research has proven that the controversial piece is genuine. In all likelihood, McReynolds stumbled upon the coin in a piece of jewelry, as it exhibits noticeable mounting marks. Schermerhorn consigned his specimen to the 1956 American Numismatic Association auction, where it realized a then-remarkable $6,000. Since then, the coin has changed hands many times, selling privately for

six figures multiple times. In addition to the two pieces mentioned earlier, a third and fourth specimen have come to light. Even with the total population reaching four, this variety still commands incredible sums of money at auction.

Designed by James B. Longacre. The obverse features an emblematic figure of Liberty wearing a coronet. The word LIBERTY is inscribed on the headband. 13 stars are engraved at the periphery. The reverse shows the legend UNITED STATES OF AMERICA engraved at the perimeter. Inside is a wreath, in the center of which is the denomination— 1 DOLLAR—and the date.

HISTORICAL VALUES
Extremely Fine

1960: $7,500	1980: $75,000	1st ed./2003: $275,000	2nd ed./2005: $325,000	3rd ed./2008: $375,000	4th edition: $450,000

1787 FUGIO CENT

STANDARDS · **Weight:** Varies from 9.72 to 10.37 grams. **Composition:** Pure copper. **Diameter:** Varies from 28 to 29 mm. **Edge:** Plain. **RARITY** · Common (although some varieties are extremely rare). Many are struck on imperfect planchets. High-grade examples are rarely seen. **CERTIFIED POPULATION** · 2,950

The Fugio cent is the first officially sanctioned U.S. coin struck in quantities large enough that collectors can afford to collect it. Much of the charm of these coins comes from the interesting design elements, some of which are attributed to the plain-speaking U.S. statesman Benjamin Franklin. The Fugio cents are very similar in appearance to the 1776 Continental dollar (No. 10).

Following the short-lived coinage of 1776 pewter dollars, the successors to the Continental Congress tried a different approach in 1787. This time, rather than try to create its own mint, Congress contracted with a private coiner to strike Fugio cents. The deal was advantageous for both parties: the government would loan the coiner more than 71,000 pounds of copper at a good price to get him started, and he would repay the loan with the coins he made. The winner of the contract was required to strike 345 tons of coins and would receive a percentage of anything he coined.

Through bribery and political machinations, James Jarvis (who had no mint, no machinery, and no employees versed in coining) won the contract. Jarvis immediately purchased a controlling interest in the company that also held the contract to produce copper coins for the state of Connecticut. To obtain additional copper to fulfill the contracts, Jarvis left for England. While he was gone, his representatives struck roughly 9,000 pounds of Fugio cents, but appropriated the rest of the government's copper to make Connecticut coppers. When Jarvis failed to obtain the necessary copper, he defaulted on the contract, never paying a cent for the rest of the metal loaned to him by the U.S. government.

According to some historians, Fugio cents were not received very well at the time they were struck. The public was wary of the new and unusual design, preferring instead the old copper coins then in circulation. However, it is likely that most—but not all—served the intended purpose. Somehow a small hoard of Fugio cents (reportedly a keg of approximately 5,000 pieces) ended up in

Benjamin Franklin's role in the creation of the Fugio cent makes it particularly significant—and desirable.

the vaults of the Bank of New York. They were released slowly over the years, even as late as the 1950s, although some remain today. A few years ago, the colonial-coin expert Tony Terranova examined them and filed a report for interested numismatists. Were it not for this hoard, Uncirculated Fugio cents would be very rare and expensive.

Today, the Fugio cent is one of the most popular and desirable of all U.S. coins. It is also one of the most affordable coins on the 100 Greatest U.S. Coins list.

Designed by James Jarvis, copying designs from the 1776 Continental Currency pewter dollar. The obverse shows a sundial with a sun and rays above. The motto **MIND YOUR BUSINESS** appears beneath the base of the sundial. **FUGIO** appears on the left side of the coin, the date 1787 on the right. The reverse shows a never-ending chain of 13 links surrounding a circular label with **WE ARE ONE** in the center and **UNITED STATES** surrounding.

HISTORICAL VALUES					
Choice Uncirculated					
1960: $50	1980: $500	1st ed./2003: $2,500	2nd ed./2005: $3,500	3rd ed./2008: $5,000	4th edition: $6,500

1907 "ROLLED EDGE" INDIAN HEAD EAGLE

STANDARDS · **Weight:** 16.718 grams. **Composition:** 90% gold, 10% copper. **Net weight:** .48375 oz. pure gold. **Diameter:** 27 mm. **Edge:** Displays 46 stars, representing the states in the Union at the time. **RARITY** · It is estimated that 35 to 40 examples remain in various Mint State grades. Although a few circulated coins are known, most survivors seen are brilliant gems. Only two certified Proof examples are currently known to exist. An NGC PF-67 example sold at auction in 2011 for $2,185,000. **CERTIFIED POPULATION** · 77

Saint-Gaudens created this head study for the Sherman Victory monument, later modifying it and adding an Indian headdress to become the design for the Indian Head eagle. Although commonly referred to as the "Indian Head," the design actually depicts Liberty wearing an Indian headdress.

To improve the design of U.S. coins, President Theodore Roosevelt personally sought the efforts of famed sculptor Augustus Saint-Gaudens. His works include some of the most important sculptures of the late 19th century. One of his most visible works is the Sherman Victory monument, a statuary group which stands in Grand Army Plaza at the southeast corner of New York's Central Park.

Roosevelt was a great admirer of classic Greek coins and wanted U.S. coinages of similar appearance. The president especially liked the high relief of the ancient coinage. Because of the difficulty in mass-producing high-relief coinage, Saint-Gaudens restricted his design work to the eagle and double eagle. The artist preferred the Indian Head design for the double eagle coinage. One pattern coin of that design was struck at the artist's request, but eventually, the Indian Head design was chosen for the eagle, with examples of the new design struck in late 1907.

The first variety of the 1907 Indian Head eagle produced is the so-called "Wire Rim, With Period." Reportedly, 500 were struck, and this design type is considered experimental per conventional wisdom, although research has revealed that, in fact, these were made as delicacies to be distributed by Mint officials, Treasury Department officials, and others. To acquire one at the time of issue, you needed a "connection"! Charles Barber, the chief engraver of the U.S. Mint, changed the design by giving the coin broad, raised borders, creating the so-called "Rolled Edge" type. According to Mint director Frank Leach, the Mint struck 31,500 pieces of this modified design on the coining press, and 50 examples were struck on the medal press. The large mintage is an important aspect of the 1907 "Rolled Edge" eagle. This clearly demonstrates that this issue was made for circulation and was not experimental. Although Charles Barber was happy with the new design, superintendent of the Mint John Landis was not. He preferred the final design, now known as the 1907 "No Periods." With

the exception of 40 to 50 coins (which, again, were privately distributed by Mint and Treasury officials), all of the "Rolled Edge" coins were melted. Most surviving examples are brilliant gems. Several circulated coins are known, probably those that were saved as pocket-piece souvenirs. Two examples have been certified as Proof, one or both of which is possibly a survivor of the 50 examples that were struck on the medal press as related by Director Leach. The 1907 "Rolled Edge" Indian Head eagle is one of the most highly desired U.S. coins struck in the 20th century.

Designed by Augustus Saint-Gaudens. The obverse displays the head of Liberty wearing an Indian headdress with 13 stars above the portrait. The reverse features a magnificent eagle perched on a bundle of arrows. Mintage for the issue is 31,550, but nearly all were melted.

HISTORICAL VALUES					
Choice Uncirculated					
1960: $3,500	1980: $40,000	1st ed./2003: $85,000	2nd ed./2005: $125,000	3rd ed./2008: $175,000	4th edition: $225,000

1893-S MORGAN SILVER DOLLAR

STANDARDS · **Weight:** 26.7 grams. **Composition:** 90% silver, 10% copper. **Diameter:** 38 mm. **Edge:** Reeded. **RARITY** · Rare. Only 100,000 1893-S silver dollars were struck for circulation. Uncirculated examples are very rare, although a handful of gems are known, and at least two superb pieces have appeared on the market. The finest seen by the author has been the Eliasberg specimen, which sold for $357,500 in 1988, a record for any Morgan dollar at the time. **CERTIFIED POPULATION** · 8,014

The 1893-S silver dollar has the lowest mintage of any of the Morgan dollars issued between 1878 and 1921, making it one of the rarest and most valuable coins in the series. In fact, the 1893-S silver dollar is the most valuable of any of the dates made for circulation. The only other date that is more valuable is the 1895, a date that is believed to have been issued only as a Proof. The Morgan dollar, because of its large size and silver content, is perhaps the most popular series of U.S. coins ever produced. Because so many people are familiar with the rarity of the 1893-S silver dollar and because so many people still need the coin to complete their set, we feel it deserves a place in the pantheon of the 100 Greatest U.S. Coins.

The very low mintage of the 1893-S Morgan dollar is a direct result of the panic of 1893. The country faced an economic crisis that caused the loss of more than four million jobs and conditions not seen again until the Great Depression of the 1930s. An imbalance in the value of gold and silver also was a contributing factor to the low mintage. Of the 100,000 coins struck, many undoubtedly were melted under the terms of the 1918 Pittman Act. Of the known 1893-S dollars seen today, most are heavily worn, and Mint State examples are very rare and desirable.

As with any rare coin, authenticity is always a concern. All 1893-S Morgan dollars were struck from a single die pairing. Genuine 1893-S silver dollars display a diagonal die scratch in the top of the T in LIBERTY. This diagnostic can be seen even on very low-grade examples.

In the midst of the Panic of 1893, President Grover Cleveland lobbied Congress for a repeal of the coinage provisions of the Sherman Silver Purchase Act, which resulted in much lower mintages of silver coins like the Morgan dollar.

Designed by George Morgan. The obverse features a large head of Liberty facing left, wearing a liberty cap banded with the word LIBERTY and a wreath of American agricultural produce. E PLURIBUS UNUM appears in an arc around Liberty's head; the date appears below. On either side of the obverse, 13 stars are divided, seven on the left and six on the right. The reverse features a plain eagle with wings raised and outstretched, holding an olive branch and arrows in its talons. IN GOD WE TRUST appears above the eagle in script. A wreath arcs around below the eagle and the legends UNITED STATES OF AMERICA and ONE DOLLAR appear in a circular arrangement on the outside of the coin. The mintmark can be seen just below the bow of the wreath on the reverse.

HISTORICAL VALUES
Choice Uncirculated

1960: $2,500	1980: $35,000	1st ed./2003: $125,000	2nd ed./2005: $135,000	3rd ed./2008: $150,000	4th edition: $175,000

1861-D INDIAN PRINCESS HEAD GOLD DOLLAR

STANDARDS · **Weight:** 1.672 grams. **Composition:** 90% gold, 10% copper. **Diameter:** 15 mm. **Edge:** Finely reeded. **RARITY** · Most researchers agree that between 50 and 60 examples of the 1861-D gold dollar have survived. Many are found well-worn, and some have traces of having been mounted for use as jewelry, probably as keepsakes because of their historical importance. A small number of very choice examples are known as well. **CERTIFIED POPULATION** · 88

The 1861-D is the second-rarest gold dollar, superseded only by the 1849-C Open Wreath. Though it is an undeniably scarce coin, its primary claim to fame is that it was struck under Confederate control. The same Congressional Act of 1835 that created the Charlotte Mint also established the Dahlonega Mint. Like its Charlotte counterpart, the Dahlonega Mint opened in 1838, striking only quarter eagles and half eagles. Though it was fairly prosperous in the 1840s and 1850s, the future of the Dahlonega Mint became uncertain in 1861. After the Confederacy took over the mint in April of that year, director George Kellogg resigned and turned the facility over to the Confederate States of America. Using what limited bullion remained, Rebel forces struck approximately 1,000 to 1,500 gold dollars in May of 1861.

The Rebel minters were obviously inexperienced. The quality of the coins they struck was poor, as the strike was incomplete and the planchets were sloppily prepared. While most of the coins they struck were released into circulation, a small quantity was likely retained by the Rebels. This would account for the relatively high number of Mint State survivors; almost all other Dahlonega gold dollars of 1861 are found well-worn and battered from use. In total, approximately 50 to 60 examples of the original mintage struck are known. Although the Dahlonega Mint also struck half eagles in 1861, these were probably minted early in the year under the auspices of Kellogg. The $1 coins, conversely, were clearly produced by Rebels after the Union employees fled. This makes the 1861-D gold dollar unique as the only U.S. coin struck by Rebels for which no federal counterpart exists (in contrast, some 1861-O silver half dollars and some 1861-C half eagles were struck under federal auspices, others after the mints fell into the hands of the Confederacy).

The 1861-D gold dollar has been a favorite among collectors since the late 19th century. When the denomination was discontinued in 1889, it became popular to try to form complete sets. As numismatists began to collect the series, the 1861-D emerged as a challenging coin to acquire. When a specimen did appear at auction, bidding was always fierce and competitive. While the 1861-D gold dollar is not the most valuable coin discussed in this text, its connection to the Confederacy makes it one of the most historically significant.

The Dahlonega Mint building is shown here circa 1877, by which time it had become the main building of North Georgia Agricultural College.

Designed by James B. Longacre. The obverse features a head of Liberty wearing a feathered headdress. The word LIBERTY is inscribed on the headband. The legend UNITED STATES OF AMERICA is engraved at the perimeter. The reverse features the denomination 1 DOLLAR, and a wreath of corn and grain encircles the date.

HISTORICAL VALUES
Uncirculated

1960: $2,000	1980: $15,000	1st ed./2003: $35,000	2nd ed./2005: $40,000	3rd ed./2008: $75,000	4th edition: $85,000

1792 SILVER-CENTER CENT

STANDARDS · **Weight:** 4.666 grams. **Composition:** Pure copper with a small plug of silver. **Diameter:** 23 mm. **Edge:** Reeded. **RARITY** · Extremely rare. Only about a dozen examples are known, two of which are permanently impounded in museum collections. **CERTIFIED POPULATION** · 15

The 1792 silver-center cent is extremely rare and represents the first bimetallic coin produced by the U.S. government. The 1792 silver-center cent was a pattern piece, struck to test both the new design and the unusual two-part alloy in anticipation of full production of cents in 1793. Historically, the 1792 silver-center cent is very important, as it was the first coin struck in the Philadelphia Mint.

In 1792, the public's perception of coins was much different from what it is today. Then, if a coin did not contain its full value in metal, merchants refused to accept it in payment or discounted it heavily. This was especially true for gold and silver coins, but copper coins were also subject to the same demands. Unfortunately, one cent of pure copper in 1792 translated into a very large and heavy coin. To reduce the size of the cent, the Mint considered adding a small amount of silver to replace a lot of the copper. In one version, the copper and silver were melted and mixed together, but it was impossible to tell by looking at the coin whether it contained any silver at all. Thus, counterfeiters could have made a lot of money simply by leaving the silver out of the mixture and making their copies out of pure copper.

To solve the problem, chief coiner Henry Voigt advocated placing a small plug of silver in the middle of a copper coin, bringing the value up to one cent. A small hole was drilled in the center of a copper blank, a plug of silver was inserted, and the coin was struck, flattening out the silver plug so that it filled the hole completely. While the concept was ingenious, the technique was inefficient and unsuitable for mass production. In the end, the Mint officials decided to make the one-cent piece out of pure copper.

The lore of the 1792 silver-center cent increased with the discovery of some interesting examples. In 1911, while the original U.S. Mint building was being demolished, workmen found some old copper planchets (blanks) with holes drilled through the centers. These were the same size as the 1792 silver-center cents and, most

Thomas Jefferson, then secretary of state, presented President Washington with the first silver-center pattern cents.

likely, the intent was to turn them into coins with the addition of a silver plug. Then, in 1994, a struck silver-center cent was discovered without the silver plug and with no traces of a plug ever having been inserted, although there was a hole in the proper position.

Designs attributed to Henry Voigt. The obverse shows a head of Liberty facing right, her disheveled hair falling loosely behind her. The date appears beneath the bust. The encircling legend reads: LIBERTY PARENT OF SCIENCE & INDUST (INDUST stands for "Industry"). The same legend is found on other 1792 pattern coins, including the Birch cent, the half disme, and disme. The reverse shows the words ONE CENT within a wreath. The fraction 1/100 appears beneath the bow of the wreath. UNITED STATES OF AMERICA makes up the outer legend.

HISTORICAL VALUES
Very Fine

1960: $1,500	1980: $25,000	1st ed./2003: $85,000	2nd ed./2005: $150,000	3rd ed./2008: $250,000	4th edition: $300,000

1933 INDIAN HEAD EAGLE

STANDARDS · **Weight:** 16.718 grams. **Composition:** 90% gold, 10% copper. **Net weight:** .48375 oz. pure gold. **Diameter:** 27 mm. **Edge:** Displays 48 stars, representing the number of states in the Union at the time.
RARITY · As a result of the presidential order, nearly the entire mintage of 1933 eagles was melted. It is estimated that only 25 to 30 examples are known today. Most are in Mint State condition and were surely obtained directly from the Mint. A few gem specimens are known to exist. The finest certified example (MS-66) sold at auction in October 2004 for more than $700,000. **CERTIFIED POPULATION** · 36

The Philadelphia Mint struck 312,500 examples of the 1933 eagle. On March 6, 1933, however, President Franklin D. Roosevelt issued an order banning the private ownership of gold and marking the end of gold-coin production in the United States. In response to the banking crisis in the United States and in an attempt to stimulate price and wage increases, the president eventually removed all gold coinage from the economy. Gold coinage had been produced on a nearly uninterrupted basis since 1795, though there were long periods of time, including 1821 to 1834 and 1861 to 1878, when gold coins were not seen in general circulation. Thus, 1933 became the last year for nearly 50 years that gold coins were produced in the United States. Eagles and double eagles minted in Philadelphia constituted the only gold coinage for the year. Until very recently, the 1933 eagle was the only gold coin struck that year which, according to a position later taken by the Treasury Department, was legal to own. Currently, the U.S. government has declared only one 1933 double eagle legal to own (see the story of the 1933 double eagle, No. 4 on the list, on page 16). The year 1933 is historically important in U.S. coinage, and the 1933 eagle is a fascinating survivor of the era.

The original mintage of the 1933 eagle was 312,500 pieces, well ahead of more than half the dates in the series, all of which are readily available and affordable today. However, once Roosevelt's order came down, virtually the entire stock of 1933 eagles was destroyed, eventually being converted back into bullion and becoming a part of the United States' huge gold reserve (think Fort Knox). Thus, a date that might once have been common and pedestrian is now a great rarity and one of the 100 Greatest U.S. Coins!

As desirable as the 1933 eagle is, it is hard to imagine that so many of the issue were simply melted into bullion. Many great coins in the U.S. series are rare today not because few were minted, but because most were just destroyed. Quite a few, such as the 1964 Peace dollar, are unknown now because every single example ended up in the melting pot. Even today many great errors and experimental coins are routinely destroyed.

With Executive Order 6102, President Franklin D. Roosevelt criminalized the possession of monetary gold and set in motion the melting of many existing gold coins, which resulted in the rarity of coins such as the 1933 eagle.

Designed by Augustus Saint-Gaudens. The obverse displays the head of Liberty wearing an Indian headdress with 13 stars above the portrait. The reverse features a magnificent eagle perched on a bundle of arrows. Mintage for the issue is 312,500, but nearly all were melted.

HISTORICAL VALUES
Choice Uncirculated

1960: $2,500	1980: $75,000	1st ed./2003: $150,000	2nd ed./2005: $250,000	3rd ed./2008: $350,000	4th edition: $450,000

1815 CAPPED HEAD HALF EAGLE

STANDARDS · **Weight:** 8.75 grams. **Composition:** 92% gold, 8% silver. **Diameter:** 25 mm. **Edge:** Reeded. **RARITY** · This coin is one of those venerated rarities that only change hands when great collections are sold. Many of the most highly celebrated collections sold over the last century have lacked this important coin—even the impressive Dunham Collection. Approximately 12 coins can be pedigreed with certainty, although the possibility remains that an additional coin or two still exist. **CERTIFIED POPULATION** · 7

John Reich also designed the 1801 Thomas Jefferson Peace medal, the reverse of which was adapted in 2004 for the Westward Journey Nickel Series™.

In the early 19th century, large U.S. gold coins were not in great demand by the general public. Since the average merchant or citizen rarely handled such grand amounts of money, there was rarely a need for large denominations. As official records indicate, there were three gold deposits at the Mint in 1815: one on June 24 from a Mr. Thomas Parker, a second on October 30 from the Bank of Pennsylvania, and a holding of earlier-dated gold still at the Mint. These three deposits were melted together, and portions of it were struck into exactly 635 half eagles. Interestingly, there was more than $3,600 worth of gold sitting in the Mint ready to be converted into coin the next year, but a fire at the Mint on January 11, 1816, damaged some rolling and cutting equipment, which precluded further production for a time.

Relatively few of the original 635 specimens minted have survived. It is estimated that a dozen coins are currently known, many of which were likely pulled from circulation long ago. Indeed, the average survival rate for an early U.S. gold coin is less than 2 percent, and more than half of the existing pieces show no wear or only minimal circulation.

The 1815 half eagle is a tried and true classic—and in the 19th century, before mintmarks were generally collected and before the true rarity of the 1822 half eagle was known, the 1815 was the most famous of all U.S. gold coins, with no close competition! This is an interesting illustration of the changing perceptions and popularity trends over the years.

The 1815 half eagle has been long considered very rare. In 1859, Dr. Montroville W. Dickeson wrote in his book *The American Numis-* *matic Manual*, "The Mint Report gives a coinage of 635 pieces for the year. We have never met one of them." That is quite a statement given that his work was the first substantial study of U.S. coinage.

Designed by John Reich. The obverse features a large portrait of Liberty surrounded by 13 stars with the date below. The reverse depicts an eagle with spread wings, holding an olive branch and arrows. Surrounding the eagle are the inscriptions UNITED STATES OF AMERICA and 5 D., with the motto E PLURIBUS UNUM above the eagle's head.

HISTORICAL VALUES					
Extremely Fine					
1960: $2,500	1980: $45,000	1st ed./2003: $100,000	2nd ed./2005: $125,000	3rd ed./2008: $200,000	4th edition: $250,000

1916 STANDING LIBERTY QUARTER DOLLAR

STANDARDS · **Weight:** 6.25 grams. **Composition:** 90% silver, 10% copper. **Diameter:** 24.3 mm. **Edge:** Reeded. **RARITY** · There were 52,000 struck for circulation. A few hundred Uncirculated examples are known, most of which fall into the MS-62 to MS-64 grade levels. Above MS-65, the 1916 Standing Liberty quarter dollar becomes extremely rare; superb pieces are virtually nonexistent. The 1916 Standing Liberty quarter has become very popular as one of the most affordable issues on the 100 Greatest U.S. Coins list. **CERTIFIED POPULATION** · 2,508

In 1916, Hermon MacNeil redesigned the quarter dollar as part of an ongoing effort begun in 1905 by then-president Theodore Roosevelt to bring a fresh look to all U.S. coins. Unfortunately, Mac-Neil's look was a bit *too* fresh; his vision included a partially nude Liberty, a first on any U.S. coin struck for circulation. MacNeil's risqué design was modified in 1917, when Liberty was given a chaste coat of mail with which to cover herself. Early conventional wisdom was that the cover-up was due to a prudish outcry against nudity. Today, however, it is thought that the change was made to depict Liberty ready for defense or war—World War I had been raging in Europe since August 1914.

The redesign of the quarter dollar should not have taken place until 1917, due to a federal law making it illegal to change coinage designs more than once every 25 years. The Barber quarter dollar debuted in 1892 and was slated for retirement no earlier than the end of 1916. However, the decision was made to implement MacNeil's new design at the end of 1916, when 52,000 examples were struck for circulation. Little or no notice was given that quarter dollars of the new design had been struck, and before anyone knew it, virtually the entire mintage was released into circulation. As a result, Uncirculated examples of the 1916 Standing Liberty quarter dollar are very scarce today.

Having itself already "broken" the law prohibiting designs changes more than once every 25 years, the Standing Liberty quarter dollar fell victim to its own set of special circumstances. In 1932, a quarter dollar commemorating the 200th anniversary of the birth of George Washington replaced the design, supposedly for one year only. Unfortunately, the new Washington quarter dollar was so popular that it was continued as a regular-issue coin, thereby completely replacing the Standing Liberty design after only 15 years!

Hermon MacNeil's original design for the Standing Liberty quarter only appeared on coins dated 1916, as the design was modified before the following year's coins were struck.

Designed by Hermon MacNeil. The obverse shows a full-length view of a partially nude Liberty in a flowing gown. She holds a shield in her left hand and an olive branch in her right and appears to be walking through some sort of gate emblazoned with IN GOD WE TRUST and stars. The word LIBERTY appears in an arc at the top of the obverse, and the date appears beneath Liberty's feet. The reverse shows an eagle in flight. The legends UNITED STATES OF AMERICA and E PLURIBUS UNUM appear above the eagle; QUARTER DOLLAR appears beneath. On the reverse, 13 stars are divided, with seven to the left of the eagle and six to the right.

HISTORICAL VALUES

Choice Uncirculated

1960: $750	1980: $2,500	1st ed./2003: $7,500	2nd ed./2005: $20,000	3rd ed./2008: $25,000	4th edition: $30,000

1844-O PROOF LIBERTY HEAD HALF EAGLE AND EAGLE

STANDARDS, HALF EAGLE · **Weight:** 8.359 grams. **Composition:** 90% gold, 10% copper. **Net weight:** .24287 oz. pure gold. **Diameter:** 21.6 mm. **Edge:** Reeded. **STANDARDS, EAGLE** · **Weight:** 16.718 grams. **Composition:** 90% gold, 10% copper. **Net weight:** .48375 oz. pure gold. **Diameter:** 27 mm. **Edge:** Reeded. **RARITY** · These incredibly rare coins were virtually unknown to the collecting community until the early 1990s. Today, only one coin each is known to exist, and it is virtually certain that no others will surface. Each of the known coins is in Choice Proof condition. **CERTIFIED POPULATION** · 1 of each

These coins' first public appearance was in the 1890 sale of Lorin G. Parmelee's collection. Both an 1844-O half eagle and an 1844-O eagle Proof were sold at the same sale. In the Parmelee auction, the $10 piece was cataloged as "Eagle: O mint sharp and perfect Proof: as it is allowable to strike Proofs only at the Philadelphia Mint, it would seem that this lot and the following (the Proof 1844-O $5 gold half eagle) must be extremely rare." The buyer of both coins was William Woodin at $16 and $9.50, respectively. The coins later appeared in Thomas L. Elder's sale of Woodin's Collection in 1911.

According to his journal entry number 57068, Virgil Brand purchased the 1844-O Proof eagle for $50 in 1911. After his death, the Brand Collection was broken up over a period of many years, and the coin did not surface for some time.

For many years, the rumored existence of the 1844-O Proof eagle only added to its mystique. The late Texas dealer Mike Brownlee heard about the coin in the 1950s while working for the legendary B. Max Mehl. He searched for the coin his entire numismatic life. His search ended in 1994 when he was finally able to purchase the 1844-O Proof eagle for an undisclosed amount. The last auction appearance of the 1844-O Proof half eagle was in the sale of the King Farouk collection. Abe Kosoff sold the coin in 1959, and it now resides in a private collection.

Why the Proof 1844-O half eagle and eagle were struck in the first place is the real mystery. It is possible the coins were struck for a dignitary of this country or some foreign head of state visiting the New Orleans Mint. Possibly a presentation set of coins was made for the outgoing Southern president John Tyler or for the incoming Southern president James K. Polk. Perhaps someday researchers will solve the puzzle of these two incredible coins.

Recent years have seen an incredible interest in "Southern gold," and these two rarities are probably the most desirable coins of the genre. Proof U.S. gold coins are some of the most highly sought-after and desirable coins ever produced. A branch-mint Proof gold coin is virtually off the charts.

The New Orleans Mint building now houses the Louisiana State Museum. Although damaged by Hurricane Katrina, it reopened in 2007.

Designed by Christian Gobrecht. The obverse portrays Liberty with a coronet facing left, surrounded by 13 stars. The reverse features an eagle with spread wings clutching arrows and an olive branch. Mintage is thought to be only one of each coin.

HISTORICAL VALUES					
Half Eagle, Choice Proof					
1960: $2,500	1980: $75,000	1st ed./2003: $850,000	2nd ed./2005: $850,000	3rd ed./2008: $1,250,000	4th edition: $1,500,000
Eagle, Choice Proof					
1960: $2,500	1980: $75,000	1st ed./2003: $1,250,000	2nd ed./2005: $1,500,000	3rd ed./2008: $1,750,000	4th edition: $2,000,000

1834–1837 PROOF CLASSIC HEAD HALF EAGLES

STANDARDS · **Weight:** 8.36 grams. **Composition:** 89.9% gold, 10.1% silver and copper; changed to 90% gold, 10% silver and copper in 1837. **Diameter:** 22.5 mm. **Edge:** Reeded. **RARITY** · As a type coin, the Classic Head half eagle must be considered a major rarity in any state of preservation. Populations of the Proof coins in this series range from 12 to 15 known for the 1834, to unique for the 1837. **CERTIFIED POPULATION** · 20

I n mid-1834, William Kneass extensively redesigned the half eagle and quarter eagle denominations, creating what is now known as the Classic Head type. On the obverse, Liberty faces left with stars surrounding her head and with the date below. On the reverse, an eagle holds a shield on its breast; it is perched on an olive branch and holds three arrows. The inscription UNITED STATES OF AMERICA, 5 D. can be found near the edges. This type is also known as the "No Motto" version because the words E PLURIBUS UNUM were eliminated. In addition to the obvious stylistic changes, the weight was reduced from 135 grains (8.75 grams) to 129 grains (8.36 grams), due to the Coinage Act of 1834. This was a badly needed weight modification, as many early gold coins were melted because their bullion value exceeded their face value. Consequently, Classic Head gold coins are more common than earlier types.

While Classic Head circulation strikes are abundant, the Proof versions are not. At most, 20 Classic Head half eagles are known

in Proof, and, of these, a few are either damaged or permanently held in museums. The 1834 is the most "common" of the group. One resides in the fabulous "King of Siam set." There are several deceptive first strikes, but probably 12 to 15 true Proofs are known. Meanwhile, the 1835 was well-represented in the Pittman Collection by two of the three known examples of the date. The third known specimen is a part of the Smithsonian Institution's National Numismatic Collection. There are also only three examples known of the 1836 half eagle in Proof. Again, the Pittman Collection contained a gem example, the National Numismatic Collection has one, and the third was contained in an original 1836 Proof set purchased by Brian Hendelson in 1996. 1837 is represented by a unique example in the Numismatic National Collection.

There are several die varieties of the 1834 Proof Classic Head half eagle. Although this would only be of interest to specialists of U.S. gold coins, on one variety of the Proof examples for this year, the eagle's tongue is missing.

As usual, such fabulous coins are only seen for sale when great collections are dispersed. The Pittman Collection was a prime opportunity, as it contained four examples of the type in the Proof format. John J. Pittman had the foresight to recognize the importance of these great coins. Many were purchased for a fraction of what they sold for when his landmark collection was sold in 1997 and 1998. Any opportunity to purchase a Proof Classic Head half eagle is a rare occasion.

CHAP. XCV.—*An Act concerning the gold coins of the United States, and for other purposes.*

Be it enacted by the Senate and House of Representatives of the United States of America, in Congress assembled, That the gold coins of the United States shall contain the following quantities of metal, that is to say: each eagle shall contain two hundred and thirty-two grains of pure gold, and two hundred and fifty-eight grains of standard gold; each half eagle one hundred and sixteen grains of pure gold, and one hundred and twenty-nine grains of standard gold; each quarter eagle shall contain fifty-eight grains of pure gold, and sixty-four and a half grains of standard gold; every such eagle shall be of the value of ten dollars; every such half eagle shall be of the value of five dollars; and every such quarter eagle shall be of the value of two dollars and fifty cents; and the said gold coins shall be receivable in all payments, when of full weight, according to their respective values; and when of less than full weight, at less values, proportioned to their respective actual weights.

An excerpt from the Coinage Act of 1834, in which Congress laid out the new specifications for U.S. gold coins.

Designed by William Kneass. The obverse features a head of Liberty facing left surrounded by 13 stars. The reverse displays a heraldic eagle clutching arrows and olive branches. Mintage for these issues is unknown.

HISTORICAL VALUES					
Choice Proof					
1960: $2,500	1980: $25,000	1st ed./2003: $65,000	2nd ed./2005: $100,000	3rd ed./2008: $150,000	4th edition: $200,000

1866 "NO MOTTO" LIBERTY SEATED SILVER DOLLAR

STANDARDS • **Weight:** 26.7 grams. **Composition:** 90% silver, 10% copper. **Diameter:** 38 mm. **Edge:** Reeded. **RARITY** • Two known. **CERTIFIED POPULATION** • 1

Salmon P. Chase, secretary of the Treasury from 1861 to 1864, responded favorably to the suggestion of the Reverend M.R. Watkinson and incorporated the name of God on several U.S. denominations.

Only two 1866 "No Motto" Liberty Seated dollars are known to exist. These special coins are identical to the regular silver dollars of 1866 except for one small detail that might easily be overlooked: there is no scroll with IN GOD WE TRUST above the eagle on the reverse. The motto was added to the reverse of most U.S. coins in 1866, including the silver dollar, following five years of development. This coin is part of our trio of "No Motto" 1866 silver coins, except that two specimens are known of the silver dollar, whereas only one each is known for the half dollar and quarter dollar (Nos. 83 and 48, respectively).

The seed for the motto came from an 1861 letter written by the Reverend Mr. M.R. Watkinson, of Ridleyville, Pennsylvania, to secretary of the Treasury Salmon P. Chase, in which Watkinson bemoaned the lack of a reference to God on U.S. coins. Chase responded favorably and quickly, and by December 1861, pattern half dollars and eagles were produced with the experimental motto GOD OUR TRUST. In 1864, the motto IN GOD WE TRUST was adopted and was introduced to the general public on the new two-cent piece. In 1866, the motto was added to all U.S. silver coins valued at 25¢ and up, and all U.S. gold coins valued at $5 and up.

Several of the "With Motto" pattern coins of 1863 to 1865 have been shown to be from dies used first in 1866 and 1867. The 1866 "No Motto" coins may have been fabricated to create deliberate rarities, a theory contrary to the previously held belief that they were transitional patterns. Whether they were made as numismatic rarities, or for whatever reason, virtually all "numismatic delicacies" are highly collectible today. While their parentage is very interesting to study, as here, most collectors concentrate on their rarity, fame, and display value!

One of the 1866 "No Motto" silver dollars was part of a three-piece set (along with the quarter dollar and half dollar) owned ultimately by the DuPont family and stolen from them in 1967 during an armed robbery. The 1866 "No Motto" quarter dollar and 1866

"No Motto" half dollar were recovered in 1999 and 2000, respectively. The 1866 "No Motto" silver dollar was recovered in February 2004. Today, all three coins are on display at the Museum of American History's rare coin exhibit.

A second 1866 "No Motto" silver dollar resurfaced in the 1970s before entering a private Midwestern collection in the early 1980s. After not meeting its auction reserve price in September 2003, the coin was sold privately for nearly $1 million some time later.

Designed by Christian Gobrecht. The obverse shows Liberty in a flowing gown sitting on a rock. Her left hand holds a staff surmounted by a liberty cap; her right hand steadies a shield and holds a band bearing the word LIBERTY. An arc of 13 stars appears around Liberty, and the date appears at the base of the obverse, below the rock. The reverse shows an eagle with a shield on its chest, an olive branch in its right talon, and a bunch of arrows in its left. The words UNITED STATES OF AMERICA appear above the eagle; the abbreviation ONE DOL. appears below.

HISTORICAL VALUES
Choice Proof

1960: $15,000	1980: $100,000	1st ed./2003: $1,000,000	2nd ed./2005: $850,000	3rd ed./2008: $1,250,000	4th edition: $2,000,000

1817, 7 OVER 4
CAPPED BUST HALF DOLLAR

STANDARDS · Weight: 13.478 grams. **Composition:** .89% silver, 11% copper. **Diameter:** 32 mm. **Edge:** Lettered FIFTY CENTS OR HALF A DOLLAR with a star between DOLLAR and FIFTY. **RARITY ·** Nine known. The finest 1817, 7 Over 4 half dollar is the coin from the Louis Eliasberg collection. This particular coin was graded EF-45 in the 1997 sale of Eliasberg's silver coins, where it reached the princely sum of $209,000. It has since been graded AU-50 by PCGS. The Eliasberg coin resold in 2009 for $356,500. The ninth example was discovered in just the last couple of years. **CERTIFIED POPULATION ·** 9

Only nine examples of the 1817, 7 Over 4 half dollar are known, earning it the title of "King of the Capped Bust half dollars" and making it one of the rarest of all U.S. coins.

The 1817, 7 Over 4 half dollar illustrates the conservative economics of the early U.S. Mint by showing how old dies were turned into "new" ones simply by changing the last digit of the date. Although there were many exceptions, it was the general policy to strike coins only in the original year shown on the die. By 1815, at least three half dollar dies were left over: one from 1812, a second from 1813, and a third from 1814. In preparation for striking 1815 half dollars, the engraver grabbed the oldest die (the 1812) and stamped a 5 over the 2. This die was then used to strike half dollars, all of which show a clear overdate.

In 1816, no half dollars were struck because of a fire at the Mint that destroyed some of the machinery. In 1817, after repairs were made and production of half dollars was ready to resume, the engraver pulled out the 1813 and 1814 dies and punched a 7 in the place of the last digits, creating two different overdates for the year. The 1817, 7 Over 3 die performed well, turning out enough coins that the variety is readily available today. On the other hand, the 1817, 7 Over 4 die broke quickly, cracking nearly in half while producing an unknown (but obviously small) number of coins.

The 1817, 7 Over 4 half dollar is so rare that it remained unknown to collectors until 1930, when E.T. Wallis of Los Angeles, California, announced the discovery in a full-page advertisement on the back of one of his auction sale catalogs. A second example turned up sometime between 1940 and 1942, mistakenly sold as one of the "Punctuated Date" varieties. Subsequent discoveries occurred in the early 1960s, another of which was a misat-

tributed "Punctuated Date." A seventh example was discovered in 1976.

Two more 1817, 7 Over 4 half dollars have been found since then. The first sold at auction in 2006 for $235,000. The second has only come to light in the last couple years.

The 1817, 7 Over 4 half dollar is one of the dream cherrypicks for an early-coin enthusiast. You can rest assured that every collector and knowledgeable dealer has been looking for this rarity with great earnest.

OCTOBER, 1930. 689

NEW VARIETY OF HALF DOLLAR OF 1817 REPORTED.

E. T. Wallis, of Los Angeles, Cal., writes that he has recently discovered a heretofore unknown variety of the 1817 half dollar, the last figure of the date being cut over a 4. A number of half dollars of 1817 over '13 are known, but this is the first one over '14 reported, Mr. Wallis says. He also says the coin is practically uncirculated and the overdate can be seen plainly. The reverse is also an unlisted variety, as both I's in United and America have the lower ceriphs broken off diagonally toward the right, and the I in United also has the left side of the top ceriph broken off. The obverse shows a die break across the coin, starting from the border to the right of the figure 7 and through the ear and between B and E of [ ] to the top of the border. Mr. Wallis thinks the die may have [ ] when the 7 was cut over the 4 and the die may have [ ] striking began.

Howard R. Newcomb, of Los Ange[ ]
[Pa?], both authorities on the [ ]
[p?]ounced it a h[ ]

In October 1930, the *Numismatist* announced E.T. Wallis's discovery of the 1817, 7 Over 4 half dollar.

Designed by John Reich. The obverse features a bust of Liberty wearing a liberty cap with the word LIBERTY on the band. The bust is circled by 13 stars; the date appears on the bottom of the obverse. The reverse features an eagle, with open wings and a shield on its chest, holding an olive branch and a bundle of arrows. A scroll with the words E PLURIBUS UNUM hovers above the eagle. UNITED STATES OF AMERICA appears near the rim; the denomination 50 C. sits beneath the eagle.

HISTORICAL VALUES
Extremely Fine

1960: $3,500	1980: $40,000	1st ed./2003: $200,000	2nd ed./2005: $250,000	3rd ed./2008: $350,000	4th edition: $350,000

1866 "NO MOTTO" LIBERTY
SEATED QUARTER DOLLAR

STANDARDS · **Weight:** 16.25 grams. **Composition:** 90% silver, 10% copper. **Diameter:** 24.3 mm. **Edge:** Reeded. **RARITY** · Unique!
CERTIFIED POPULATION · 1

The 1866 "No Motto" Liberty Seated quarter dollar is considered unique. The "Motto" refers to the scroll bearing the words IN GOD WE TRUST added to the backs of quarter dollars beginning in 1866. Thus, some experts consider the 1866 "No Motto" quarter dollar to be a transitional pattern, a sort of missing link that bridges the old "No Motto" quarter dollars and the new "With Motto" quarter dollars. Without any other evidence, such a conclusion is perfectly logical and implies exceptional value and desirability. However, the 1866 "No Motto" quarter dollar was probably not made in 1866, but years later! Its history is unknown, and this and related "No Motto" high-denomination silver coins were not known to the collecting community until the 20th century.

According to Walter Breen, the 1866 "No Motto" quarter dollar is a "fantasy piece, struck in a set with the half dollar [J-538] and silver dollar [J-540], long after authorization to adopt the new design with motto (Act of March 3, 1865). This set was made up for the Mint's favorite druggist, Robert Coulton Davis. Calling them transitional pieces destroys the meaning of the term; the true transitionals are the 1865 coins with motto as adopted in 1866."

The three coins mentioned by Breen remained together as they passed through some significant collections, including those of William Woodin (secretary of the Treasury), Colonel E.H.R. Green, and King Farouk of Egypt. Eventually, the set became part of the Willis H. DuPont family's collection. Then, in 1967, five masked gunmen robbed the DuPont family in their Florida home and took the set of 1866 "patterns" and other valuable coins.

For more than 30 years, the whereabouts of many of the stolen DuPont coins remained a mystery. While some coins were recovered over the years, the 1866 "patterns" remained hidden until late 1999, when a Los Angeles coin company purchased the quarter dollar in "a lot of junk and old electrotype colonial coins." The significance of the coin was soon discovered, the proper owners were notified, and the coin was returned to the DuPont family. They, in turn, loaned the

Starting in 1866, all quarter dollars, like the 1874 example shown above—as well as half dollars, silver dollars, eagles, and double eagles—incorporated the motto IN GOD WE TRUST. However, Robert Coulton Davis made one quarter, half dollar, and silver dollar dated 1866 without the motto as "fantasy pieces."

coin to the American Numismatic Association, which proudly (and securely) displayed the 1866 "No Motto" quarter dollar, along with the DuPont's 1866 "No Motto" half dollar, at the Edward T. Rochet Money Museum in Colorado Springs, Colorado. Today, all three coins now reside in National Numismatic Collection of the Smithsonian in Washington, D.C.

The last sale record for an 1866 "No Motto" quarter dollar was in 1961, when the DuPont family acquired the coin from the Edwin Hydeman collection for $24,500 (a huge price at the time). Hydeman, from York, Pennsylvania, was a long-time collector who operated Wiest's Department Store in that city. He also had some other 100 Greatest U.S. Coins, including an 1804 dollar, a 1913 Liberty Head nickel, and, not to be overlooked, an 1894-S dime!

Designed by Christian Gobrecht. The obverse shows Liberty in a flowing gown sitting on a rock. Her left hand holds a staff surmounted by a liberty cap; her right hand steadies a shield and holds a band bearing the word LIBERTY. An arc of 13 stars appears around Liberty, and the date appears at the base of the obverse, below the rock. The reverse shows an eagle with a shield on its chest, an olive branch in its right talon, and a bunch of arrows in its left. The words UNITED STATES OF AMERICA appear above the eagle; the abbreviations QUAR. DOL. appear below.

HISTORICAL VALUES
Choice Proof

1960: $25,000	1980: $75,000	1st ed./2003: $350,000	2nd ed./2005: $375,000	3rd ed./2008: $500,000	4th edition: $750,000

1854 AND 1855 PROOF
INDIAN PRINCESS HEAD GOLD DOLLARS
TYPE II

STANDARDS • **Weight:** 1.672 grams. **Composition:** 90% gold, 10% copper. **Diameter:** 15 mm. **Edge:** Finely reeded. **RARITY** • Four examples of the 1854 Proof are known, including an impaired example in the Smithsonian Institution. It is estimated that seven or eight Proof 1855 dollars still survive. **CERTIFIED POPULATION** • 17

The Mint experimented with ring-form gold dollars, but the concept never developed into a circulating coin. (Actual size 16 mm.)

The "Type I" gold dollar, released in 1849, was successful in commerce (mainly because many silver dollars were melted for their metallic content at this time), and many were struck. However, they were found to be inconvenient in size. At a tiny 12.7 millimeters in diameter, it was easily lost and too small to handle. Moreover, the small and simple design was susceptible to counterfeiting. In 1852, U.S. Mint officials began to experiment with annular (ring-form) gold dollars, thus enlarging the coin to a more manageable size.

Still, no change occurred until James Ross Snowden took the place of Robert M. Patterson as Mint director. Snowden was then free to change Patterson's gold dollar. Physically, the new coin was wider and thinner, and intended to make the coin more convenient. However, the "Type II" was a failure due to its design. The relief on the obverse was much too high, making it extremely difficult to strike with detail on Liberty's hair. The reverse was poorly executed because the inscription THE UNITED STATES OF AMERICA was directly opposite the wreath. The thinner planchet only aggravated the overall predicament.

The Type II gold dollar lasted only three years: 1854 to 1856 (with those of 1856 struck only in San Francisco). During two of those three years, Proofs of this design were minted at the Philadelphia Mint (1854 and 1855), although very few still exist. It is believed that only 11 or 12 Type II gold dollars survived as Proofs, with the 1854 represented by just four coins. In 1997, an 1854 coin realized a stunning $193,600 at auction. The coin had been purchased by the legendary collector John J. Pittman for $525 in 1956. Later, an 1855 from the Pittman collection realized an incredible $373,750 when it crossed the auction block in 2008.

The Proof Type II gold dollar is considered one of the most desirable gold type coins in the U.S. series. Mint State examples of the Type II gold dollar are quite scarce. Proof examples of the type are coins most collectors dream of owning. Only the most serious and well-heeled collectors include this rarity on their want list.

Designed by James B. Longacre. The obverse features a bust of Liberty wearing a feathered headdress. The words UNITED STATES OF AMERICA are found at the periphery. The reverse shows the words 1 DOLLAR with the date beneath, and a wreath encircles the denomination and date.

HISTORICAL VALUES					
1854, Choice Proof					
1960: $3,500	1980: $35,000	1st ed./2003: $150,000	2nd ed./2005: $250,000	3rd ed./2008: $350,000	4th edition: $400,000
1855, Choice Proof					
1960: $3,500	1980: $35,000	1st ed./2003: $125,000	2nd ed./2005: $165,000	3rd ed./2008: $225,000	4th edition: $275,000

1861-S "PAQUET REVERSE" LIBERTY HEAD DOUBLE EAGLE

STANDARDS · **Weight:** 33.436 grams. **Composition:** 90% gold, 10% copper. **Net weight:** .96750 oz. pure gold. **Diameter:** 34 mm. **Edge:** Reeded.

RARITY · Today, there are probably 200 to 300 examples known in all grades of the 1861-S Paquet reverse double eagle. Most are well-worn and very baggy in appearance. It is obvious that the entire mintage was placed into extensive circulation. There are no Mint State examples known.

CERTIFIED POPULATION · 151

In 1860, Anthony Paquet, an engraver at the Philadelphia Mint, modified the reverse design for the double eagle. The new design was very similar to the standard issue, but the reverse letters were much taller and more slender in appearance. There were also several technical variations with regard to the positioning and size of the lettering. In late 1860, the Paquet reverse became the standard design adopted for the regular-issue coinage of 1861 double eagles. Dies were shipped to the branch mints of New Orleans and San Francisco. Actual coinage on high-speed presses began in January 1861 in Philadelphia, but Mint director James Ross Snowden felt that the die would be unsuitable for high-speed production, so he recalled the new design and ordered the Philadelphia Mint issue to be melted. The entire Philadelphia run was destroyed, with the exception of a few coins. Snowden also ordered production to cease in New Orleans and San Francisco. The order reached New Orleans in time to prevent any coinage. But because the transcontinental railroad was still several years away from completion, and the telegraph did not extend past St. Joseph, Missouri, the directive to stop coinage did not reach San Francisco until 19,250 coins had been struck, and no effort was made to recall the issue.

Today, the 1861-S Paquet double eagle ranks as one of the most desirable of the denomination. Prices for the issue have surged in recent years. About Uncirculated examples have nearly tripled in price since the first edition of *100 Greatest U.S. Coins* was published. The interest in double eagles has never been higher, and with gold prices rising, prices for this coin will most likely continue their steady rise.

Mint director James Ross Snowden, who recalled Paquet's new reverse design for the double eagle, is depicted here on a medal—also by Paquet.

As mentioned on several occasions in this book, it is always very exciting when a new example of rarity is discovered. Shortly before this writing, author Jeff Garrett handled an 1861-S Paquet that had been sold in a small coin shop in a piece of jewelry for around melt value. Luckily, the coin was identified as a rarity before it was damaged. Every day is an adventure in the world of rare coins!

Designed by James B. Longacre and Anthony C. Paquet. The obverse features a portrait of Liberty wearing a coronet, facing left, surrounded by 13 stars. The reverse features an outspread eagle and shield design. Mintage for this issue is 19,250 coins.

HISTORICAL VALUES					
		About Uncirculated			
1960: $1,500	1980: $7,500	1st ed./2003: $35,000	2nd ed./2005: $45,000	3rd ed./2008: $85,000	4th edition: $100,000

1921 PROOF SAINT-GAUDENS DOUBLE EAGLE

STANDARDS • **Weight:** 33.436 grams. **Composition:** 90% gold, 10% copper. **Net weight:** .96750 oz. pure gold. **Diameter:** 34 mm. **Edge:** Lettered, includes E PLURIBUS UNUM with the words divided by stars. **RARITY** • Two known examples **CERTIFIED POPULATION** • 1

The numismatic fraternity was stunned in the summer of 2000 when Sotheby's auction house offered a previously unknown example of a Proof Roman-finish presentation-strike 1921 double eagle. That coin traces its pedigree to Raymond T. Baker, who was director of the U.S. Mint in 1921. Reportedly, the piece was struck for the director's nephew, Joseph Baker, on his birth. The coin, which is lightly cleaned, sold for $203,500. In 2006, a second example of this incredible rarity surfaced. This time, it was offered at auction incorrectly attributed as an MS-63. Two very knowledgeable numismatists battled until the hammer fell at $1,495,000. The newly discovered coin is nearly identical to the Sotheby's specimen, but it is original and unmolested. These two coins rank among the most interesting issues of the Saint-Gaudens series. The auction record for business-strike examples of the 1921 double eagle has now crossed the million-dollar mark, so one can only guess what these two rarities would bring on today's market.

There has been quite a debate regarding how these coins should be designated. The surfaces of these two coins very closely resemble the surfaces of Roman-finish Proof gold coinage minted in 1909 and 1910. Side-by-side comparison makes a strong case for the Proof moniker. They were clearly made under special circumstances for presentation by Mint officials. There is no doubt in our opinion that these two coins were not intended for circulation. Since the coins have only been discovered in recent years, more research could shed light on the circumstances of their striking. For now, they surely rank among the most interesting and great U.S. coins in the gold series.

In terms of the circulation-strike issues of this coin, 528,500 1921 Saint-Gaudens double eagles were struck, but the vast majority were destroyed in the great gold coin melts of the 1930s. Very few remain in all grades, and there have been no hoards or small groups to have surfaced in the multitude of double eagles

Raymond T. Baker, director of the U.S. Mint from 1917 to 1922, had a 1921 Proof double eagle struck for his new-born nephew, Joseph Baker. That coin crossed the auction block in 2000, and another example surfaced in 2006.

that have migrated back to the United States from Europe. For more information of the fascinating history of Saint-Gaudens double eagles and the financial panic that resulted in the melting of the majority of U.S. gold coins in circulation, we highly recommend David Tripp's book *Illegal Tender*. The main subject of the book is the 1933 double eagle, but the background story of the banking crisis and its effect on coinage is a must read.

Designed by Augustus Saint-Gaudens. The obverse depicts Liberty draped in Romanesque clothing and holding a torch. The reverse features an eagle in flight. Mintage for circulation strikes of this issue was 528,500, but nearly all examples were melted.

HISTORICAL VALUES					
Proof					
1960: n/a	1980: n/a	1st ed./2003: —	2nd ed./2005: —	3rd ed./2008: $2,500,000	4th edition: $3,500,000

1804 "13 STARS" CAPPED BUST QUARTER EAGLE

STANDARDS · **Weight:** 4.37 grams. **Composition:** 92% gold, 8% copper. **Diameter:** 20 mm. **Edge:** Reeded. **RARITY** · About eight or nine examples are currently known. **CERTIFIED POPULATION** · 7

In 1804, the Philadelphia Mint struck two varieties of the quarter eagle: one with 14 stars on the reverse and a second with 13 stars. One of the most intriguing aspects of the "13 Stars" quarter eagle is its connection to the ten-cent denomination. In the early 19th century, the U.S. Mint made every effort to conserve steel for dies. Thus, many dies were overpunched from one year to another. In the case of early quarter eagles and dimes, the two denominations were approximately the same size and had an identical reverse motif, so the Mint conveniently used one reverse die for both denominations. The reverse die found on the 1804 "13 Stars" quarter eagle, interestingly, was first used on the 1802 quarter eagle. The Mint saved it until 1804, when it was put into action to strike dimes. It was used yet again to strike the 1804 "13 Stars" quarter eagle. Such a cross-denomination link is extremely rare in U.S. numismatics, but it does occur with a few other dimes and quarter eagles.

The reverse used for the 1804 quarter eagle—both the 13- and 14-star varieties—was also used for 1804 dimes (and before that, for 1802 quarter eagles)!

It had been suggested by Walter Breen that the mintage for the 1804 "13 Stars" quarter eagle was from a delivery of 1,003 coins in 1804. It has now been concluded by researchers that these were of the "14 Stars" variety, and his mintage estimate is incorrect. The 1804 "13 Stars" is actually the rarest early quarter eagle and one of the rarest early federal coins produced.

Only eight or nine 1804 "13 Stars" quarter eagles are known. Their conditions range from Very Fine to About Uncirculated. At least one coin we have seen had the number 10 scratched in the right obverse field. The coin had once belonged to the legendary collector John J. Pittman, who purchased the coin in 1960 for $620. This was quite high for the time, and illustrates the constant demand for the incredible rarity. The damage was very expertly removed, and the coin later was certified by PCGS as AU-50, although an image of the damage appears in the catalog of the John J. Pittman collection. This specimen's most recent appearance was in January 2004, when it sold for $92,000.

The auction record for this variety was shattered in July 2008 when the collection of Bust dimes and quarter eagles formed by Ed Price was auctioned. At that time, the Price example sold for $322,000. That specimen, which traces its pedigree to a 1912 Henry Chapman sale, grades AU-55 and is one of the finest known.

Designed by Robert Scot. The obverse features Liberty wearing a liberty cap surrounded by stars. The word LIBERTY is featured at the top with the date located at the bottom. The reverse features an eagle surrounded by the words UNITED STATES OF AMERICA. Above the eagle's head is a field of stars and six clouds.

HISTORICAL VALUES					
Extremely Fine					
1960: $2,500	1980: $7,500	1st ed./2003: $75,000	2nd ed./2005: $85,000	3rd ed./2008: $250,000	4th edition: $275,000

1856-O LIBERTY HEAD DOUBLE EAGLE

STANDARDS · **Weight:** 33.436 grams. **Composition:** 90% gold, 10% copper. **Net weight:** .96750 oz. pure gold. **Diameter:** 34 mm. **Edge:** Reeded

RARITY · With a mintage of only 2,250 coins, this date is very rare by any standard. Only 20 to 25 are known today in all grades. The lone Mint State example known is a choice prooflike example, considered by many to be a presentation strike. The coin sold for just $542,000 in 2004. An About Uncirculated example sold for $431,250 one year later. Today the MS-63 coin would most likely sell for millions. **CERTIFIED POPULATION** · 22

Southern gold coinage has been very popular with collectors for many years. One of the "crown jewels" of the market is the 1856-O double eagle. Just 2,250 examples were struck in New Orleans for the year. Only one set of dies is thought to have been used for the production of 1856-O double eagles. The coins were circulated extensively, as most of the survivors are well-worn. Many of the higher-grade examples exhibit partially prooflike surfaces. The finest known example is fully prooflike, and considered by many experts to be a Proof or presentation piece. It is one of the most spectacular rarities in the U.S. gold series. This date is the rarest New Orleans double eagle and is one of the rarest non-Proof coins of the series.

Considerable collector interest has focused on double eagles in recent years. Rarities have surged in value. The 1856-O double eagle has more than tripled in price since the first edition of *100 Greatest U.S. Coins* was published. The discovery of the SS *Central America* and the SS *Republic* has focused tremendous attention on double eagles. As noted earlier, with the rise in world gold prices and huge demand for these large collectibles, prices will probably continue to rise. The ranking of the 1854-O and 1856-O double eagle on the list of 100 Greatest U.S. Coins will most likely rise as well.

Designed by James B. Longacre. The obverse features a portrait of Liberty wearing a coronet, facing left, surrounded by 13 stars. The reverse features an outspread eagle and shield design. Mintage for this issue is 2,250 coins.

This mid–19th-century coin press was used at the New Orleans Mint and is now on display in the old mint building as part of the Louisiana State Museum.

HISTORICAL VALUES
Extremely Fine

1960: $500	1980: $35,000	1st ed./2003: $85,000	2nd ed./2005: $135,000	3rd ed./2008: $275,000	4th edition: $300,000

1798, 8 OVER 7 CAPPED BUST EAGLES
TWO VARIETIES

STANDARDS · Weight: 17.50 grams. **Composition:** 92% gold, 8% silver and copper. **Diameter:** 33 mm. **Edge:** Reeded. **RARITY ·** The 9 × 4 stars is rare, and fewer than 100 are known in all grades. Several Mint State examples remain. The 7 × 6 stars is extremely rare and seldom encountered. It is estimated that fewer than 20 examples exist, with a couple of Mint State examples at the high end of the condition scale. Auction records for the issue exceed $275,000 for a PCGS-graded MS-62 that sold in 2003. **CERTIFIED POPULATION ·** 72

Because early U.S. gold coins became worth more for their bullion than for their face value, most of these issues were destroyed. Only 135,592 eagles were struck from 1795 to 1804. From 1797 to 1804, the heraldic eagle design was produced. The great rarities of this design are two varieties dated 1798, 8 Over 7. One variety has nine stars on the left and four on the right of the obverse. The other variety has seven stars on the left and six stars on the right. Records indicate that 900 eagles were delivered from the Mint on February 17, 1798. It is thought that these were the 9 × 4 variety. On February 28, only 842 of the 7 × 6 variety were delivered, these figures being the estimates of Walter Breen. Both of these historic coins are rare, but the 7 × 6 is one of the major rarities of the era. Most examples seen of both varieties are well-worn or damaged, though a few Mint State examples do exist. The early gold eagles, minted from 1795 to 1804, are rare, but completing a set is possible. There are no "stoppers" like the early

The 9 x 4 Stars variety of 1798, 8 Over 7 eagle, while not as rare as the 7 x 6 Stars variety, is still a very valuable coin.

half eagle issues. For this reason, gold eagles minted from 1795 to 1804 are very popular coins.

The 7 x 6 is a very rare and unusual coin for a couple of reasons: (1) it's an overdate and (2) it's the only early eagle or early half eagle with the word LIBERTY completely above the cap. This unusual situation began when the diesinker punched the head of Liberty into the die too low (the bottom curl and the tip of the bust are closer to the edge than on any other early eagle). This gave the engraver room enough to put the stars and the word LIBERTY in a continuous arc around the head.

The National Numismatic Collection contains two examples each of these popular rarities in Mint State condition. This is a result of the merger of the Mint Cabinet and Lilly Collection.

John Adams was president of the United States when these coins were struck. During his administration, the federal government was moved from New York City to Washington City, now known as Washington, D.C.

Designed by Robert Scot. The obverse features a capped Liberty facing right, surrounded by 13 stars. The reverse displays a heraldic eagle clutching arrows and olive branches. Mintage for the issue is 900 of the 9 × 4 variety and 842 of the 7 × 6 variety.

HISTORICAL VALUES

9 x 4 Stars, About Uncirculated					
1960: $1,000	1980: $12,500	1st ed./2003: $35,000	2nd ed./2005: $40,000	3rd ed./2008: $75,000	4th edition: $85,000
7 x 6 Stars, About Uncirculated					
1960: $2,500	1980: $25,000	1st ed./2003: $95,000	2nd ed./2005: $100,000	3rd ed./2008: $175,000	4th edition: $185,000

1825, 5 OVER 4 CAPPED HEAD HALF EAGLE

STANDARDS · **Weight:** 8.75 grams. **Composition:** 92% gold, 8% silver. **Diameter:** 25 mm. **Edge:** Reeded. **RARITY** · Two coins are known: an Uncirculated specimen and an AU-50. The Eliasberg coin, the finer of the two, brought $220,000 in 1982. Both had been off the market for more than a decade, but the Kaufman specimen was auctioned in July 2008 and sold for $690,000. **CERTIFIED POPULATION** · 22

At the first U.S. Mint in Philadelphia (1792–1832), reusing dies over several years was not uncommon. The Mint operated on a tight budget, so it was necessary to recycle dies for as long as possible. In the case of the 1825, 5 Over 4 half eagle, a leftover 1824 die was repunched, thus changing the date from 1824 to 1825. However, the underlying digit "4" was still quite obvious, hence the moniker "1825, 5 Over 4 half eagle."

As a variety, the 1825, 5 Over 4 half eagle is one of the rarest of all U.S. gold coins. A surprise hit the numismatic world in 1978 when a long-lost 1825, 5 Over 4 half eagle reappeared on the market. That year, RARCOA auctioned the Nathan M. Kaufman Collection, a group of coins that had gone untouched for decades. Unfortunately, the coins had been displayed in a bank conference room in Marquette, Michigan, in a most unsafe manner: they were tacked to the wall, creating unsightly rim bumps on some (but not all) of the specimens. Luckily, Kaufman's 1825, 5 Over 4 half eagle escaped unscathed and fetched a strong $140,000 in the sale. The Kaufman specimen would come up for auction again in July 2008, when it sold for an astonishing $690,000.

There are two varieties known of the 1825, 5 Over 4 half eagle. What was previously known as the 1825, 5 Over 1 half eagle has now been proven to be a second variety of the 1825, 5 Over 4. The undertype is less obvious, and for many years attributed as an 1825, 5 Over 1. Harry W. Bass Jr. never owned an example of the 1825, 5 Over 4, even though he had the opportunity on two occasions to purchase one. It has been speculated that he may have declined to pursue the 1825, 5 Over 4 because he felt the two may be different die states of the same variety. The cost may have been a factor as well, because the two coins sold for incredible prices at the time—as they continue to do, judging by the 2008 auction of the Kaufman coin!

The practice of reusing dies (and thereby creating overdates) was most common when the U.S. Mint was young and still in its original facility in Philadelphia.

Designed by John Reich. The obverse depicts a large portrait of Liberty surrounded by 13 stars with the date below. The reverse features an eagle with spread wings, holding an olive branch and arrows. Surrounding the eagle are the inscriptions UNITED STATES OF AMERICA and 5 D., with the motto E PLURIBUS UNUM above the eagle's head.

HISTORICAL VALUES
About Uncirculated

1960: $2,500	1980: $125,000	1st ed./2003: $250,000	2nd ed./2005: $275,000	3rd ed./2008: $350,000	4th edition: $400,000

1796 AND 1797 DRAPED BUST HALF DOLLARS

STANDARDS · Weight: 13.478 grams. **Composition:** 89% silver, 11% copper. **Diameter:** 32.5 mm. **Edge:** Lettered FIFTY CENTS OR HALF A DOLLAR. **RARITY ·** The total mintage of all 1796 and 1797 amounted to only 3,918 coins! Mint State examples are extremely rare. **CERTIFIED POPULATION ·** 278

A 15-star die was used for the obverse of both the 1796 and 1797 half dollar. A 16-star die (with one additional star added to the left of the bust) was also used for the 1796 half dollar.

The 1796 and 1797 half dollars are a classic U.S. rarity. The mintages of the 1796 and 1797 half dollars were comingled in the Mint records, and the total number of coins for both dates is a mere 3,918 pieces. Their minuscule mintages reflect the scarcity of silver in the early days of the Mint. Factor in the coins that were lost or destroyed, and the number of survivors becomes significantly small. At the time, depositors of silver bullion at the Mint could request the denomination(s) desired, and most requests were for silver dollars, to the detriment of half dollars.

Mint records indicate that no half dollars were delivered in 1796. Numismatic historians speculate that half dollars may have been struck in 1796, but not delivered by the coiner until early 1797, when 934 half dollars were recorded. The coins in the later delivery of half dollars, in May of 1797, are all believed to be 1797-dated coins. The earliest 1796 half dollars show 15 stars on the front of the coin, representing each of the states then in the Union. Later versions show 16 stars, reflecting the expected admission of Tennessee as a state in 1797.

Most 1796 and 1797 half dollars known today are well circulated. Collectors are willing to accept examples in just about any grade, including coins that have been professionally repaired (holes filled, scratches removed)—coins they would not accept were the 1796 and 1797 half dollar more available. A few Uncirculated 1797 half dollars are known to exist, but they are not as common as Mint State 1796 half dollars, nor do they come as nice. For instance, the finest 1797 half dollar rates a grade of MS-63, while there are a couple of 1796 half dollars at that grade and higher, one even having been certified as MS-66.

Curiously, the Draped Bust, Small Eagle Reverse half dollar was the first silver U.S. coin to bear a denomination on the reverse, despite that the denomination was already stated by the edge lettering. The practice was not carried over when the design of the half dollar changed in 1801. Denominations first appeared on the reverse of silver coins in the following order: 1809 for dimes, 1815 for quarter dollars, 1829 for half dimes, and 1836 for silver dollars!

Designed by Robert Scot. The obverse features a draped bust of Liberty with some of her hair tied back in a bow. LIBERTY appears above, the date below, and stars are divided up on the sides (one variety has 15 total stars, the other 16 stars). The reverse features a plain eagle standing on clouds with outstretched wings within a wreath of palm and olive branches. The outer legend reads UNITED STATES OF AMERICA. The denomination appears as the fraction "1/2" beneath the bow of the wreath.

HISTORICAL VALUES					
1796, 15 Stars, Extremely Fine					
1960: $2,000	1980: $15,000	1st ed./2003: $45,000	2nd ed./2005: $55,000	3rd ed./2008: $125,000	4th edition: $150,000
1796, 16 Stars, Extremely Fine					
1960: $2,000	1980: $16,500	1st ed./2003: $50,000	2nd ed./2005: $60,000	3rd ed./2008: $125,000	4th edition: $150,000
1797, Extremely Fine					
1960: $2,000	1980: $15,000	1st ed./2003: $45,000	2nd ed./2005: $65,000	3rd ed./2008: $125,000	4th edition: $150,000

1856 FLYING EAGLE CENT

STANDARDS · Weight: 4.666 grams. **Composition:** 88% copper, 12% nickel. **Diameter:** 19 mm. **Edge:** Plain. **RARITY ·** Rare. Probably 1,500 or so exist today. The estate of Colonel John A. Beck had 731 pieces that were dispersed in the 1970s by Abner Kreisberg and Jerry Cohen—remarkably, without even a wiggle in the market price, so strong was the demand for such pieces. The 1856 Flying Eagle cent is available in both Uncirculated and Proof formats. **CERTIFIED POPULATION ·** 1,484

Prior to 1857, one-cent pieces were large pieces of pure copper, almost the size of today's half dollar. Because of rising copper prices and the ever-increasing costs of production, the U.S. Mint began in 1850 to search for a cheaper and smaller alternative. Finally, in 1856, the Mint chose an alloy mixture of copper and nickel that gave the finished product a whitish color, completely unlike any other coins then in production. For the diameter of the coin, government officials settled on a size that has remained ever since, one identical to that of the cent in your pocket. To differentiate the new coins from the previous cents, these smaller coins became popularly known as "small" cents.

James B. Longacre painted this water-color self-portrait in 1845. He depicted himself with his engraving tools.

Technically, the 1856 Flying Eagle cent is a pattern piece, meant to illustrate how the design would look as an actual coin. However, unlike most pattern coins, which are normally produced in small quantities for in-house use, the 1856 Flying Eagle cents were struck in large quantities (some experts estimate that as many as 2,000 to 3,000 were minted). The reason for the inordinately high mintage was twofold: to influence the passage of pending legislation authorizing the new small cent, and to satisfy collector demand.

The 1856 Flying Eagle cent is essentially a "copycat" coin. The engraver, James Barton Longacre, placed a flying eagle design on the front of the coin, borrowing heavily from the back of the 1836 to 1839 Gobrecht dollars (classed together as No. 73). For the reverse, Longacre used the wreath design from the back of the $3 gold piece, simply reducing the size to fit the cent die. The "borrowing" was done for the sake of expediency, for the Mint had to get coins into the hands of Congressmen who were debating the legislation and arguing over the final alloy mixture.

Hundreds of the new small cents were given to lawmakers, VIPs, and anyone who could influence the passage of the bill. The campaign succeeded, the new small cent was authorized, and the public met its newest coin. To make the transition even easier, the Mint produced both large cents and small cents in 1856 and 1857.

The new coins were an immediate success. Demand was high, especially for Flying Eagle cents dated 1856. Thus, in 1857 and 1858, the Mint restruck the 1856 Flying Eagle cent and sold them to collectors, a somewhat questionable practice for which numismatists give thanks today. Unfortunately, this beautiful design was short-lived, ending after only two years, in 1858.

There are several different die-varieties known of the 1856 Flying Eagle cent. The 1856 Flying Eagle cent is also known in Proof and non-Proof issues. It is very difficult to determine the striking status for this issue. Many examples are struck with polished dies but are poorly made. When purchasing a coin that is offered as a circulation strike, it is best to consult with an expert.

Designed by James B. Longacre. The obverse shows an eagle flying left through a plain field. UNITED STATES OF AMERICA appears in an arc above the eagle and the date appears below. The reverse shows the words ONE CENT within a wreath made of ears of corn and other grains.

HISTORICAL VALUES					
Choice Proof					
1960: $1,250	1980: $3,500	1st ed./2003: $15,000	2nd ed./2005: $17,500	3rd ed./2008: $18,500	4th edition: $20,000

1870-S LIBERTY SEATED HALF DIME

STANDARDS • **Weight:** 1.231 grams. **Composition:** 90% silver, 10% copper. **Diameter:** 15.5 mm. **Edge:** Reeded. **RARITY** • Unique! The only known example is an MS-64 that last sold at public auction in July 2004 for $661,250. It is worth far more today. **CERTIFIED POPULATION** • 2

Numismatic treasures await us in the most unlikely places. Take the 1870-S half dime, for example. According to official Mint records, none were ever struck, even though six pairs of half dime dies were on hand at the San Francisco Mint. Then, in early 1978, a single example of this previously unrecorded date was purchased as a common type coin. The exciting news of the discovery of an 1870-S half dime stunned the numismatic world, and following its exhibition at the 1978 convention of the American Numismatic Association, this previously unappreciated coin sold for $425,000 to Michigan dealer John Abbott. How was the selling price for this unique rarity determined? By a formula agreed to in advance by all parties in which $25,000 was added to the hammer price of the 1804 silver dollar sold as part of the John Work Garrett collection!

Accounts of the discovery of the 1870-S half dime vary. One account claims the coin was found in a "junk tray," another says a "junk box" (same thing, actually), and a third says it was bought over the counter as a common type coin by a Cook County, Illinois, dealer.

The cornerstone of the second San Francisco Mint may contain another example of the 1870-S half dime along with an 1870-S $3 gold piece (believed to have been placed there), and possibly other 1870-S-dated coins of different denominations.

Coinage from the San Francisco Mint in 1870 varies greatly from modestly scarce to unique. The double eagles were the most plentiful, with 982,000 coins struck. Today, they are readily available in circulated condition. Like the 1870-S half dime, no Mint records survive for the 1870-S silver dollar, though there are currently 12 known examples of the coin. Both the 1870-S half dime and the 1870-S $3 coin are unique. Many of the other issues from this year are quite scarce and seldom encountered.

Although the 1870-S half dime is a true giant of numismatics, the coin's value is diminished for a couple of reasons. First, the coin was only recently discovered and has not received the publicity that many of the 100 Greatest U.S. Coins have. The coin's size is also a major issue. Half dimes are very tiny coins. We recall an amusing story about this coin from the mid-1980s. A prominent dealer wanted to offer the coin to a client. The owner went to great expense and trouble to have the coin delivered to a convention for his consideration. When presented with the coin, the dealer merely said, "It's too small," and handed it back. If the coin were a silver dollar, it would probably be one of the most desirable U.S. coins.

The cornerstone of the second San Francisco Mint reputedly holds several rare coins, including a second example of the 1870-S half dime.

Designed by Christian Gobrecht (obverse) and James Barton Longacre (reverse). The obverse shows Liberty in a flowing gown sitting on a rock. Her left hand holds a staff surmounted by a liberty cap; her right hand steadies a shield and holds a band bearing the word LIBERTY. The legend UNITED STATES OF AMERICA appears near the outer rims and the date appears at the base of the obverse, beneath the rock. The reverse shows the words HALF DIME within a wreath. The mint-mark appears below the word DIME.

HISTORICAL VALUES					
Choice Uncirculated					
1960: n/a	1980: $425,000	1st ed./2003: $750,000	2nd ed./2005: $1,000,000	3rd ed./2008: $2,000,000	4th edition: $2,000,000

1875 INDIAN PRINCESS HEAD $3 GOLD PIECE

STANDARDS · **Weight:** 5.015 grams. **Composition:** 90% gold, 10% copper. **Diameter:** 20.6 mm. **Edge:** Reeded. **RARITY** · The 1875 $3 gold coin is very rare in any condition. Although all coins of the issue were originally struck as Proofs, circulated examples are known to exist. There are also a tiny number of pattern 1875 $3 coins that were struck in aluminum or copper and have been gold-plated. These pattern coins are worth substantially less than the regular Proof examples. In all, probably 20 to 30 specimens are believed to exist today. **CERTIFIED POPULATION** · 23

In the field of U.S. gold coinage, the year 1875 has a magical allure. Indeed, the 1875 gold dollar, quarter eagle, $3 gold piece, half eagle, and eagle are all formidable rarities. However, the 1875 $3 gold piece has been a long-time favorite among numismatists, given its tiny mintage and perennial fame. In the early 1880s, when it was realized that the $3 denomination might be discontinued (which did happen in 1889), numismatists began to collect the soon-to-be defunct series with vigor. As more and more enthusiasts began to focus on the $3 denomination, the 1875 emerged as a prime rarity.

The 1875 $3 gold piece gained additional notoriety in 1974, when a specimen sold for the then-astounding sum of $150,000. By comparison, an MCMVII (1907) Ultra High Relief double eagle—a coin now worth around $2 million—changed hands in 1974 for $200,000. In fact, the 1875 $3 piece was the first federal gold coin to break the $100,000 mark.

Although official U.S. Mint records indicate that only 20 specimens were minted of the 1875 $3 gold piece, many numismatic researchers feel that more were actually struck. There is no accurate census for the coins of this date, and it is possible that more than 20 remain. Although only Proofs were struck, there are a few examples known that had been placed into circulation. Because of the tiny mintage and the historic appeal of the date, the 1875 $3 gold coin is a famous and desirable rarity to this day.

Proof gold coins are considered the ultimate in U.S. coinage by many. Only the very wealthiest collectors can attempt to complete a series of Proof U.S. gold coins. One notable collector who assembled a complete collection was the late Ed Trompeter. At one time, he owned three 1875 $3 gold coins. Part of his collection was sold at auction in 1992; the remainder sold via private treaty some years later for more than $15 million.

Longacre's design for the $3 gold piece obverse is echoed in other works by the engraver: the gold dollar of 1856 to 1889 (right), and his sketch for the obverse of the pattern dollars of 1870 and 1871 (above).

Designed by James B. Longacre. The obverse features the head of Liberty wearing a feathered headdress. The word LIBERTY is inscribed on the headband. The legend UNITED STATES OF AMERICA is engraved at the perimeter. The reverse depicts the denomination 3 DOLLARS, and the date is encircled by a wreath of corn and grain.

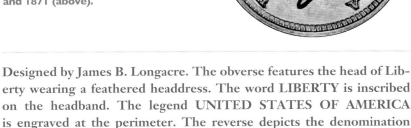

HISTORICAL VALUES					
Choice Proof					
1960: $7,500	1980: $75,000	1st ed./2003: $125,000	2nd ed./2005: $145,000	3rd ed./2008: $175,000	4th edition: $200,000

U.S. ASSAY OFFICE
$50 GOLD SLUGS

STANDARDS · **Weight:** Varies from 83.50 to 85.50 grams, depending on fineness. **Composition:** Varies from 88% to 90% gold, the remainder silver and trace metals. **Diameter:** 41 mm edge to edge. **Edge:** Reeded or lettered, depending on the variety. **RARITY** · Very scarce. Uncirculated examples are very rare. A few Proofs are known, including a piece that brought $500,000 more than 20 years ago! The Smithsonian Institution's exhibit at the Museum of American History features a Proof example, and seeing this coin is highly recommended. **CERTIFIED POPULATION** · 286

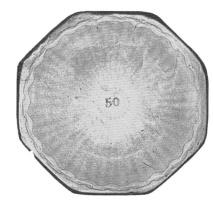

Various issues of the slugs featured different reverse designs, such as a simple "50" in the center.

The 1848 discovery of gold in California created special problems for certain of the state's inhabitants. The massive influx of people, coupled with inflation and a lack of coins with which to conduct business, led to great difficulties. Gold dust became a de facto currency, but measurements varied, often to the detriment of the owner of the dust (the size of a "pinch" of gold was directly related to the size of a man's finger and thumb). Private minters moved in to fill the void, producing a variety of gold coins of somewhat suspect quality and purity.

To help solve the problem, a U.S. Assay Office was created in 1851 in San Francisco under the direction of Augustus Humbert. He contracted with the firm of Moffat & Company to produce massive $50 coins (legally termed "ingots") with eight sides and nearly 2.75 troy ounces of pure gold. Known today as "slugs," these big, heavy coins created a new level of confidence with the general public, essentially driving the underweight and impure coins out of circulation. Unfortunately, the slugs failed to address the need for smaller-denomination coins.

Because they were technically ingots and not coins, the $50 slugs were not required to be of the same 90 percent purity as federal gold coins. Thus, four different finenesses appear on the $50 slugs: .880, .884, .887, and .900. The earliest versions had lettered edges; later versions had reeded edges. Some varieties required as many as 14 steps to produce a single coin!

Although they were produced in large quantities, most of the $50 slugs were melted down and converted into U.S. gold coins once the San Francisco Mint began operations in 1854. Today, $50 slugs are prized, impressive reminders of an important part of our U.S. heritage. Although thousands of U.S. double eagles were found in the wreckage of the steamer SS *Central America*, which sank in 1857, very few of the slugs were discovered, most of which were Augustus Humbert issues. When the great treasure was first discovered, it was speculated that slugs would become much more available. The opposite has occurred because the publicity of the SS *Central America* has created increased demand for all territorial gold coins.

Designs by **Charles Cushing Wright** and **Augustus Humbert**. The obverse shows an eagle on a rock, clutching a shield, a bundle of arrows, and an olive branch. The eagle holds a scroll in its beak. A scroll above the eagle states the fineness of the coins (e.g., 800 **THOUS.**); **UNITED STATES OF AMERICA** and the denomination surround the eagle. The outer margins are plain or lettered, depending on the variety. The reverse is an engine-turned design, sometimes with a target in the center and sometimes with the number 50 (for the denomination) punched in the center.

HISTORICAL VALUES					
Extremely Fine					
1960: $1,500	1980: $6,500	1st ed./2003: $15,000	2nd ed./2005: $18,000	3rd ed./2008: $30,000	4th edition: $50,000

1793 "STRAWBERRY LEAF" FLOWING HAIR, WREATH REVERSE LARGE CENT

STANDARDS · **Weight:** 13.478 grams. **Composition:** Pure copper. **Diameter:** 27 mm. **Edge:** Vine and bars. **RARITY** · Only four examples are known. The finest sold at auction in 2004 for $414,000. A second example has a unique reverse; a third is in the ANS's collection. The fourth appeared on the market in 1992, when it and the second example were sold as part of the Naftzger collection of large cents; both are now in a complete collection of Sheldon varieties. The nicest specimen known is only in Fine condition, and the next best in Good! **CERTIFIED POPULATION** · 3

The Strawberry Leaf large cent is an extremely rare variety of the 1793 Flowing Hair Wreath cent type. Years ago, conventional wisdom was that these were patterns and not circulation strikes, never mind that all known pieces are extensively worn (unlikely for a pattern coin). Either way, Strawberry Leaf cents have a rich tradition in U.S. numismatics that goes back many years.

In place of the normal, three-leaved sprig just above the date, the Strawberry Leaf cent sports a curious cluster that looks, to many people, like a clump of three strawberries. No one knows why the engraver made this change, but the front and back of the Strawberry Leaf cent are sufficiently different from the normal Wreath cent to suggest that a different person made each. The extreme rarity, interesting stories, and high degree of popularity make it one of the most sought-after of all U.S. coins. Just mention the words "Strawberry Leaf" to large-cent collectors and watch their expressions.

A Guide Book of United States Coins attributes the Wreath cent design to Henry Voigt, while Walter Breen assigns it to Adam Eckfeldt. In spite of some hearsay evidence to the contrary, we doubt if either man engraved the dies, since neither had the requisite skill, nor was either man trained as an engraver. However, because the die work on the Strawberry Leaf cents is somewhat cruder than that on the other Wreath cents and if, indeed, we look

The obverse of the standard Flowing Hair Wreath cent, showing the normal three-leaved sprig above the date.

at the Strawberry Leaf cents as patterns of some sort, then it is distinctly possible that Voigt had a hand in these dies.

Designed by Voigt, Eckfeldt, or some other artist. The obverse depicts a head of Liberty facing right, with a sprig of "strawberry" leaves just above the date. Above the head is the word LIBERTY. The reverse features the words ONE CENT surrounded by a wreath within the legend UNITED STATES OF AMERICA. The fraction 1/100 appears beneath the bow of the wreath.

HISTORICAL VALUES					
Fine					
1960: $2,500	1980: $30,000	1st ed./2003: $200,000	2nd ed./2005: $245,000	3rd ed./2008: $450,000	4th edition: $450,000

1854-S LIBERTY HEAD HALF EAGLE

STANDARDS · **Weight:** 8.359 grams. **Composition:** 90% gold, 10% copper. **Net weight:** .24287 oz. pure gold. **Diameter:** 21.6 mm. **Edge:** Reeded. **RARITY** · The 1854-S half eagle may not be the most famous rarity in the U.S. gold series, but it certainly is one of the most elusive. Only three examples are known, two of which are in private hands. The rank of this coin will surely rise when the Eliasberg example is sold along with the rest of the Texas collection in which it currently resides. **CERTIFIED POPULATION** · 1

The earliest collectors of U.S. coins formed their collections with virtually no regard to mintmarks. It was not until after Augustus G. Heaton's *Treatise on the Coinage of the United States Branch Mints* was published in 1893 that collecting branch-mint coinage became popular. The famous Texas dealer B. Max Mehl once stated that when he began his career, he paid little attention to where a coin was struck. When numismatists finally began to pay attention to branch-mint coins, it became apparent that many issues were very rare. The 1854-S half eagle is a star among the many scarce coins that were identified. Only 268 examples were struck for the year. Today, just three coins survive. The reason for the low mintage is still a mystery. It has been speculated that acid needed to part or refine gold was in short supply and that this may have resulted in the low mintage of quarter eagles and half eagles. However, a more probable reason is that depositors preferred larger-denomination coins, as they were easier to store and count. At the time, coins were struck specifically to the order of holders of bullion. Double eagles, eagles, and gold dollars were made in large quantities in 1854, so the "lack of acid" theory can be dismissed, although the idea was unchallenged until recent times. Whatever the reason, today the 1854-S half eagle is a great rarity.

The first auction appearance of an 1854-S half eagle was in the F.C.C. Boyd collection. The Numismatic Gallery (Abe Kosoff and Abner Kreisberg) sold Boyd's collection in 1945 and 1946. The 1854-S half eagle was sold for the then-astounding sum of $5,250 to Louis Eliasberg. The coin remained in his collection until it was sold in 1982. It now resides in a prominent Texas collection that is scheduled to be sold in the next year or so. The Boyd 1854-S half eagle was graded Extremely Fine in 1946, but by today's standard would be called Uncirculated by most dealers and is considered the finest of the three survivors.

Another example of the 1854-S half eagle was obtained privately by B. Max Mehl, who later sold the coin to Colonel E.H.R.

Christian Gobrecht designed the Liberty Head obverse, as well as the eagle reverse, that was used on quarter eagles, half eagles, and eagles until the first decade of the 20th century.

Green (son of Hetty Green, the "Witch of Wall Street"), one of the greatest collectors of his time. Later, the coin changed hands several times and finally became part of the Samuel W. Wolfson collection. Stack's sold the Wolfson collection in 1962, when it realized $16,500. Today, a private collector owns the coin.

The third example of this incredible rarity surfaced in 1919 and became part of the Waldo Newcomer collection. When the Newcomer estate was distributed in the 1930s, B. Max Mehl again sold a specimen to the insatiable Colonel Green, who at one time owned two examples. This coin was later part of the Josiah K. Lilly collection, which was donated to the Smithsonian Institution and is now part of its National Numismatic Collection.

Designed by Christian Gobrecht. The obverse portrays Liberty with a coronet, facing left and surrounded by 13 stars. The reverse features an eagle with spread wings clutching arrows and olive branches. Mintage is 268 coins.

HISTORICAL VALUES					
About Uncirculated					
1960: $5,000	1980: $200,000	1st ed./2003: $750,000	2nd ed./2005: $1,000,000	3rd ed./2008: $2,000,000	4th edition: $2,500,000

1848 "CAL." LIBERTY HEAD QUARTER EAGLE

STANDARDS · **Weight:** 4.18 grams. **Composition:** 90% gold, 10% copper. **Diameter:** 18 mm. **Edge:** Reeded. **RARITY** · Fewer than 75 1848 CAL. quarter eagles are believed to exist. There are a couple of amazing survivors for the issue. An NGC MS-67 sold in 2008 for $345,000. **CERTIFIED POPULATION** · 108

The California gold rush began on January 24, 1848, when James Marshall discerned a gleaming gold nugget at Sutter's Mill on the American River. This had a profound impact on U.S. numismatics, when one considers that a new mint was established in San Francisco (in 1854), that countless assayers and refiners began to strike their own coinage, and that the double eagle became a staple of the United States' currency system because of this gold discovery. One of the more interesting by-products of the gold rush is the 1848 CAL. quarter eagle.

On December 9, 1848, California's military governor, Colonel R.B. Mason, sent 230 ounces of the yellow metal to secretary of War William L. Marcy. Secretary Marcy, in turn, had the bullion delivered to Philadelphia Mint director Robert M. Patterson, who was instructed to use some of the gold for specially marked quarter eagles. In commemoration of the important discovery in California, 1,389 pieces were produced, all stamped with the abbreviation CAL. on the upper reverse, just above the eagle's head. Due to this special inscription, many numismatists rightfully consider the 1848 CAL. quarter eagles the nation's first commemorative coin.

Because the 1848 CAL. quarter eagle was a direct result of the California gold rush, it is a highly coveted issue. Not only does the coin have a direct link to U.S. history, but also it is one of the rarest regular-issue Liberty Head quarter eagles. Because many examples are deeply reflective, some old listings suggest that a few 1848 CAL. quarter eagles were struck in Proof format. However, modern study has revealed that all were struck from the same pair of dies at the same time and that the dies had prooflike, not Proof, finishes.

Apparently, the word CAL. was punched into the dies while the coins were still in the press, preventing any flattening on the opposite side of the coin. At least one coin shows evidence of having been punched three times! All of the coins were stamped with

"Forty-niners," as they were called, were individuals who moved to California from both the Eastern United States and abroad in 1849 to capitalize on the discovery of gold the year prior.

the same punch, but the position of the punch sometimes varies. Nefarious individuals, wishing to capitalize on this rarity, have attempted to create counterfeits by making their own "CAL." punch and stamping it into the back of regular-issue 1848 quarter eagles from Philadelphia. Fortunately, no one has yet been able to duplicate the CAL. punch exactly, but certification of any 1848 CAL. quarter eagle is a must.

Designed by Christian Gobrecht. The obverse features a bust of Liberty wearing a coronet. The word LIBERTY is inscribed on the headband. The portrait is encircled by 13 stars, with the date at the bottom. The reverse depicts a spread eagle located in the center with the words UNITED STATES OF AMERICA written towards the edge. The denomination 2 1/2 D. is featured at the base of the reverse.

HISTORICAL VALUES
Uncirculated

1960: $1,500	1980: $20,000	1st ed./2003: $45,000	2nd ed./2005: $75,000	3rd ed./2008: $85,000	4th edition: $100,000

1927-D SAINT-GAUDENS DOUBLE EAGLE

STANDARDS · **Weight:** 33.436 grams. **Composition:** 90% gold, 10% copper. **Net weight:** .96750 oz. pure gold. **Diameter:** 34 mm. **Edge:** Lettered, includes E PLURIBUS UNUM with the words divided by stars. **RARITY** · Extremely rare. Only a dozen or so examples are known to exist, most of which are in Choice Uncirculated to Gem Uncirculated condition. A few are permanently impounded in museum collections. With the discovery of 10 Israel Swift 1933 double eagles, the 1927-D is now the rarest regular-issue Saint-Gaudens double eagle. **CERTIFIED POPULATION** · 14

Despite a mintage of 180,000 coins, the 1927-D is one of the rarest dates in the entire double eagle series. Though 1927 was too early for the coins to have been affected by the gold recall of 1933, it seems that the entire mintage was destroyed, except for a handful of survivors.

Millions of U.S. gold coins were shipped to Europe from around 1879 to 1933 for international payments. Often, foreign banks, merchants, and other interests wanted gold or "hard money," not printed paper bills. After the United States stopped paying out gold coins in 1933 and later asked for their return from the U.S. public, the foreign banks held on to them more tightly than ever! Following World War II, many long-stored double eagles and other coins were found in vaults in Switzerland (in particular), France, Venezuela, and elsewhere, much to the delight of numismatists. Later, word spread and a modern gold rush was on! In the case of the 1927-D, fewer coins may have gone to Europe because of the lower initial mintage; in any case, no quantities of this date have yet been discovered there.

At one time, the true rarity of the 1927-D double eagle went unrecognized. Several other dates were considered much rarer, including the 1924-D and 1926-D, both later found by the hundreds in Europe. However, unlike those other dates, the 1927-D double eagle *remains* a great rarity. As time passes and the European gold stocks dwindle, the likelihood of any 1927-D coins showing up becomes smaller and smaller.

To illustrate that rarities can show up in the strangest places, we cite the appearance of two 1927-D double eagles in 1995, following their discovery in the Museum of Connecticut History in Hartford, Connecticut. The museum's core collection was formed by Joseph Mitchelson and donated to the museum in 1911. Later, curators continued to expand the collection with newly released coins. Apparently, two 1927-D double eagles were purchased at their time of issue in 1927, and then squirreled away in the collection. Although researchers were aware of this fabulous collection (some had even visited the site), these two coins escaped detection until their discovery in 1995, when the Museum decided to sell off some duplicates.

The Museum of Connecticut History—where two examples of the 1927-D double eagle were found in 1995—is housed, along with the State Library and State Supreme Court, in a historic building in downtown Hartford.

Designed by Augustus Saint-Gaudens. The obverse depicts standing Liberty draped in Romanesque clothing and holding a torch. The reverse features an eagle in flight. Mintage for this issue was 180,000, but nearly all examples were melted.

HISTORICAL VALUES

Gem Uncirculated

1960: $1,500	1980: $150,000	1st ed./2003: $500,000	2nd ed./2005: $1,100,000	3rd ed./2008: $2,000,000	4th edition: $2,000,000

1873-CC "NO ARROWS" LIBERTY SEATED DIME

STANDARDS · **Weight:** 2.462 grams. **Composition:** 90% silver, 10% copper. **Diameter:** 17.9 mm. **Edge:** Reeded. **RARITY** · Unique! The only known example is an MS-65 that last sold at public auction in July 2004 for $891,250. **CERTIFIED POPULATION** · 1

Only one 1873-CC "No Arrows" Liberty Seated dime is known to exist. Although Mint records indicate a mintage of 12,400 pieces, all were presumed melted in mid-1873 and were most likely turned into dimes with arrowheads on either side of the date (indicating a slight change in the weight of the coins). The sole survivor is a coin sent to Philadelphia in 1873 to be evaluated by the annual Assay Commission. For some unexplained reason, the coin was saved from destruction and added to the National Numismatic Collection (then known as the Mint Cabinet). Once there, it disappeared from memory until it resurfaced in 1909 as part of the biggest coin trade ever to take place!

In 1909, future secretary of the Treasury William Woodin purchased a pair of gold $50 patterns (No. 19) from dealers Stephen Nagy and John Haseltine. The transaction created a furor at the Mint, which claimed that the unique patterns were its property. To reverse the transaction, the Mint swapped crates of rare coins and patterns for the two $50 gold pieces. Included in the trade was the unique 1873-CC "No Arrows" dime.

The coin was exhibited at the 1914 American Numismatic Society exhibit and over the next several decades passed hands among a few prominent collectors. The rarity was offered at auction as part of the Adolph Menjou Collection in 1950 by Abe Kosoff. Although Louis Eliasberg had traveled from Baltimore to purchase the coin, he was denied by dealer Jim Kelly, who took down the coin with a winning bid of $3,650. Kelly must have been buying on speculation, as Louis Eliasberg purchased the 1873-C C "No Arrows" dime later that year, on November 7, 1950 (it was the last coin he needed to complete his collection of U.S. coins). The silver coins from Eliasberg's collection were sold 46 years later, and his 1873-CC "No Arrows" dime fetched $550,000. Since then, the coin reappeared at auction in 2004, selling for $891,250; and again in 2012 for $1,840,000. The 1873-CC "No Arrows" dime is one of only four Carson City Mint coins to appear in the 100 Greatest U.S. Coins. The others are the 1876-CC twenty-cent piece (No. 26), the 1873-CC "No Arrows" quarter dollar (No. 75), and the 1870-CC double eagle (No. 79), all of which are extremely rare (but none except the 1873-CC "No Arrows" dime is unique).

Today, the importance of the 1873-CC "No Arrows" Liberty Seated dime is quite apparent, but that has not always been the case. It must be remembered that early collectors of U.S. coinage paid very little attention to mintmarks. It was not until the 1950s that the true rarity of this great coin was really known.

Designed by Christian Gobrecht (obverse) and James B. Longacre (reverse). The obverse shows Liberty in a flowing gown sitting on a rock. Her left hand holds a staff surmounted by a liberty cap; her right hand steadies a shield and holds a band bearing the word LIBERTY. The legend UNITED STATES OF AMERICA appears near the outer rim, and the date appears at the base of the obverse, beneath the rock. The reverse shows the words ONE DIME within a wreath. The mintmark appears below the wreath.

The building of the Carson City Mint—which operated for a total of 19 years in the late 1800s—now serves as the home of the Nevada State Museum.

HISTORICAL VALUES
Choice Uncirculated

1960: $25,000	1980: $250,000	1st ed./2003: $750,000	2nd ed./2005: $1,000,000	3rd ed./2008: $1,500,000	4th edition: $2,000,000

1884 PROOF TRADE DOLLAR

STANDARDS · **Weight:** 27.216 grams. **Composition:** 90% silver, 10% copper. **Diameter:** 38 mm. **Edge:** Reeded. **RARITY** · Extremely rare. Only 10 examples were struck, all in Proof format. **CERTIFIED POPULATION** · 17

The 1884 trade dollar is shrouded in mystery and intrigue. Unknown until 1907, the 1884 trade dollar first appeared when a small hoard of six pieces came on the market, all from the same source. Those six pieces have since been dispersed, along with several other pieces that have appeared on the market. Whenever an 1884 trade dollar comes up for sale, it always creates considerable excitement.

Tradition has placed the mintage of the 1884 trade dollar at 10 coins (all Proofs), a figure that is actually supported by Mint records. Thus, the 1884 trade dollar has a somewhat greater claim to legitimacy than does the 1885 trade dollar (No. 8), for which no Mint records exist. The late Carl W.A. Carlson, a talented researcher who at different times worked for Paramount, NASCA, and Stack's, felt that the 1884 trade dollar was a "legitimate" issue, a regular Proof, but that only 10 were made.

A small number of copper 1884 trade dollars are known, two of which were silver-plated. One of these now resides in the National Numismatic Collection, housed in the Smithsonian's Museum of American History.

For the last several years, the 1884 trade dollar has appeared at auction at the rate of one coin per year. However, this frequency is elevated because of the sale and resale of one coin that had been off the market for decades. Most of the 1884 trade dollars sold in recent years have gone into strong hands, and it is unlikely that they will reappear any time soon.

All 10 of the 1884 trade dollars are currently accounted for. Several of the coins have lengthy pedigrees and/or have been part of famous coin collections of the past. The finest example, illustrated here, came out of the collections of William Forester Dunham (1941) and Floyd T. Starr (1992). Currently graded PF-67 by the Professional Coin Grading Service, this coin sold at auction in October 2000 for more than $500,000. It sold again in recent years for more than $1 million.

Chester Alan Arthur, the "Gentleman Boss," was president of the United States when the 1884 trade dollar was minted.

Designed by William Barber. The obverse shows Liberty in a flowing gown facing left and sitting on a bale of cotton and American produce. Her right arm is extended and holds an olive branch. In her left hand, she holds a banner with the word LIBERTY. A small scroll below the bale (just above the date) bears the motto IN GOD WE TRUST. Liberty is surrounded by 13 stars. The reverse shows a plain eagle with outstretched wings, an olive branch in its left talon, and a bunch of arrows in its right. The words UNITED STATES OF AMERICA and a scroll bearing the motto E PLURIBUS UNUM appear above the eagle. The weight and fineness (420 GRAINS .900 FINE) and the denomination (TRADE DOLLAR) appear beneath the eagle.

HISTORICAL VALUES
Choice Proof

1960: $7,500	1980: $50,000	1st ed./2003: $200,000	2nd ed./2005: $225,000	3rd ed./2008: $500,000	4th edition: $750,000

1833 PROOF CAPPED HEAD HALF EAGLE

STANDARDS · **Weight:** 8.75 grams. **Composition:** 90% gold, 10% copper. **Diameter:** 25 mm. **Edge:** Reeded. **RARITY** · The Capped Head half eagles minted from 1813 until 1834 represent one of the most challenging issues of coins in the U.S. series. Some of the greatest coins ever produced are found among the half eagles of this period. The William Kneass modification design, which was struck from 1829 through 1834, comprises extremely rare coins. Four examples of the 1833 are known in Proof, two of which are in superb condition. **CERTIFIED POPULATION** · 5

The 1833 Proof half eagle is considered one of the greatest U.S. coins mainly on the merits of the magnificent specimen from the John Jay Pittman collection, brought to market by David W. Akers. Pittman, an employee of Eastman Kodak in Rochester, New York, collected coins over a long period of time and was able to acquire many rarities that others overlooked. This 1833 half eagle is deeply mirrored, well struck, and in virtually the same state as the day it was made. This wonderful half eagle is also richly toned and fully original. It is simply a breathtaking example of early U.S. gold coinage.

As a date, the 1833 half eagle is also very rare. Fewer than 75 circulation-strike examples are thought to have survived. Early U.S. gold coins were worth more for their bullion value than for the coins' face value, so the survival rate for these early issues is minuscule. For the year 1833, there are two varieties: the Large Date and Small Date. There are four Proofs known for the year, all of which are the Large Date variety. Besides the Pittman coin, there is also an example of this rare issue in the National Numismatic Collection, housed in the Smithsonian Institution. Two impaired examples have been certified at the PF-58 level.

The Pittman coin has a long and illustrious pedigree. It was once a part of the collections of J. Colvin Randall, Lorin G. Parmelee, James Flanagan, Jake Bell, and King Farouk. John Jay Pittman purchased the coin in Egypt in 1954 when the collection of the deposed Farouk was sold at public auction. The coin realized 210 Egyptian pounds, the equivalent at the time of about $600. In 1997, the coin was sold for $467,500 at the Pittman estate auction! The coin crossed the auction block again in 2005 for $977,500.

Like the Pittman example of this great coin, the specimen that resides in the National Numismatic Collection is of gem quality. It is quite lucky that the coin has remained so nice. For many years over the last two centuries, the gold coins were kept very nice, but silver coins in the collection were harshly cleaned when some well-meaning employees of the museum would occasionally polish the tarnished silver coins. Luckily, the gold coins did not discolor and were spared such harsh treatment.

The year of this Proof rarity—1833—is also the year that the Mint moved into new headquarters. The design of the second Mint building incorporated a courtyard to allow more sunlight to illuminate the workrooms inside.

Designed by William Kneass, a modification of the John Reich design. The obverse features a capped Liberty, facing left and surrounded by 13 stars. The reverse displays a heraldic eagle clutching arrows and olive branches. Mintage is unknown.

HISTORICAL VALUES
Gem Proof

1960: $3,500	1980: $100,000	1st ed./2003: $500,000	2nd ed./2005: $750,000	3rd ed./2008: $1,000,000	4th edition: $1,000,000

1916-D MERCURY DIME

STANDARDS · **Weight:** 2.50 grams. **Composition:** 90% silver, 10% copper. **Diameter:** 17.9 mm. **Edge:** Reeded. **RARITY** · Scarce, but still one of the more affordable coins in the 100 Greatest U.S. Coins. The true scarcity of the 1916-D dime has been masked by the presence of numerous fakes, most of which were created by the addition of a small mintmark on the back of a Philadelphia dime. Certification remains a must to prevent the disappointment of discovering, sometimes years later, that your beloved 1916-D dime is a fake! **CERTIFIED POPULATION** · 10,413

Although the 1916-D dime is no great rarity, it remains one of the most popular coins of the 20th century, thus warranting inclusion as one of the 100 Greatest U.S. Coins.

The story of the 1916-D dime began more than a decade earlier, when President Theodore Roosevelt ordered the redesign of all U.S. coins. Gold coins underwent facelifts in 1907 and 1908, the cent in 1909, and the nickel in 1913. The dime, quarter dollar, and half dollar were forced to wait until 1916 because a law required coin designs to be in place for 25 years before they could be changed.

Adolph A. Weinman was chosen to redesign the dime and half dollar. For the dime, Weinman chose a head of Liberty wearing a winged cap. The artist intended for the wings to represent freedom of thought, but because so many people confused the image with the Roman messenger-god, Mercury, the coin became known popularly as the Mercury dime.

In keeping with tradition, the Philadelphia Mint bore the brunt of dime production in 1916, followed closely by the San Francisco Mint. The third mint, at Denver, was hardly a factor in 1916, producing only 264,000 dimes, barely one hundredth of the dimes produced at Philadelphia. This tiny mintage was to be the lowest of any Mercury Head dime produced from the beginning of the series in 1916 until the demise of the design in 1945.

Thus, it is easy to understand why this date has become so popular with collectors; every school-kid in the United States needed the date to complete a set. Even when silver coins were still in circulation, the 1916-D dime seemed to be the one date that could not be found in loose change. Nevertheless, most 1916-D dimes known today are well-worn, indicating that the scarcity of this date was not initially recognized. Indeed, finding a nice Very Fine or better example is difficult (and expensive).

It should also be noted that the 1916-D Mercury Dime is one of the most counterfeited of all U.S. coins. Thousands of Philadelphia issues have been altered by adding the "D" mintmark to the reverse. It is highly recommended to only buy certified coins of this issue.

Adolph A. Weinman, designer of the so-called Mercury dime.

Designed by A.A. Weinman. The obverse features a head of Liberty wearing a winged cap, LIBERTY above, IN GOD WE TRUST at lower left, and the date below. The reverse shows a fasces (ax and bundle of sticks tied together) in front of an olive branch, UNITED STATES OF AMERICA in an arc above, ONE DIME in an arc below, and E PLURIBUS UNUM in the right field.

HISTORICAL VALUES
Choice Uncirculated

1960: $750	1980: $3,500	1st ed./2003: $10,000	2nd ed./2005: $14,000	3rd ed./2008: $17,500	4th edition: $20,000

1804 "PLAIN 4"
CAPPED BUST EAGLE

STANDARDS · **Weight:** 17.50 grams. **Composition:** 92% gold, 8% silver and copper. **Net weight:** .56587 oz. pure gold. **Diameter:** 33 mm. **Edge:** Reeded. **RARITY** · Four examples are currently thought to exist. One still resides in the fabulous "King of Siam set," and another is part of the Harry W. Bass Jr. Reference Collection, which is on long-term loan to the museum of the American Numismatic Association in Colorado Springs, Colorado. The remaining two are in private collections, one of which sold privately for $5 million in recent years. **CERTIFIED POPULATION** · 3

In 1804, the production of eagles halted. The high intrinsic value of gold made the coins worth more than their face value. Regular production of reduced-weight eagles did not resume until 1838. In 1834, however, a very interesting issue of coins was specially minted. A November 11, 1834, letter to Samuel Moore, director of the Mint, from John Forsyth of the State Department explains why these coins were struck: "Sir: The President has directed that a complete set of the coins of the United States be sent to the king of Siam, and another to the sultan of Muscat. You are requested, therefore, to forward to the Department for that purpose, duplicate specimens of each kind now in use, whether of gold, silver, or copper." In due course, the instructions were followed, and Proof sets, each fitted into a special presentation case, were struck for diplomatic purposes for the Far East.

The problem arose that the silver dollar and the eagles were no longer being struck and therefore were not current. In an effort to include all denominations that had been struck by the U.S. Mint, it was decided to check production records to determine when the last coins of those denominations were made. Mint records indicated that 19,570 silver dollars and 3,757 eagles had been made in 1804. Mint officials in 1834 who created new versions of the coins did not realize that the silver dollars had been struck with earlier-dated dies; thus they inadvertently created a classic rarity. New dies were made for an 1804 silver dollar and gold eagle for inclusion in the 1834 Proof sets. The newly designed eagle differed slightly from the original, the most notable changes being the last digit of the date and the arrangement of the denticles inside the rim. The original 1804 eagles were struck with a Crosslet 4, while the 1834 restrikes, dated 1804, were made with a Plain 4. Moreover, unlike the eagles originally struck in 1804,

the new 1804-dated eagles were struck as a brilliant Proof, giving them a stunning appearance.

Today, one of the 1834 diplomatic presentation sets still exists, complete except for two coins. Numismatists call this the "King of Siam Set" and consider it to be one of the crown jewels of coin collecting. Three other examples of the 1804 "Plain 4" variety exist. Several examples of this fascinating rarity are also known in silver, but it is not certain that they were made in 1834. Perhaps they were struck at a later date, possibly 1859 (when extensive restriking began) or later. The Proof 1804 eagle is one of the earliest dated examples of Proof gold coinage from the United States and is highly desirable for that reason. The coins are also closely related to the legendary 1804 silver dollar, assuring their status as some of the greatest U.S. coins.

These closeup views show the Crosslet 4 and Plain 4 varieties of the eagle.

Designed by Robert Scot. The obverse features a capped bust of Liberty facing right, surrounded by 13 stars. The reverse displays a heraldic eagle clutching 13 arrows and an olive branch.

HISTORICAL VALUES					
Choice Proof					
1960: $3,500	1980: $50,000	1st ed./2003: $150,000	2nd ed./2005: $750,000	3rd ed./2008: $3,000,000	4th edition: $5,000,000

1796 LIBERTY CAP HALF CENTS

WITH POLE AND NO POLE

STANDARDS · Weight: 5.443 grams. **Composition:** Pure copper. **Diameter:** 23.5 mm. **Edge:** Plain. **RARITY** · Very rare (With Pole) or extremely rare (No Pole). An unusually high percentage of 1796 half cents are known in excellent condition, including several Uncirculated examples. This may indicate that their rarity was recognized early on by collectors, who deliberately set aside nice examples. Interestingly, a superb MS-66 example of the With Pole variety surfaced in England in the last year or so. Amazing discoveries occur in numismatics each year. **CERTIFIED POPULATION** · 82

The obverse of the "No Pole" variety.

Nearly every series of U.S. coins contains a classic rarity. In half cents, it's the 1796.

The mintage for the 1796 half cent is a mere 1,390 pieces. Compare this to the 139,690 half cents bearing the 1795 date and the 128,840 from 1797. Why were so few half cents made in 1796? The answer has to do with the availability of copper and the allocation of the resources available at the Mint.

In the early years of the U.S. Mint, finding copper for half cents and large cents was a constant problem. Native sources of copper were as yet largely untapped, and smelting operations in the United States were virtually nonexistent. Thus, the Mint resorted to unorthodox (but ingenious) methods of procuring planchets (blanks) for its coins. In April 1795, the Mint purchased 1,076 pounds of cent-size copper tokens already stamped with the advertising message of Talbot, Allum & Lee, merchants of New York City. These were cut down in size and used to produce 1795 half cents. The Mint also made use of misstruck or defective large cents, which were similarly cut down, then stamped with half-cent dies. Often, half cents dated from 1795 through 1797 show portions of the designs of the original Talbot, Allum & Lee tokens and, less often, large cents.

Once the Talbot, Allum & Lee tokens were used on the 1795 half cents, there was no copper, except for a few spoiled cents, with which to make 1796 half cents. Fortunately, the additional purchase of a small quantity of sheet copper from a local source enabled the Mint to strike some 1796 half cents.

Regarding the allocation of resources, by 1796 the Mint had already turned its attention to more lofty coins. Instead of worrying about copper for half cents, the Mint focused its attention on introducing three new denominations: the dime, quarter dollar, and quarter eagle ($2.50 gold); and on producing the bedrocks of the United States' monetary system, the large cent and silver dol-

lar (in fact, 1796 was the first year that the Mint produced every possible denomination under the system then in place). With the attention focused on producing this wide variety of coins, scant effort was exerted on producing 1796 half cents.

Two varieties of the 1796 half cent exist: the normal version and another, unfinished version that lacks the staff that normally supports the liberty cap (this variety also features a heavy, nearly horizontal crack that bisects the front of the coin). Not surprisingly, the two varieties are known as the 1796 "With Pole" and "No Pole" half cents. Both are very rare, the "No Pole" variety being the rarer of the two.

Designed by Robert Scot, engraved by John Smith Gardner. The obverse features a bust of Liberty facing right, her hair flowing loosely behind her head. A liberty cap and supporting pole (on the "With Pole" variety) appear behind her head. LIBERTY appears above the bust, the date below. The reverse shows the words HALF CENT within a plain wreath, the fraction "1/200" below and UNITED STATES OF AMERICA surrounding.

HISTORICAL VALUES					
With Pole, Very Fine					
1960: $750	1980: $7,500	1st ed./2003: $25,000	2nd ed./2005: $45,000	3rd ed./2008: $75,000	4th edition: $85,000
No Pole, Very Fine					
1960: $1,250	1980: $15,000	1st ed./2003: $75,000	2nd ed./2005: $95,000	3rd ed./2008: $150,000	4th edition: $200,000

1796 "NO STARS" CAPPED BUST QUARTER EAGLE

STANDARDS · Weight: 4.37 grams. **Composition:** 92% gold, 8% copper. **Diameter:** 20 mm. **Edge:** Reeded. **RARITY** · The exact number of specimens known is often debated. At least 100 coins survived, although there is the possibility that as many as 200 exist. **CERTIFIED POPULATION** · 98

When the founding fathers created the United States' coinage system in 1792, three gold denominations were included: the quarter eagle, half eagle, and eagle. However, demand for high-denomination coins was extremely limited. With the average worker making only a few dollars per week, one can imagine how infrequently large coins were used. Whereas the first copper coins were produced in 1793 and silver coins in 1794, it was not until 1795 that the Philadelphia Mint began to strike gold coins. The quarter eagle, in fact, was not introduced until 1796.

The 1796 "No Stars" quarter eagle is known mostly for its unusual obverse design. All 1796-dated gold and silver coins display stars on the front, with the sole exception of the "No Stars" quarter eagle. The reason for this remains uncertain. Some have suggested that the star punch used to engrave the dies broke. Another theory is that the Mint employees were reluctant to engrave the stars because new states were in the process of being admitted. With some states still in limbo, perhaps the Mint did not want to put an inaccurate number of stars on the coin.

The question of how many stars to place on coins was a common one in the early years of the Mint. Initially, the goal was to honor the original 13 colonies. Thereafter, it was felt that each new state should be honored with its own star. However, the rule does not seem to have been applied consistently; engravers sometimes forgot to add an extra star, or they may simply have run out of room on the dies. By 1798, the question appears to have been settled in favor of 13 stars, but that was not necessarily the end of any mistakes. The 1817 "15 Stars" large cent and 1828 "12 Stars" half cent (neither of which was ranked in the 100 Greatest U.S. Coins list) are glaring examples of how easily mistakes can be made.

Later in 1796, the Philadelphia Mint struck an updated version of the quarter eagle featuring 16 stars on the obverse. After striking 963 pieces without stars, the Mint produced an additional

The standard obverse of the 1796 quarter eagle featured a total of 16 stars along the left and right periphery of the obverse.

432 with the traditional stars. Even though the "With Stars" variety is significantly scarcer, the "No Stars" version has always been more popular. In 1995, the finest known 1796 "No Stars" quarter eagle was sold in a New York auction. After fierce bidding, the coin was hammered down for $602,000. The coin resold at an auction in early 2008 for $1,725,000.

Which U.S. coin features the largest number of stars? The 1839 "Starry Field Reverse" Gobrecht dollar is a candidate with 39 stars, but the real winner is the 1794 "Starred Reverse" large cent, with 94 (coincidentally, one for each year)!

Designed by Robert Scot. The obverse features Liberty wearing a liberty cap. The word LIBERTY is featured at the top with the date located at the bottom. The reverse depicts an eagle surrounded by the words UNITED STATES OF AMERICA. Above the eagle's head is a field of stars and six clouds.

HISTORICAL VALUES
About Uncirculated

1960: $2,500	1980: $20,000	1st ed./2003: $75,000	2nd ed./2005: $85,000	3rd ed./2008: $150,000	4th edition: $175,000

1792 QUARTER DOLLAR PATTERN

STANDARDS · **Weight:** Varies from 11.34 to 11.66 grams for copper; 25.92+ grams for white metal. **Diameter:** 28 mm or larger; metal content either pure copper or white metal. **Edge:** Reeded on the normal-sized pieces; plain on the oversized examples. **RARITY** · Extremely rare. Only two copper examples are known, the finest of which is in the National Numismatic Collection at the Smithsonian Institution. Four white metal pieces are known, as well as a pair of uniface white metal examples. **CERTIFIED POPULATION** · 0

One of the most beautiful and finely executed of all U.S. coins is the 1792 quarter dollar pattern.

The 1792 quarter dollar pattern was created as part of a series of pattern coins meant to pave the way for the regular production of coins in 1793. Unfortunately, no "real" quarter dollars were struck until 1796, and then with a completely different design. Credit for the design of the 1792 quarter dollar pattern goes to Joseph Wright, a U.S. artist who became the first engraver of the U.S. Mint. His delicate hand can also be seen on the Liberty Cap large cents issued in the last part of 1793. Unfortunately, Wright's tenure as engraver was cut short by yellow fever, a dreaded and deadly disease that afflicted Philadelphians in 1793 and several years thereafter. Both Wright and his wife died in 1793, just as the Mint was finding its footing.

For many years, the 1792 pattern quarter dollar remained a mystery because, unlike all of the other 1792 patterns, this one bore no markings as to its intended denomination or value. At various times and by various numismatists, this has been called a pattern cent, pattern quarter dollar, or pattern half eagle.

The confusion is justified. The diameter of the 1792 pattern quarter dollar matches closely that of the first cents made in 1793, but the reeded edge indicates that the intent was to produce a coin of gold or silver (copper coins had lettered or ornamented edges). The diameter was also similar to (but slightly larger than) that of the first half eagles. The combination of an eagle reverse with no denomination made a tempting comparison.

Contemporary evidence revealed the true intention behind these coins. Before his death, Wright asked his neighbor to submit a bill to the Mint for work he had performed on "Two Essays of a Quarter Dollar." The only coin that could possibly fit the evidence is the 1792 pattern quarter dollar.

The 1792 pattern quarter dollars are found in a variety of different metals and formats, including normal-sized copper pieces,

Joseph Wright's engraving of George Washington was widely copied and served as the basis for many 19th-century medallic portraits of the first president.

Joseph Wright's design for the quarter dollar was unfortunately never used on a regular-issue coin. The first regular-issue quarters did not appear until 1796, and those used the Draped Bust design.

oversized white-metal (pewter?) examples, and one-sided examples in white metal. All of them are either extremely rare or unique.

Designed by Joseph Wright. The obverse shows a delicate bust of Liberty facing right, her hair tied up neatly with a ribbon. The word LIBERTY hovers above her head and the date appears beneath. The border is a simple raised circle. The reverse features an eagle with outstretched wings standing on a round mound (perhaps a globe) surrounded by UNITED STATES OF AMERICA. The border consists of 87 tiny stars.

HISTORICAL VALUES
Extremely Fine

1960: $2,500	1980: $30,000	1st ed./2003: $175,000	2nd ed./2005: $250,000	3rd ed./2008: $500,000	4th edition: $650,000

1836, 1838, AND 1839 GOBRECHT SILVER DOLLARS

STANDARDS · Weight: Varies from 26.697 to 27.021 grams, depending on the variety. **Composition:** Varies from 89.2% to 90% silver, the balance in copper, depending on the year and variety. **Diameter:** 38 mm. **Edge:** Plain or reeded, depending on the year and the variety. **RARITY ·** Very rare to extremely rare. Surprisingly, Gem Proofs of any date are extremely rare, whether as an original or a restrike. **CERTIFIED POPULATION ·** 253

The silver dollars designed by Christian Gobrecht that were minted between 1836 and 1839 are among the most beautiful U.S. coins ever produced.

For many years, the Gobrecht dollars were considered to be patterns, but the large number of circulated 1836 and 1839 silver dollars, plus some deeper research into the Mint Archives, prove that some of these two dates were, indeed, intended for circulation. On the other hand, all 1838 Gobrecht dollars are unquestionably patterns.

Gobrecht dollars are found in an interesting variety of configurations. The obverses of the 1836 Gobrecht dollars can be found with the artist's name in the field below the base or on the base (it was moved there after Gobrecht was criticized for featuring his name so prominently). The "skies" on the reverses of the 1836 Gobrecht dollars are either empty or filled with 26 stars. Edges come plain or reeded. Although 600 Gobrecht silver dollars were struck in 1837, they bore the date 1836. Accordingly, there is no such thing as an 1837-dated dollar. Stars were added to the obverses of the 1838 and 1839 silver dollars; Gobrecht's name was deleted; the edges are found either plain or reeded; and the reverses are either plain or starred.

A confusing array of restrikes was made in later years, beginning in the spring of 1859. Planchet weights vary, as does the alignment of the obverse and reverse dies relative to each other. Even today, experts are trying to develop better ways of classifying these rare and interesting coins. Very recently, coin researcher John Dannreuther discovered that *all* Gobrecht dollars originally featured the designer's name on the base, but the dies were effaced before striking. This interesting series is sure to yield new information as serious study of the Gobrecht dollars continues.

Gobrecht silver dollars of 1838 and 1839 featured a slightly different obverse design, with stars added around the figure of Liberty and Gobrecht's name removed.

The Gobrecht dollars were the first silver dollars produced at the Mint since 1804 (when some were struck from earlier-dated dies; also, we're not counting the 1804-dated silver dollars that were specially made in 1834 for diplomatic presentation purposes). While the design eventually transformed into the Liberty Seated silver dollar in 1840, the Gobrecht dollars continue to command the respect and admiration of collectors.

Designed by Christian Gobrecht. The obverse shows Liberty in a flowing gown sitting on a rock. Her left hand holds a staff surmounted by a liberty cap; her right hand steadies a shield and holds a band bearing the word LIBERTY. The date appears at the base of the obverse, below the rock. Depending on the year and variety, the designer's name will either be missing from the coin, below the base of the rock, or on the base of the rock, and stars may surround the figure of Liberty. The reverse features an eagle in flight heading towards the left side of the coin. Surrounding the eagle are the legends UNITED STATES OF AMERICA and ONE DOLLAR. Depending on the year and variety, the fields surrounding the eagle will be either plain or filled with 26 stars.

HISTORICAL VALUES					
1836, Choice Proof					
1960: $1,750	1980: $5,500	1st ed./2003: $15,000	2nd ed./2005: $25,000	3rd ed./2008: $45,000	4th edition: $45,000
1838, Choice Proof					
1960: $2,500	1980: $7,500	1st ed./2003: $40,000	2nd ed./2005: $65,000	3rd ed./2008: $85,000	4th edition: $85,000
1839, Choice Proof					
1960: $2,500	1980: $7,500	1st ed./2003: $40,000	2nd ed./2005: $55,000	3rd ed./2008: $80,000	4th edition: $85,000

1955 DOUBLED-DIE OBVERSE LINCOLN CENT

STANDARDS · **Weight:** 3.11 grams. **Composition:** 95% copper, 5% tin and zinc. **Diameter:** 19 mm. **Edge:** Plain. **RARITY** · Scarce, with probably 10,000 to 20,000 known in all grades. Mint State examples are much more difficult to locate, and of these nearly all have brown surfaces. Full red coins are very rare. Caution is advised when purchasing mint red examples, as many have been artificially toned. **CERTIFIED POPULATION** · 7,347

Doubled-die error coins are actually quite common in the field of error coinage. There are many dates in the Lincoln cent series that are known with some degree of multiple impressions on either the obverse or reverse. The 1955 Doubled-Die Obverse Lincoln cent, however, is one of the most dramatic errors on U.S. coinage seen in the 20th century. The obverse numerals and lettering are very clearly doubled and easily seen with the naked eye. Modern coin dies are created when they are struck from a working hub, which stamps the incuse image onto the die that will subsequently strike the coins. This usually requires more than one blow, and in 1955, one of the working obverse dies at the Philadelphia Mint was misaligned on the second blow from the hub. The result of this misalignment was the double image seen on 1955 Doubled-Die Obverse cents. The dies for the 1955 cent escaped the quality controls in place at the time. According to contemporary accounts, the cents were struck during the night shift, and by morning they had already been mixed with 10 million other cents. The decision was made to let the coins circulate.

It is thought that the first 1955 Doubled-Die Obverse cents appeared in Massachusetts and upstate New York within a short period. The coins at first sold for a very small premium, but soon traded for more than $10 each. By 1960, they were listed in the *Guide Book of United States Coins* (the "Red Book") and became a well-known collectible in the Lincoln series. Later the error was included as a space to be filled in coin albums, and the popularity of the issue continued to rise. Today the 1955 Doubled-Die Obverse cent has been known to sell for more than $50,000 in gem condition.

Although it is not the most expensive Lincoln cent error (this honor goes to the 1943 bronze cent and the 1969-S Doubled-Die Obverse cent), it is one of the most popular. Collectors dream of finding one in a roll of "wheaties" or in an unsearched hoard of Lincoln cents. The reality is that because of the very clear dou-

President Abraham Lincoln was the first U.S. president to have his likeness used on a U.S. coin. The Lincoln cent remains a popular and collectable design today.

bling seen on the obverse, to our knowledge none have been "cherrypicked" in many years.

There is a much less expensive error seen on 1955 cents that is the result of die deterioration. It is known as the "poor man's doubled die." The doubling is much less pronounced, and these coins usually sell for just a few dollars.

Designed by Victor David Brenner. The obverse depicts a bust of Abraham Lincoln facing right, **IN GOD WE TRUST** above, **LIBERTY** to the left, and the date to the right. The reverse is plain and understated (but impressive), with stylized ears of wheat on either side and a big **ONE CENT** in the middle. A smaller **E PLURIBUS UNUM** appears above, and **UNITED STATES OF AMERICA** appears below **ONE CENT**.

HISTORICAL VALUES
Uncirculated

1960: $50	1980: $550	1st ed./2003: —	2nd ed./2005: —	3rd ed./2008: $3,000	4th edition: $3,500

1873-CC "NO ARROWS" LIBERTY SEATED QUARTER DOLLAR

STANDARDS · **Weight:** 6.221 grams. **Composition:** 90% silver, 10% copper. **Diameter:** 24.3 mm. **Edge:** Reeded. **RARITY** · Five known. The finest known 1873-CC "No Arrows" quarter dollar, an MS-64, sold for $460,000 in August 2012. One well-worn example is also known.

CERTIFIED POPULATION · 6

The standard obverse of the 1873 quarter dollar featured arrows at the date to signify that the coin's weight had changed from 6.22 to 6.25 grams.

The 1873-CC "No Arrows" quarter dollar was supposedly made in a quantity of 4,000 pieces, yet only five examples are known to have survived. Most assuredly, the quarter dollar suffered the same fate as the 1873-CC "No Arrows" dime (now unique), essentially being wiped out in a melt in 1873. At least one of the quarter dollars came from the same package of 1873-CC coins sent to the Assay Commission for analysis, plus a few more of the quarter dollars must have been spared from destruction by some other means.

In looking at the price trends for major rarities, a reasonable conclusion is that these special coins increase in price over time. However, the air at the top is rarified, and many factors affect the price of "blue-chip" coins. Factors include economic conditions, market timing, the simultaneous appearance of more than one example of a rarity, auction fever, auction venue, and a buyer's or seller's decision to hold the coin for an extended period. When the MS-62 Eliasberg 1873-CC "No Arrows" quarter dollar reentered the market in 1997, it realized $187,000 after spirited bidding. Exactly two years later, the same coin sold for $106,375—a rather substantial loss for the seller, but a relative bargain for the buyer, as the finest known 1873-CC "No Arrows" quarter dollar (an MS-64) had sold in the meantime for $209,000! Timing is everything. For rarities, including the majority of pieces in the 100 Greatest U.S. Coins, handsome price increases have been the rule, and hardly ever the exception, if quality pieces are bought with care and held for the long term. However, in the short term, as illustrated above, profits are sometimes elusive.

Although the 1873-CC "No Arrows" quarter dollar is a great rarity, as recently as 1996 a previously unknown example surfaced. The coin had belonged to an antique dealer in the 1940s and 1950s, and it had been handed down without recognition of the coin's true rarity.

Designed by Christian Gobrecht (obverse) and James B. Longacre (reverse). The obverse shows Liberty in a flowing gown sitting on a rock. Her left hand holds a staff surmounted by a liberty cap; her right hand steadies a shield and holds a band bearing the word LIBERTY. An arc of 13 stars appears above Liberty, and the date appears below the rock at the base of the obverse. The reverse shows an eagle with a shield on its chest, an olive branch in its right talon, and a bunch of arrows in its left. A scroll with the words E PLURIBUS UNUM hovers above the eagle. The words UNITED STATES OF AMERICA appear above the eagle; the abbreviations QUAR. DOL. appear below. The mintmark appears between the bottom of the eagle and the denomination.

HISTORICAL VALUES
Uncirculated

1960: $3,500	1980: $75,000	1st ed./2003: $175,000	2nd ed./2005: $185,000	3rd ed./2008: $250,000	4th edition: $300,000

1796 DRAPED BUST QUARTER DOLLAR

STANDARDS · **Weight:** 6.739 grams. **Composition:** 89% silver, 11% copper. **Diameter:** 27.5 mm. **Edge:** Reeded. **RARITY** · 6,146 struck. While most 1796 quarter dollars are well-circulated, a surprisingly large number of Mint State pieces exist, including several gems. The amazing NGC MS-67 example that was part of the famed Eric Newman collection sold for $1,527,500 in November 2013. **CERTIFIED POPULATION** · 525

The 1796 quarter dollar possesses the attributes required of a great coin: the mintage is tiny, it is a one-year type coin, plus it is the first year of issue for both the design *and* the denomination.

The rarity of the 1796 quarter dollar is partly a result of priorities, partly a result of demand, and partly a result of what metal was available. A look at the various denominations issued in 1796 indicates that most of the Mint's energies were focused on large cents. Silver dollars were next, followed by the new dime, then the half dime, the half eagle, and finally the quarter dollar and other denominations. Apparently, there was little demand for a quarter dollar in 1796, quite possibly because none had ever been minted before, and depositors of silver bullion did not think to request them!

Many of the 1796 quarter dollars were preserved in high grade. Allegedly, Colonel E.H.R. Green owned a hoard of more than 200 Uncirculated 1796 quarter dollars, many of which were prooflike. Supposedly, this hoard was distributed in the 1940s, but either the grades were overstated or they remain hidden, as nowhere near that number of high-grade 1796 quarter dollars exists today. Legendary numismatist Eric Newman of St. Louis was deeply involved in the disposal of the Green collection in the 1940s. We asked Mr. Newman if he remembered a large number of 1796 quarters in the Green estate. He stated that the number 200 was an exaggeration.

Some 1796 quarter dollars exhibit what appear to be deep scratches at the edges or on the high points. These so-called "adjustment marks" were caused when overweight planchets were literally filed down to remove some of the excess silver. In many cases, the cuts from the file were so deep that they remained even after the coin was struck. Adjustment marks were a part of the normal process of making coins in the late 1700s and should not be confused with scratches and marks that occurred after the coins were struck.

Most 1796 quarter dollars show weakness on the eagle's head. Because this high point on the reverse is opposite a high point on the obverse, the pressure used to strike the 1796 quarter dollars was incapable of forcing the metal into the deepest recesses of the die, except in rare instances.

Some of the prooflike 1796 quarter dollars have been called Proofs or presentation strikes in the past. These exceptional coins were early strikes from fresh dies, minus any adjustment marks on the planchets, and they were struck sharply enough that the details on the eagle's head are full and complete. While no records confirm these special strikes, it is quite possible that they were made for presentation purposes to commemorate the beginning of the new denomination.

Deceptive counterfeits exist, primarily of low-grade examples. Because of the high value of any 1796 quarter dollar, we recommend authentication or certification of any contemplated purchase. In fact, it is a good rule of thumb to have *any* high-value federal coin certified by one of the leading grading services.

Designed by Robert Scot. The obverse features a draped bust of Liberty with some of her hair tied back in a bow. LIBERTY appears above, the date below, and 15 stars are divided up to either side (eight on the left, seven on the right). The reverse features a plain eagle with outstretched wings within a wreath of palm and olive branches. The outer legend reads UNITED STATES OF AMERICA. No denomination appears anywhere on the coin.

HISTORICAL VALUES						
Extremely Fine						
1960: $1,250	1980: $7,500	1st ed./2003: $17,500	2nd ed./2005: $25,000	3rd ed./2008: $50,000	4th edition: $50,000	

1802 DRAPED BUST HALF DIME

STANDARDS · **Weight:** 1.35 grams. **Composition:** 89% silver, 11% copper. **Diameter:** 16.5 mm. **Edge:** Reeded. **RARITY** · Extremely rare. Fewer than 50 examples are known, the finest of which is a single AU-55. **CERTIFIED POPULATION** · 13

Of the 3,060 half dimes struck in 1802, only about 50 have survived. Until the discovery of the unique 1870-S half dime in 1978, the 1802 ruled the roost as "king" of the half dime series.

The story of the 1802 half dime is the classic story of attrition. Here's a coin that started out with a very low mintage, most of which was decimated over time as coins were lost or destroyed through various silver melts. The first appearance of an 1802 half dime at public auction was not until 1859 (even then, the condition of the coin was listed as "Poor"). By 1863, only three 1802 half dimes were known to exist. However, once the spotlight focused on this rarity, more examples began to appear. By 1883, 16 different examples were known. In the 1930s, dealer James G. Macallister claimed he knew of 35 examples. Today, the total population has risen to approximately 40 to 50 different examples. Certainly, a few others may exist in as-yet-undiscovered collections, but the rate at which new discoveries are being made has slowed dramatically.

Despite listings of Uncirculated examples in old auction catalogs, no truly Mint State 1802 half dimes are known to exist. At least two examples have been certified at the About Uncirculated level, both of which had been called Uncirculated in the past. Most 1802 half dimes are found in low grade, often bent or battered.

The difficulty in determining the exact population of the 1802 half dimes illustrates the problems researchers encounter using old auction records. Tracking a coin by its grade is useless because of the evolution of grading standards and terminology over the years. For instance, a Very Good coin from a century ago may be Very Fine today, and vice versa. Despite the promises of "standardized" grading, the simple truth is that even certified coins are broken out, resubmitted, and often regraded at a different level. Tracking a coin by its photograph is also dangerous because, in some instances, coins (even important ones) were not plated at all, and in other instances, stock photographs were used over and over again to illustrate the type of coin, not the actual coin. Thus, today's researcher must rely instead on new tools such as scanning technologies, the Internet, computers, and more sophisticated (and better written) auction catalogs.

On average, collectors can expect to see but one 1802 half dime appear at auction in any given year. This means that the collector seeking to acquire one of these rarities must be patient, yet ready to act quickly or wait a year for another one!

Ownership of any 1802 half dime is a mark of distinction and an accomplishment that many "big name" collectors have failed to achieve.

Designed by Robert Scot. The obverse features a draped bust of Liberty with some of her hair tied back in a bow. LIBERTY appears above, the date below, and 13 stars are divided up on the sides (seven on the left, six on the right). The reverse features a heraldic eagle with outstretched wings (similar to that seen on the Great Seal of the United States). In its beak, the eagle holds a scroll with the words E PLURIBUS UNUM. In its left talon, the eagle grasps an olive branch; in its right talon, it holds a bunch of arrows. Clouds and 13 stars appear above the eagle. The outer legend reads UNITED STATES OF AMERICA. No denomination appears anywhere on the coin.

HISTORICAL VALUES
Extremely Fine

1960: $2,000	1980: $25,000	1st ed./2003: $75,000	2nd ed./2005: $100,000	3rd ed./2008: $150,000	4th edition: $175,000

1795 "NINE LEAVES" CAPPED BUST EAGLE

STANDARDS · **Weight:** 17.50 grams. **Composition:** 92% gold, 8% silver and copper. **Diameter:** 33 mm. **Edge:** Reeded. **RARITY** · Fewer than 20 examples of the 1795 "Nine Leaves" eagle are known. Of those, four or five are Mint State coins. The finest coin certified is Choice Uncirculated MS-63. **CERTIFIED POPULATION** · 24

The Coinage Act of 1792, which established the Mint, called for various denominations, including several in gold. However, it was not until 1795 that the first U.S. gold coins were made. It is believed that George Washington wanted gold coins struck before his presidential term ended (he had been in office since 1789, accepted a second term in 1793, but had no desire for a third term). It is said that in October of 1795, Mint director Henry DeSaussure delivered 100 gold eagles to President Washington, who lived in Philadelphia at the time, as it was the seat of the federal government. The coins had been designed by Robert Scot, and, similar to the half eagles, featured a capped bust portrait of Liberty facing right. A Roman onyx cameo may have inspired the design. The reverse, an eagle with a wreath in its beak and palm branches grasped by its talons, may also have been inspired by early Roman art. The majority of 1795 gold eagles have palm branches with 13 leaves. A very few examples are known with only nine leaves. Today, the "Nine Leaves" variety is considered a major rarity. The variety was not recognized until the last few decades, and fewer than 20 can now be traced. The Harry W. Bass Jr. Reference Collection, on display at the museum of the American Numismatic Association, contains the finest known Mint State example. At least one or two repaired coins are also known. The 1795 eagles are a historic link to the early formation of the United States. President Washington took a personal interest in the striking of these coins. The 1795 eagle is also a very scarce and popular first year of issue. The so-called "Small Eagle" design was produced for only three years. The "Nine Leaves" variety can only be described as the best of the best.

The 1795 "Nine Leaves" eagle is considered a major variety for the series. Many lesser-known varieties exist of the 1795 to 1804 eagle issues, but are unrecognized in the standard catalogs.

On the standard reverse of the 1795 eagle, the eagle holds a 13-leaf palm branch.

John Dannreuther and Harry W. Bass Jr. have written an excellent study of the subject called *Early U.S. Gold Coin Varieties, 1795–1834*.

Unlike the stars on the obverse, the number of leaves in the palm branch was not tied to the number of states in the Union. Thus, it was coincidental that most of the reverses on 1795 eagles (with the exception of this "Nine Leaves" rarity) counted 13 leaves, while the obverses showed 15 stars. In 1796, one eagle variety is known with 16 stars (to show the admission of Tennessee as the 16th state), but only 11 leaves! Thus, the number of leaves in the palm branch depended not on some official edict but on the ambition, or laziness, of the engraver.

Designed by Robert Scot. The obverse features a capped bust of Liberty, facing right, surrounded by 13 stars. The small eagle reverse shows an outstretched eagle with wings spread, holding a circular wreath in its beak. Mintage for the issue is unknown.

HISTORICAL VALUES
About Uncirculated

1960: $1,000	1980: $12,500	1st ed./2003: $75,000	2nd ed./2005: $100,000	3rd ed./2008: $175,000	4th edition: $200,000

1870-CC LIBERTY HEAD DOUBLE EAGLE

STANDARDS · **Weight:** 33.436 grams. **Composition:** 90% gold, 10% copper. **Net weight:** .96750 oz. pure gold. **Diameter:** 34 mm. **Edge:** Reeded.

RARITY · Between 35 and 45 examples are believed to exist in all grades. Most are very well-worn, with extensive bagmarks. Just a few are known in relatively high-grade condition, and they command a solid six-figure price when they appear on the market. The finest known example was discovered a few year ago: a lustrous, Choice About Uncirculated example. It was lost while in transit from the grading companies. Another numismatic mystery in the making! **CERTIFIED POPULATION** · 67

In 1870, a new U.S. branch mint opened at Carson City, Nevada. Because of the Comstock Lode and other mineral discoveries, the West was producing an abundance of precious metals. It was felt that a coining facility in Carson City, only about 15 miles from the Comstock Lode, would be useful to the inhabitants of the territory. On March 10, 1870, the first Carson City double eagles were delivered by the coiner. A total of only 3,789 was struck for the year. Most were used for commercial purposes in Nevada and the surrounding territory. The key word is "used," for the average 1870-CC double eagle is well-worn and heavily abraded, with signs of extensive circulation, and so is seldom seen above Very Fine condition. There are no known Mint State examples of the 1870-CC double eagle.

The 1870-CC double eagle is highly sought after for several key reasons. First, Carson City coinage is very popular. Many individuals collect only coinage from that mint. There is a great interest in the early West and relics from that part of U.S. history. Collecting U.S. double eagles is also very popular. They are the largest and most substantial regular-issue U.S. gold coin. With the exception of the 1870-CC, a complete set of Carson City double eagles can be completed relatively easy. The 1870, however, is a real "stopper." The demand far exceeds the supplies of the "king of Carson City gold." It is by far the best-known and most highly sought-after gold coin from the Carson City Mint.

Nearly all examples of this great rarity are owned by serious collectors and are seldom offered for sale. The demand for scarce-date double eagles is at an all-time high, prompted in part by the availability of 1856-S and, in particular, 1857-S coins from the SS *Central America* hoard brought to market from 2000 to 2002. New price records are broken nearly every time a nice 1870-CC appears at auction. It has been reported that an About Uncirculated example traded hands privately for in excess of $500,000. The pressure to maximize the grade of this issue is incredibly high. Many examples have been resubmitted over the last few years, and population information from the grading services does not always take into account resubmissions.

While most examples of the 1870-CC double eagle are genuine, fakes are known to exist. Unscrupulous individuals could very easily add the tiny "CC" mintmark to the far more common 1870 double eagle. As with most great coins, authentication is an important issue.

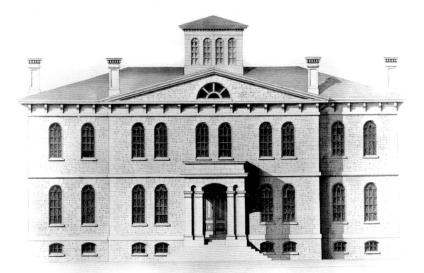

During its 19 years of operation, the Carson City Mint produced a number of numismatic rarities, including the 1870-CC double eagle.

Designed by James B. Longacre. The obverse features the portrait of Liberty facing left, wearing a coronet, and surrounded by 13 stars. The reverse features an outspread eagle and shield design. Mintage for this issue is 3,789 coins.

HISTORICAL VALUES
Extremely Fine

1960: $2,500	1980: $25,000	1st ed./2003: $125,000	2nd ed./2005: $165,000	3rd ed./2008: $285,000	4th edition: $325,000

1801, 1802, AND 1803 PROOF DRAPED BUST SILVER DOLLARS

STANDARDS · Weight: Around 27.2 grams. **Composition:** 90% silver, 10% copper. **Diameter:** Varies from 39 to 40 mm. **Edge:** Lettered HUNDRED CENTS ONE DOLLAR OR UNIT. **RARITY ·** Extremely rare. Exact mintages are unknown but cannot be more than a few of each date. Most of the 1801–1803 Proof silver dollars have survived in excellent condition. Those that have appeared on the market in recent years have all graded PF-64 or better. **CERTIFIED POPULATION ·** 26

The Proof silver dollars of 1801, 1802, and 1803 are all extremely rare, valuable, and desirable, although none of them were made anywhere near the dates on the coins, nor do they share any die characteristics with any real silver dollars made from 1801 to 1803. On the other hand, they share a close kinship with the "King of Coins," the 1804 silver dollar (No. 1)—although they are actually rarer than the 1804 silver dollar.

Exactly when the 1801 to 1803 Proof dollars were made is unclear. It may have been around 1834, when the first 1804 silver dollars were made. Or they may have been created (or the dies finished) around 1870. The weights of the coins may help to place or confirm the striking date; at around 420 grains (27.2 grams) each, they are closer in weight to the trade dollars (minted from 1873 to 1885) than either Draped Bust dollars or Liberty Seated dollars. As with other interesting coins on the 100 Greatest U.S. Coins list, all of the Proof Bust dollars of 1801, 1802, and 1803 originated from the same source. Captain John W. Haseltine revealed the coins to the numismatic community in 1876.

The Proof dollars of 1801 to 1803 all feature unusual characteristics:

1. They share a reverse die with the "original" (Class I) 1804 silver dollars.
2. The edge border on both sides is beaded, an invention credited to William Kneass in 1828.
3. The edge lettering appears to have been added to the coins after they were struck.

Today, the Proof silver dollars of 1801 to 1803 rarely appear on the market. In fact, in recent years, five 1804 silver dollars have

The fact that the 1801, 1802, and 1803 Proof silver dollars weigh approximately the same as the trade dollars struck between 1873 and 1885 may well be a hint for the rarities' actual year of origin.

appeared at auction, compared to no Proof 1801s, two Proof 1802s, and only three Proof 1803s during the same time period! Recently, a Gem Proof 1802 sold at auction for $920,000. It has also been reported that a superb 1803 sold for in excess of $1 million in a private sale.

These silver dollars are now among the most popular U.S. coin series. Several collectors have made serious attempts to assemble sets of the series by date and die variety. Draped Bust dollars remain a tangible link to the early commerce of the United States. Because of their considerable size, these dollars are among the most physically impressive coins and are always in demand.

Designed by Robert Scot. The obverse features a draped bust of Liberty with some of her hair tied back in a bow. LIBERTY appears above, the date below, and 13 stars are divided up on the sides (seven on the left, six on the right). The reverse features a heraldic eagle with outstretched wings (similar to the one on the Great Seal of the United States). In its beak, the eagle holds a scroll with the words E PLURIBUS UNUM. In its left talon, the eagle grasps an olive branch; in its right talon, it holds a bunch of arrows. Clouds and 13 stars appear above the eagle. The outer legend reads UNITED STATES OF AMERICA. No denomination appears anywhere on the coin.

HISTORICAL VALUES					
1801, Choice Proof					
1960: $4,500	1980: $35,000	1st ed./2003: $150,000	2nd ed./2005: $225,000	3rd ed./2008: $750,000	4th edition: $1,000,000
1802, Choice Proof					
1960: $4,500	1980: $35,000	1st ed./2003: $150,000	2nd ed./2005: $225,000	3rd ed./2008: $650,000	4th edition: $750,000
1803, Choice Proof					
1960: $4,500	1980: $35,000	1st ed./2003: $150,000	2nd ed./2005: $225,000	3rd ed./2008: $600,000	4th edition: $700,000

1829 CAPPED HEAD HALF EAGLES
LARGE AND SMALL PLANCHETS

STANDARDS • **Weight:** 8.75 grams. **Composition:** 92% gold, 8% silver. **Diameter:** 25 mm (Large Planchet) or 23.8 mm (Small Planchet). **Edge:** Reeded. **RARITY** • Recent estimates suggest that seven or eight Large Planchet specimens are known and about 10 examples of the Small Planchet are still in existence. In fact, some of the greatest U.S. rarities, such as the 1815 and 1822 half eagles (Nos. 42 and 17, respectively), are siblings of the 1829 half eagles. **CERTIFIED POPULATION** • 9

The United States is not the only country whose coinage depicts Liberty as a woman in a liberty cap. Coins from France (left) and Ecuador (bottom) have also used this iconography. (Actual sizes 21 mm and 37 mm.)

In 1829, Chief Engraver William Kneass modified the obverse motif on the half eagle, and the diameter was reduced to 23.8 millimeters. In addition, half eagles were struck with a close collar and beaded borders from that point onward. This modified format was continued from 1829 until the summer of 1834, at which time the Classic Head design was unveiled. This subtle change created not just one formidable rarity, but two: the 1829 Large Planchet and 1829 Small Planchet half eagles. The two coins are comparable in overall scarcity; about eight exist of each variety, although forming an exact roster of known specimens is exceedingly difficult.

An incredible Gem Uncirculated 1829 Large Planchet half eagle was auctioned by Bowers and Merena Galleries in October 1999 as part of the Harry W. Bass Jr. collection. The coin was hammered down at $241,500—a record for the variety. A technically inferior 1829 Small Planchet half eagle was sold in the same auction for $80,500, a price more indicative of the individual coin's quality than the variety's desirability. The finest 1829 Small Planchet half eagle is the Byron Reed specimen, a beautiful gem coin that sold for a remarkable $374,000 in 1996. Although opinions regarding its exact grade vary, it is undisputedly the finest example of the date and variety.

The reason for the half eagle's size reduction in 1829 was to take advantage of new minting technologies. In particular, the "close" collar created perfectly uniform diameters by preventing the spread of the planchets allowed by the "loose" collar. The close collar also allowed for perfect centering of the dies on the planchet, yielding secondary benefits—a beaded border and a raised, circular rim. A loose collar required dies with borders that extended beyond the edges of the planchet, because the loose collar allowed some movement of the planchet beneath the dies. Thus, the often crude, tooth-like denticles gave way to the cleaner look of a circle of beads within a raised border.

Designed by John Reich. The obverse features a large head of Liberty surrounded by 13 stars, with the date below. The reverse shows an eagle with spread wings, holding an olive branch and arrows. Surrounding the eagle are the inscriptions UNITED STATES OF AMERICA and 5 D., with the motto E PLURIBUS UNUM above the eagle's head.

HISTORICAL VALUES

Large Planchet, Uncirculated

1960: $3,500	1980: $50,000	1st ed./2003: $150,000	2nd ed./2005: $165,000	3rd ed./2008: $250,000	4th edition: $300,000

Small Planchet, Uncirculated

1960: $3,500	1980: $45,000	1st ed./2003: $125,000	2nd ed./2005: $135,000	3rd ed./2008: $250,000	4th edition: $300,000

1853-O "NO ARROWS"
LIBERTY SEATED HALF DOLLAR

STANDARDS · **Weight:** 13.349 grams. **Composition:** 90% silver, 10% copper. **Diameter:** 30.6 mm. **Edge:** Reeded. **RARITY** · Extremely rare. Only three 1853-O "No Arrows" half dollars are known to exist. The finest example is Very Fine; the others grade only Good and Very Good. In October 2006, the Very Fine example sold for more than $368,000 at auction. **CERTIFIED POPULATION** · 4

Only three examples of the 1853-O Liberty Seated half dollar "Without Arrows and Rays" are known today. While this number is extremely low, one might also consider it extremely high, considering that Mint records indicate that none were struck!

The story of this rarity begins with the Coinage Act of 1853, which reduced the weight of the half dollars from 206 grains (13.35 grams) to 192 grains (12.44 grams). In order to make the public aware of this change, special features were added to the lighter-weight coins; arrowheads were placed on either side of the date, and rays were placed around the eagle on the reverse. These marks made it easy for the government and the public to identify the new coins and to differentiate them from the older, heavier coins that were worth more than their face value. Many millions of the older coins were melted down and converted into lighter-weight coins or bullion. Thus, the survival of any pre-1853 silver coin depended on coin collectors (few in number at the time), hoarders, and just plain luck.

In late 1852 or early 1853, the New Orleans Mint received a shipment of dies from the Philadelphia Mint, just as it did every year, to prepare for the new year's coinage. These dies bore no arrowheads on either side of the date, nor rays on the reverse. Quite possibly, the New Orleans Mint struck a quantity of 1853-O half dollars with no arrows or rays early in 1853, before the new Coinage Act went into effect. Presumably, they were all destroyed (or were believed to have been destroyed) after the effective date of the act, thus explaining why none are recorded in the Mint's records.

Regardless of how, when, or why they were made, 1853-O half dollars without the arrowheads or rays most certainly exist.

Had the law not been changed in 1853, the 1853-O "No Arrows" half dollar would be a very common coin, indeed, as indicated by the one-million-plus mintage of the 1853-O "With Arrows" half dollar. However, such are the twists of fate through

In addition to arrows on either side of the coin's date, half dollars of the reduced weight also incorporated rays around the eagle on the obverse.

which great rarities are born. Often, the difference between being "common" and "rare" hinges on a single circumstance; other times, rarity is caused by a number of factors occurring at the same time. Yes, rarities are sometimes deliberate creations (such as the 1913 Liberty Head nickel or any of the 1866 "No Motto" silver coins). The purist, however, would argue that the most important rarities are those, like the 1853-O "No Arrows" half dollar, that occurred as naturally as possible.

Designed by Christian Gobrecht. The obverse shows Liberty in a flowing gown sitting on a rock. Her left hand holds a staff surmounted by a liberty cap; her right hand steadies a shield and holds a band bearing the word LIBERTY. An arc of 13 stars appears above Liberty, and the date appears at the base of the obverse, below the rock. The reverse shows an eagle with a shield on its chest, an olive branch in its right talon, and a bunch of arrows in its left. The words UNITED STATES OF AMERICA appear above the eagle; the abbreviation HALF DOL. appears below.

HISTORICAL VALUES
Fine

1960: $3,500	1980: $25,000	1st ed./2003: $175,000	2nd ed./2005: $185,000	3rd ed./2008: $250,000	4th edition: $300,000

1866 "NO MOTTO" LIBERTY SEATED HALF DOLLAR

STANDARDS · Weight: 12.441 grams. **Composition:** 90% silver, 10% copper. **Diameter:** 30 mm. **Edge:** Reeded. **RARITY** · Unique! **CERTIFIED POPULATION** · 1

The story of the 1866 "No Motto" Liberty Seated half dollar is very similar to that of the 1866 "No Motto" quarter dollar (No. 48; see its listing for the full story). Both coins are unique, both were part of the same three-piece set (with the 1866 "No Motto" silver dollar), and both were stolen from the DuPont family collection in 1967. From that point, however, their paths separated, only to meet again more than 30 years later, under very similar circumstances. This coin was purchased over the counter in a coin shop, later returned to the DuPont family, and later given on loan to the American Numismatic Association for display.

The word "Motto" refers to the scroll bearing the words IN GOD WE TRUST, authorized by a congressional act in March 1865 but not added to the backs of half dollars until 1866. Some experts consider the 1866 "No Motto" half dollar to be a transitional pattern, but others believe they were made years later at the request of a Mint "insider." Some collectors even speculate that a special set of the quarter dollar, half dollar, and silver dollar was made for Robert Coulton Davis, a druggist-turned-informant for the Mint, whose help enabled the Mint to recover 1804 dollars in an 1858 operation. Thus, the words "fantasy coin" and *pièce de caprice* can be used to describe this unique rarity, similar to the 1866 "No Motto" quarter dollar, which is also now on display at the Museum of American History of the Smithsonian Institution.

The restriking of known rarities and the creation of fantasy pieces were somewhat common occurrences at the Philadelphia Mint in the 1850s and 1860s. When the Mint opened up the sale of Proof coins to the general public in 1858, collectors besieged the Mint with requests for coins from previous years, especially the rare ones that were hard to find in circulation or in dealers' inventories. Recognizing an opportunity for profit, enterprising individuals in the Mint restruck old rarities (sometimes with official sanction, sometimes not) and created a number of never-

The Mint began experimenting with adding a motto to the nation's coinage as early as 1861, as reflected in this pattern (Judd-277) from that year. It features the phrase **GOD OUR TRUST** in a scroll above the eagle.

before-seen delicacies with which to pry open the purses of eager collectors. This was the source of the Class II and Class III 1804 silver dollars (No. 1), the 1866 "No Motto" quarter dollar and silver dollar (Nos. 48 and 46), some of the "missing link" pattern coins that bridged the transition from "No Motto" to "With Motto," and others. The sudden appearance of these rarities did not go unnoticed, and after several collectors complained, measures were taken at the Mint to end the practice.

The last sale record for an 1866 "No Motto" half dollar was in 1961, when the DuPont family acquired the coin from the sale of the Edwin Hydeman collection for $15,500 (an extremely high price for the time).

Designed by Christian Gobrecht. The obverse shows Liberty in a flowing gown sitting on a rock. Her left hand holds a staff surmounted by a liberty cap; her right hand steadies a shield and holds a band bearing the word LIBERTY. An arc of 13 stars appears above Liberty, and the date appears at the base of the obverse, below the rock. The reverse shows an eagle with a shield on its chest, an olive branch in its right talon, and a bunch of arrows in its left. The words UNITED STATES OF AMERICA appear above the eagle; the abbreviation HALF DOL. appears below.

HISTORICAL VALUES
Choice Proof

1960: $20,000	1980: $75,000	1st ed./2003: $350,000	2nd ed./2005: $375,000	3rd ed./2008: $500,000	4th edition: $750,000

1918-D, 8 OVER 7 BUFFALO NICKEL

STANDARDS · Weight: 5 grams. **Composition:** 75% copper, 25% nickel. **Diameter:** 21.2 mm. **Edge:** Plain. **RARITY** · Scarce in all grades and very rare in Mint State. Probably fewer than 2,000 to 3,000 examples of the 1918-D, 8 Over 7 nickel are known in all grades. **CERTIFIED POPULATION ·** 2,033

The 1918-D, 8 Over 7 Buffalo nickel is another very popular Mint error of 20th-century coinage. It was produced when a hub from 1917 was switched for another during the annealing process required to harden the working dies. This error was first discovered sometime in the 1930s, and over the years it has remained quite scarce. By the time the overdate was discovered, the coins had been in circulation for nearly two decades. This probably explains why most examples seen are well-worn. Mint errors are found on almost every series of U.S. coinage, but overdates hold a special place of interest in the field of numismatics. Some, but not all, are collected as part of the series and are listed in standard references, such as the *Guide Book of United States Coins* (the "Red Book"). The 1918-D, 8 Over 7 Buffalo nickel is also found in many coin albums, and thus is more famous and collectible. This is another of the popular coins that collectors would love to discover unattributed. Because the error is somewhat subtle to the naked eye, low-grade examples have been found in recent years in dealer junk boxes.

During the last few years of the First World War, there was a nationwide shortage of small-denomination coinage. In response, the U.S. Mint began to produce much larger quantities of the Lincoln cent and Buffalo nickel. It is thought that this increased production workload led to confusion, which caused this error to occur. It is also interesting to note that other popular overdate mint errors of the 20th century, the 1918-S, 8 Over 7 quarter dollar and the 1942, 2 Over 1 and 1942-D, 2 Over 1 dimes, were also struck during war years.

As noted, most 1918-D, 8 Over 7 Buffalo nickels are well-worn. Finding one with nice details is quite difficult and expensive. Mint State coins are very rare, and there are probably fewer than 100 known. Just a few gem examples are known, with the price record for an MS-65 example currently at $350,750.

The sculptor James Earle Fraser created the design for the Buffalo nickel. In *Numismatic Art in America,* author Cornelius Vermeule suggests the artist may have used his own likeness for inspiration when designing the Native American chief for the obverse.

The overdate, while noticeable with close inspection, can be missed by the untrained eye.

Designed by James Earle Fraser. The obverse features an American Indian facing right with two feathers and ribbons placed in the hair. The word LIBERTY is also found on the obverse. The reverse depicts a bison or buffalo standing on a mound, with the words UNITED STATES OF AMERICA and E PLURIBUS UNUM above the bison. FIVE CENTS and the mintmark are below the bison.

HISTORICAL VALUES					
Extremely Fine					
1960: $375	1980: $1,850	1st ed./2003: —	2nd ed./2005: —	3rd ed./2008: $9,500	4th edition: $10,000

1874 BICKFORD
$10 GOLD PATTERN

STANDARDS · Weight: 16.718 grams. **Composition:** Gold. **Diameter:** 34 mm. **Edge:** Reeded. **RARITY** · Two examples are known in gold. One is now a part of the incredible collection of U.S. patterns that changed hands for around $30 million. Beware of deceptive copies from unofficial modern dies. **CERTIFIED POPULATION** · 4

The idea for this unusual, internationally denominated pattern came from Dana Bickford, who, upon his return from a trip abroad, proposed that the United States needed a coin that could be easily converted into the currencies of other nations. Bickford—an entrepreneur who devised many products, including hand-operated knitting machines—believed that travelers needed an easy way to convert money as they traveled from country to country. The back of "Dana Bickford's International Coin," as it was called in 1876, bore the weight of the coin (in gold), the fineness (or purity), plus the value in six different international currencies. Unfortunately, because of the ever-changing relationship of world currencies, the Bickford pattern proved unworkable and "died on the vine." Examples are known in a variety of metals, including two in gold.

At one time, the Bickford "Ten" was only known in copper. The two known gold examples are thought to have been part of

the enormous trade of patterns between A.L. Snowden and William Woodin as payment for the return of the 1877 half unions that are also discussed in this book (No. 19). The gold pattern coins were later included in the illustrious collections of Brand, Boyd, Wilson, and others. Both specimens were a part of the fabulous Wilkison collection of gold patterns that was sold to Paramount International Coin Corporation in 1973.

The concept of a truly international coin continues to intrigue politicians and economists alike. The "Stellas" of 1879 and 1880 were failed attempts at an international coin, partly because the coins didn't really fit into our own coinage system. Today's euro is perhaps the most successful international coin, allowing travelers to move from country to country within the European Union without having to change currencies or convert the prices of goods and services. A subtle aspect of the 1874 Bickford $10 pattern is the use of grams for the weight. Prior to 1873, standards for U.S. coins were measured using the English troy system of weights (in which 5,760 grains made up one pound). Accordingly, the standard weight for an eagle was 258 grains, as legislated by the Coinage Act of 1837. Then, in 1873, the Mint decided to convert to the metric system, requiring a recalculation of (but not a change in) the weights of the coins. Thus, for the eagle, 258 grains became 16.72 grams. While this difference is subtle, it marked a significant change in scientific policy in the United States. The Bickford $10 gold piece was one of the first coins to incorporate this change in a stated form.

DANA BICKFORD'S
NEW IMPROVED FAMILY
KNITTING MACHINE.
$1,000 to $5,000 a year
Agents can make in almost any section of the country, selling Dana Bickford's New and Improved FAMILY KNITTER. This Machine is guaranteed in its present completeness, to meet every want of the household, for either domestic or fancy work. Price $25. Send stamped envelope, with full directions, for an illustrated book.
Address DANA BICKFORD, Vice-President and General Agent, 689 Broadway, N. Y. s-6:

This advertisement for Dana Bickford's home knitting machine appeared in the 1871 *Herald of Health.*

Designed by Dana Bickford and William Barber. The obverse has the head of Liberty facing left, with a coronet bearing the word LIBERTY inscribed below six stars. The reverse has a continuous rope divided into six sections with a conversion of various world currencies.

HISTORICAL VALUES
Choice Proof

| 1960: $3,500 | 1980: $100,000 | 1st ed./2003: $350,000 | 2nd ed./2005: $350,000 | 3rd ed./2008: $600,000 | 4th edition: $1,000,000 |

1918-S, 8 OVER 7 STANDING LIBERTY QUARTER DOLLAR

STANDARDS · **Weight:** 6.22 grams. **Composition:** 90% silver, 10% copper. **Diameter:** 24.3 mm. **Edge:** Reeded. **RARITY** · Mintage unknown. Probably only 2,000 to 3,000 coins are known in all grades. Gem examples have traded for more than $100,000. **CERTIFIED POPULATION** · 993

The 1918-S, 8 Over 7 Standing Liberty quarter dollar is another of the great 20th-century error coins. Like the 1918-D, 8 Over 7 Buffalo nickel and the 1955 Doubled-Die Obverse Lincoln cent, they are collected as part of the series. This is an important distinction, as there are many error coins found in nearly every series of U.S. coins. Many are minor, but some are quite major. The popular 1918, 8 Over 7 error quarters were created in sufficient quantities to actually stimulate demand. Very shortly after they were discovered, these errors were listed in the standard references and included in many of the coin albums popular before the advent of coin certification and slabbing. This interesting variety was caused when two obverse hubs with different dates were used to create the single obverse working die. It is quite visible to the naked eye, and the underlying numeral 7 is very clear beneath the 8 of the date.

The 1918-S, 8 Over 7 Standing Liberty quarter was discovered around 1937, and the first specimen appeared at auction in the Barney Bluestone sale of December 4, 1937, when an Uncirculated example sold for $25.25. This was quite high for the time (during the depths of the Great Depression), and was due to the fact that the coin was thought to be unique. Others soon were discovered, but since the coins had been in circulation for many years, most were well-worn. Type II Standing Liberty quarters are also notorious for dates that quickly wear off. The date on the coin was later recessed (in 1925) to alleviate the problem. Today, Mint State examples of the 1918-S, 8 Over 7 are very rare. Fully struck examples are nearly unheard of. A Mint State coin with the very desirable full head would bring a very large premium.

Because of the rarity and popularity of this issue, counterfeits are often seen. Certification is highly recommended on any example.

At right, a closeup shows the overdate; above, the bronze casting of Hermon MacNeil's approved obverse design for the Standing Liberty quarter shows some striking differences from the final coin. (Actual size of design 130 mm.)

Designed by Hermon MacNeil. The obverse shows a full-length view of Liberty in a flowing gown. She holds a shield in her left hand and an olive branch in her right and appears to be walking through some sort of gate emblazoned with IN GOD WE TRUST and stars. The word LIBERTY appears in an arc at the top of the obverse, and the date appears beneath Liberty's feet. The reverse shows an eagle in flight. The legends UNITED STATES OF AMERICA and E PLURIBUS UNUM appear above the eagle; QUARTER DOLLAR appears beneath. On the reverse, 13 stars are divided, with five to the left of the eagle, five to the right, and three below.

HISTORICAL VALUES
Uncirculated

1960: $525	1980: $6,000	1st ed./2003: —	2nd ed./2005: —	3rd ed./2008: $20,000	4th edition: $25,000

1827 "ORIGINAL" CAPPED BUST QUARTER DOLLAR

STANDARDS · Weight: 6.739 grams. **Composition:** 89% silver, 11% copper. **Diameter:** 29 mm. **Edge:** Reeded. **RARITY ·** Extremely rare. Fewer than 10 originals known, all originally struck as Proofs. The finest known original is PF-66. **CERTIFIED POPULATION ·** 12

Whereas the overdate on the 1827 quarter dollar is less noticeable, others—such as this, seen on the 1823, 3 Over 2 quarter dollar—are quite visible to the naked eye.

Mint reports indicate that 4,000 1827 quarter dollars were struck, but this number appears to be erroneous, as no examples struck for circulation have ever been found. Joseph J. Mickley received four Proofs in change from the Mint in 1827, and for several decades, these were the only ones known to exist. Now, however, there are believed to be as many as eight or nine Proof examples. One circulated example is known that traces its pedigree to 1893, when the coin was paid out to a railroad ticket clerk.

Because of this date's rarity, restrikes were made in later years (1858–1859) using a different reverse. Restrikes have been found made of copper, on regular silver planchets, and even struck over an 1806 quarter dollar! In 1860, to prevent further restrikes, Mint director James Ross Snowden seized all of the old dies and placed them in his personal vault.

The difference between originals and restrikes is easy to determine. Originals used a reverse die of 1828 with a curled base on the 2 of the denomination, while restrikes used a reverse die of 1819 with a flat base on the 2 of the denomination. Also, restrikes are usually found with heavy die rust (now in the form of raised pimples) on both sides.

The original 1827 quarter dollar has always been recognized as a classic rarity. Early collector demand is probably the reason restrikes were produced in the 1850s. The original 1827 quarter dollar is usually only available when great collections are sold. The last examples to have crossed the auction block were from the collections of Louis E. Eliasberg and John J. Pittman!

All 1827 quarter dollars, whether originals or restrikes, are also overdates, with remnants of a 3 clearly visible beneath the 7 of the date. Overdating was a common practice in the early 1800s because of the high cost of die production. Rather than waste leftover dies from earlier years, the Mint engravers simply punched a new number over the old one. Thus, in the early quarter dollar series, interesting overdates such as 1806, 6 Over 5, 1818, 8 Over 5, 1823, 3 Over 2, 1824, 4 Over 2, 1825, 5 Over 2 (there must have been a lot of 1822 dies left over), and 1825, 5 Over 4 exist to tempt the collector. Overdates are not necessarily rarer than normal dates, but they are certainly popular items, especially when the date is 1827.

Designed by John Reich. The obverse features a draped bust of Liberty facing left, wearing a liberty cap banded with the word LIBERTY. Along the edge, 13 stars appear (seven on the left side, six on the right). The date appears below the bust. The reverse features an eagle with outstretched wings and a shield on its chest. In its talons, the eagle holds an olive branch and a bunch of arrows. A scroll with E PLURIBUS UNUM hovers above the eagle's head. The outer legend reads UNITED STATES OF AMERICA, and the denomination 25 C. appears beneath the eagle.

HISTORICAL VALUES					
Choice Proof					
1960: $7,000	**1980:** $40,000	**1st ed./2003:** $100,000	**2nd ed./2005:** $115,000	**3rd ed./2008:** $175,000	**4th edition:** $200,000

1974 ALUMINUM LINCOLN CENTS

PHILADELPHIA AND DENVER ISSUES

STANDARDS · **Weight:** .93 grams. **Composition:** 96% aluminum with trace metals mixed in. **Diameter:** 19 mm. **Edge:** Plain. **RARITY** · Fewer than 20 are thought to remain. **CERTIFIED POPULATION** · 1

The 1974 aluminum cent has been voted for inclusion in the fourth edition of the 100 Greatest U.S. Coins. This issue has been an intriguing numismatic rarity since it was produced in the early 1970s. The coin's interesting story is closely related to those of the 1943 copper cent (which it was proposed to replace) and the 1933 double eagle (which has also been the focus of recent litigation).

During the early 1970s, the price of copper rose to a point that the cost of producing a cent nearly exceeded the resultant coin's face value. Since the U.S. Mint produces billions of examples each year, an alternative metal for production was explored. A composition of 96 percent aluminum was chosen, and beginning in late 1973 and early 1974, the Philadelphia Mint produced 1,571,167 examples.

In order to promote the idea of changing the cent's composition, a small quantity of coins were given to various members of the House Banking and Currency Committee. Several special-interest groups opposed the idea, including the copper mining and vending machine industries. What's more, the price of copper began to fall, and the idea was eventually abandoned.

According to William Hubert, Chief of the Mint's Internal Audit Staff at the time, all but about 100 coins were destroyed of the original mintage for 1974 aluminum cents. Mary Brooks, the Mint Director at the time, requested the return of the coins given out as samples. Most were returned, but nearly a dozen remained unaccounted for. The Federal Bureau of Investigation was asked to look into the situation, but the matter was eventually dropped.

In 2001, an example of the 1974 aluminum cent surfaced and was attributed to U.S. Capitol police officer Albert Toven. He claimed the coin had been dropped by an unnamed Congressman who, thinking the coin was a dime, told Officer Toven to keep the coin. To date, no government agency has attempted to confiscate the coin.

Finally, though the U.S. Mint has no record of 1974 aluminum cents being produced at the Denver Mint, apparently a small number were struck there, as an example of the 1974-D aluminum cent surfaced in San Diego earlier this year. The owner's father was a former deputy superintendent of the Denver Mint. The coin was certified as genuine by PCGS and consigned to auction. This basically forced the Mint's hand, as the coin is officially illegal to own for private citizens. The U.S. Mint filed legal action against the owners, and the coin was withdrawn from the auction.

The ultimate fate of the 1974 and 1974-D aluminum cents remains in question. Luckily, one example of the Philadelphia issue was donated to the Smithsonian's National Numismatic Collection and can now be seen on display in Washington, D.C. There are probably other examples still in private hands, but it is unlikely they will surface until the matter of legal ownership has been resolved.

Thus, the story of the 1974 aluminum cents is sure to be an ongoing saga for the next few years as the Mint battles for their return.

Designed by Victor David Brenner (obverse) and Frank Gasparro (reverse). The obverse continues the design of 1909, featuring a bust of Lincoln facing right, the word LIBERTY to this left, and the date in the field in front of his coat. The legend IN GOD WE TRUST appears above his head. The reverse shows a frontal view of the Lincoln Memorial with UNITED STATES OF AMERICA and E PLURIBUS UNUM appearing above and ONE CENT below.

HISTORICAL VALUES
Uncirculated

1960: n/a	1980: n/a	1st ed./2003: —	2nd ed./2005: —	3rd ed./2008: —	4th edition: $500,000

1867 PROOF "WITH RAYS" SHIELD NICKEL

STANDARDS · Weight: 5 grams. **Composition:** 75% copper, 25% nickel. **Diameter:** 21 mm. **Edge:** Plain. **RARITY ·** Extremely rare. A few Gem Proofs represent the finest examples of this rare nickel. **CERTIFIED POPULATION ·** 87

The 1867 Proof "With Rays" Shield nickel is a mysterious, major rarity. According to one account, A.L. Snowden, chief coiner at the time, refused to strike any Proofs of the 1867 "With Rays" nickels, citing difficulties caused by the presence of the rays. However, the existence of some three to four dozen specimens indicates that somebody decided to strike them.

The "nickel" (as we now know our five-cent piece) was a new invention in 1866. From 1794 to the early 1860s, the silver half dimes served admirably as our five-cent denomination, but in 1862, the uncertain outcome of the Civil War caused hoarding of anything of value, including the silver coins then in circulation. To make up for the shortage of half dimes, the Treasury issued small five-cent notes called Fractional Currency. Fractional Currency circulated widely and was produced in such quantities that the Treasury was unable to redeem them all with gold and silver. Thus, the nickel was born; its primary purpose was to replace the five-cent Fractional Currency notes.

"Nickel" is a misnomer, for the main metal in a five-cent piece is copper, with nickel making up only 25% of the alloy. Nor were nickels meant to replace the half dime. In fact, nickels and half dimes were minted simultaneously until 1873, when the half dime was finally phased out.

The first nickels had an alternating series of 13 stars and 13 rays surrounding the numeral "5" on the back of the coin. Because the copper and nickel alloy was so hard, the Mint had problems with dies cracking and breaking prematurely. In early 1867, the decision was made to remove the rays from the reverse to improve the life of the dies. Yet, in spite of this change, most Shield nickels continued to show cracks and breaks.

The exact mintage of the 1867 Proof "With Rays" nickels is unknown and unrecorded. *A Guide Book of United States Coins* lists a mintage of 25-plus. The experts at PCGS list a mintage of 35 pieces in their population report, yet they report having certified

The rays on the reverse of the Shield nickel were removed in early 1867, resulting in a very small mintage of the "With Rays" variety.

50 examples. Assuming that some of these may represent resubmissions of the same coin, one must still factor in the coins graded by other certification services, leading to the conclusion that as many as 50 to 65 examples may exist. Examination of the coins themselves indicates that at least three varieties exist. One variety could be Proofs that were actually struck in 1867; Proofs of the other two varieties were restruck in later years.

While we may never know the exact mintage for this important coin, a significant rarity it remains, earning it a place in the 100 Greatest U.S. Coins.

Designed by James B. Longacre. The obverse shows a Union Shield with a pair of crossed arrows behind and near the base of the shield, somewhat similar to that used on the 1864 two-cent piece. The motto **IN GOD WE TRUST** appears in an arc above the shield, and the date appears at the bottom of the obverse. The reverse shows a large 5 within a circle of stars and rays. The legend **UNITED STATES OF AMERICA** appears in an arc above the circle, and the word **CENTS** appears beneath.

HISTORICAL VALUES					
Choice Proof					
1960: $1,500	1980: $5,000	1st ed./2003: $45,000	2nd ed./2005: $45,000	3rd ed./2008: $60,000	4th edition: $75,000

1854-S LIBERTY HEAD QUARTER EAGLE

STANDARDS · **Weight:** 4.18 grams. **Composition:** 90% gold, 10% copper. **Diameter:** 18 mm. **Edge:** Reeded. **RARITY** · Approximately 12 coins are known, all of which are worn to varying degrees. The issue is unknown in Mint State. **CERTIFIED POPULATION** · 14

The 1854-S quarter eagle is one of the rarest regular-issue U.S. coins ever produced. For years, the issue had largely been forgotten by most numismatists, although it has an incredibly low mintage of only 246 and only a dozen survivors are known. In 1982, a specimen changed hands for less than $10,000, representing an astounding value considering its overall rarity. One researcher stated in 1952 that the 1854-S quarter eagle is "one of the most underrated United States coins in any metal . . . and [is] completely free of the stigma of Mint experimentation and chicanery." However, with a recent auction price of nearly $350,000, it appears that gold specialists have indeed rediscovered the 1854-S quarter eagle. A previously unknown example surfaced in the San Francisco area in the summer of 2005. The coin had been held in the same family since the 1850s. The coin was certified by NGC as EF-45 and auctioned for $253,000. It is exciting that coins of this magnitude still await discovery.

It is unknown why only 246 quarter eagles were minted in 1854. Purportedly, the Mint could not obtain the necessary acids to remove silver from the impure California gold. But the San Francisco Mint was able to strike an ample supply of double eagles and eagles. Actually, depositors of gold requested higher and lower denominations; as the quarter eagle and half eagle were between denominations, few were made. Interestingly, not a single 1854-S quarter eagle was known until 1910, when Edgar Adams discovered a specimen. Since then, numerous other examples have surfaced, though the total population known does not exceed 12. Most pieces are heavily worn; the AU-50 Bass coin ranks as the finest known. The National Numismatic Collection contains one of the finest survivors, an Extremely Fine example that was donated to the institution as part of the incredible Lilly gold holdings.

With only a dozen examples known, the 1854-S quarter eagle compares closely with many of the top-ranked coins in this book. There are fewer examples known of this issue than some of the multi-million-dollar rarities, such as the 1804 dollars, 1933 double eagles, and 1907 Ultra High Relief double eagles. As interest in Western Americana rises, prices for such tangible links to the California gold rush as the 1854-S quarter eagle will very likely increase.

Designed by Christian Gobrecht. The obverse depicts a figure of Liberty wearing a coronet. The word LIBERTY is inscribed on the headband. The portrait is encircled by 13 stars, with the date at the bottom. The reverse features a spread eagle located in the center with the words UNITED STATES OF AMERICA written at the edge. The denomination 2 1/2 D. is featured at six o'clock.

The California gold rush is immortalized in a frieze by Constantino Brumidi at the U.S. Capitol building.

HISTORICAL VALUES
Very Fine

1960: $1,500	1980: $15,000	1st ed./2003: $75,000	2nd ed./2005: $85,000	3rd ed./2008: $225,000	4th edition: $300,000

1864 PROOF "SMALL MOTTO" TWO-CENT PIECE

STANDARDS · Weight: 6.221 grams. **Composition:** 95% copper, 5% tin and zinc. **Diameter:** 23 mm. **Edge:** Plain. **RARITY** · Extremely rare. There are probably 20 to 30 examples known. Gem examples today sell for nearly $100,000. **CERTIFIED POPULATION** · 25

Today, the 1864 Proof "Small Motto" two-cent piece is represented by a mere handful of pieces and ranks as one of the rarest major varieties in all of U.S. numismatics. Two significant varieties are recognized of the 1864 two-cent piece: the Small Motto and Large Motto variants. The size difference refers to the motto IN GOD WE TRUST. The difference is subtle, but easily recognized when the two varieties are compared side-by-side. Collectors soon discovered that the Small Motto variety was considerably rarer than the Large Motto variety.

The two-cent piece was an odd, short-lived denomination. The two-cent piece first appeared during a period of coin shortages caused by the Civil War. Attempts to introduce the two-cent denomination occurred in 1806 and 1836, but both efforts failed due to technical considerations. In 1863, Mint officials revived the idea of a two-cent coin simultaneous with their plans to reduce the weight and metal content of the bulky, copper-nickel Indian Head cent. The new coin featured a patriotic design (a Union Shield) and the first instance of the religious motto IN GOD WE TRUST on a circulating coin.

In anticipation of an eager demand and wide circulation for the new coin, the Mint struck nearly 20 million 1864 two-cent pieces, mostly of the Large Motto variety, plus several hundred Proofs, of which only a few were of the Small Motto variety. In later years of the series, the number of coins struck for circulation decreased while the number of Proof coins struck for collectors increased. In 1865, approximately 14 million two-cent pieces were struck; in 1866, only three million were struck; and in 1872, the last year circulating pieces were made, only 65,000 were struck. In the final year (1873), no two-cent pieces were struck for circulation at all and only Proof examples were made! Mike Kliman's 1977 book *The Two-Cent Piece and Varieties* remains a standard reference guide for these coins.

All circulation-strike two-cent pieces and the majority of the Proofs were of the Large Motto variety (bottom). An unknown—but very small—number of Proofs of the Small Motto variety (top) have emerged.

The high value of the Proof 1864 Small Motto two-cent piece indicates the success and importance of variety collecting. When numismatics took root in the United States (circa the 1850s), collectors were happy to obtain just one coin from each year. Mintmarks were of little concern, and interest in collecting coins by subtle changes in the dies (varieties) was unheard of. In 1864, collectors did not even notice the size differences in the mottos, nor did they care. The people who were prescient enough to obtain Proof examples of the new two-cent denomination were not given a choice of a Small or a Large Motto version; they took what the Mint gave them. It was only years later, after some eagle-eyed collector noticed the size differences, that the extreme rarity of the Small Motto Proofs was recognized.

Designed by James B. Longacre. The obverse shows a Union Shield with a pair of crossed arrows behind. The motto IN GOD WE TRUST appears on a scroll above the shield; strands of leaves are draped on either side of the shield. The date appears at the bottom of the obverse. The reverse shows the denomination 2 CENTS within a wreath, all surrounded by the legend UNITED STATES OF AMERICA.

HISTORICAL VALUES					
Choice Proof					
1960: $1,500	**1980:** $5,000	**1st ed./2003:** $35,000	**2nd ed./2005:** $45,000	**3rd ed./2008:** $65,000	**4th edition:** $70,000

1808 CAPPED BUST QUARTER EAGLE

STANDARDS · **Weight:** 4.37 grams. **Composition:** 92% gold, 8% copper. **Diameter:** 20 mm. **Edge:** Reeded. **RARITY** · Between 125 and 150 specimens are known from an original mintage of 2,710. **CERTIFIED POPULATION** · 98

A popular method of collecting U.S. coins is to buy one coin of each design type, one of each date or mint variety. The 1808 quarter eagle has the distinction of being a one-year type. As such, it is a coin sought by both type collectors and quarter eagle specialists. It is also an extremely scarce coin, with approximately 125 to 150 pieces known in total. Of those, many are well-worn, with only a few high-grade specimens in existence. Author Jeff Garrett has seen several expertly repaired coins, and certification is highly recommended.

The 1808 quarter eagle was designed by John Reich and is the only issue of the denomination attributed to him. Only 2,710 coins were struck, and it is thought that only one set of dies was used. Most coins were lost or destroyed, and locating an example in any condition is quite difficult. After this striking, the denomination was discontinued until 1821.

The finest known 1808 quarter eagle, generally considered an MS-65 by today's standards, was sold in the mid-1980s for a figure close to $100,000. It was once part of the collection built by former congressman Jimmy Hayes of Louisiana (whose specialty was collecting first-year of issue type coins) and traces its pedigree to the collection of J. Hewitt Judd. The coin now resides in a prominent Texas collection. The most recent auction record for a Mint State coin is an NGC-graded MS-63 that sold for $223,250 in August 2012.

Designed by John Reich. The obverse features Liberty wearing a liberty cap. There are 13 stars present at the obverse periphery. The date is located below the truncation of the portrait. The reverse portrays a spread eagle at the center with the motto E PLURIBUS UNUM inscribed above the eagle's head. The words UNITED STATES OF AMERICA are written at the circumference with the denomination 2 1/2 D. at six o'clock.

The liberty cap, also known as a Phrygian cap or freedman's cap, was traditionally shown with a peaked top, as in the 1807 quarter eagle shown at left; with the 1808 Capped Bust design (right), the cap took on a much more formless shape; a band with **LIBERTY** prominently displayed was also added.

HISTORICAL VALUES
About Uncirculated

1960: $2,000	1980: $17,500	1st ed./2003: $35,000	2nd ed./2005: $55,000	3rd ed./2008: $95,000	4th edition: $100,000

1842 "SMALL DATE" LIBERTY SEATED QUARTER DOLLAR

STANDARDS · Weight: 6.674 grams. **Composition:** 90% silver, 10% copper. **Diameter:** 24.3 mm. **Edge:** Reeded. **RARITY ·** Extremely rare. The 1842 Small Date quarter was only struck as a Proof, and in an extremely limited quantity. Only seven examples are known today. **CERTIFIED POPULATION ·** 3

The 1842 "Small Date" Liberty Seated quarter dollar is a rarity known only in Proof format and represented by just seven demonstrably different examples.

In the 1840s, Proof coins were sold individually or as part of complete sets. The opportunity to purchase Proof coins was not advertised by the Mint, nor were most collectors aware of the possibility. It was not until the late 1850s that the Mint standardized the regulations concerning the sale of Proof sets and began to make a regular business out of it. (A similar situation occurred in the 1940s, when the Treasury tired of filling individual orders for Uncirculated coins and began offering official Mint Sets.)

Of the seven known Proof 1842 "Small Date" quarter dollars, two are in institutional collections (the Smithsonian's National Numismatic Collection and the American Numismatic Society). Others include one from the celebrated Louis Eliasberg collection, which sold in July 2002 for $87,400 (an $11,400 increase in just more than five years); the Kaufman PF-64 example, which sold in early 2008 for $126,500; and an example that once belonged in the famed Norweb collection. As can be seen, this issue usually only becomes available when great collections are sold.

The quarter dollar was not the only denomination to undergo changes in the size of the date in 1842. "Small Date" and "Large Date" varieties are known also for large cents, half dollars, half eagles, and eagles, but none compare with the rarity of the 1842 "Small Date" quarter dollar (with the possible exception of the 1842 "Small Date, Small Letters" half dollar). Virtually every

Tweaks made to several denominations' designs during the 1840s created several rarities, including the 1842 "Small Date" quarter dollar (top). Note the bolder face used for the date on the "Large Date" variety (bottom).

denomination was "tweaked" at some time in the 1840s, all with the goal of improving the coin and adding uniformity to its appearance. The success of this program was expressed in the long life of the Liberty Seated design on silver coins and the Liberty Head design on gold coins.

Designed by Christian Gobrecht. The obverse shows Liberty in a flowing gown sitting on a rock. Her left hand holds a staff surmounted by a liberty cap; her right hand steadies a shield and holds a band bearing the word LIBERTY. An arc of 13 stars appears above Liberty, and the date appears at the base of the obverse, below the rock. The reverse shows an eagle with a shield on its chest, an olive branch in its right talon, and a bunch of arrows in its left. The words UNITED STATES OF AMERICA appear above the eagle; the abbreviations QUAR. DOL. appear below.

HISTORICAL VALUES					
Choice Proof					
1960: $2,500	1980: $15,000	1st ed./2003: $85,000	2nd ed./2005: $85,000	3rd ed./2008: $125,000	4th edition: $150,000

1797 "16 STARS OBVERSE" CAPPED BUST, HERALDIC REVERSE HALF EAGLE

STANDARDS · Weight: 8.75 grams. **Composition:** 92% gold, 8% copper. **Diameter:** 25 mm. **Edge:** Reeded. **RARITY ·** Unique. Because the only known specimen has not changed hands in recent decades—and may never again—it is difficult to assign a value to the coin. However, it is comparable in rarity to the 1870-S $3 gold piece and 1822 half eagle, both of which are valued in excess of $1 million. **CERTIFIED POPULATION ·** 0

When the half eagle first debuted in 1795, the coin featured Robert Scot's Small Eagle reverse design. However, the public criticized the image, opining that the eagle appeared scrawny and weak. In response to the public disapproval, Scot revamped the design and introduced the Heraldic Eagle reverse, which was used for the entire coinage of half eagles in 1796.

The half eagle issues of 1797 were not so uniform in appearance, though, as some were struck using the Small Eagle reverse die, while a smaller number were struck using the Heraldic Eagle reverse die. Of the latter group, the most common variety features an overdate (as 1795 obverse dies were repunched with a 7 over the 5) and a total of 15 stars around the bust of Liberty. However, there also exists a single example that not only does not feature an overdate, but includes 16 stars on the obverse.

The original reverse design for the half eagle or $5 coin, featured the unpopular small eagle.

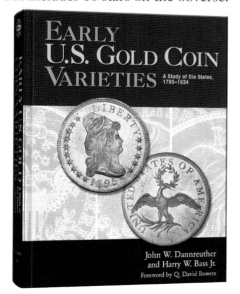

This unique coin is permanently housed in the Smithsonian Institution, having been donated by the executors of the Josiah K. Lilly estate. Legendary gold coin collector Harry W. Bass Jr., who assembled one of the finest collections of early U.S. coinage, was never able to own this variety. The coin was purchased for $2,500 in the late 1910s or early 1920s by Waldo Newcomer. The coin made several appearances at auction in the 1940s and 1950s and at one time was owned by Colonel Green and, later, King Farouk. Perhaps another is awaiting discovery, but for now this incredibly rare coin ranks as one the most important die varieties of early U.S. coinage.

For those with an interest in early U.S. coinage, a very important reference work on the subject, John Dannreuther and Harry W. Bass Jr.'s *Early U.S. Gold Coin Varieties, 1795–1834*, is highly recommended. Because of this important work, interest in the 1797 "16 Stars Obverse" Heraldic Reverse half eagle and many other early U.S. gold coins will undoubtedly increase.

Designed by Robert Scot. The obverse depicts Liberty wearing a soft liberty cap and facing right. The stars are placed around the edge of the obverse, and the date is located at the base. The heraldic eagle reverse features an outstretched eagle that wears a 13-stripe shield. The wings are partially covered by a flowing scroll inscribed E PLURIBUS UNUM. Clouds are placed above the eagle's head.

HISTORICAL VALUES					
Extremely Fine					
1960: $2,500	1980: $50,000	1st ed./2003: $300,000	2nd ed./2005: $325,000	3rd ed./2008: $750,000	4th edition: $1,000,000

1857-S LIBERTY HEAD DOUBLE EAGLES

FROM THE WRECK OF THE SS CENTRAL AMERICA

STANDARDS · Weight: 33.436 grams. **Composition:** 90% gold, 10% copper. **Net weight:** .96750 oz. pure gold. **Diameter:** 34 mm. **Edge:** Reeded. **RARITY ·** The SS *Central America* hoard contained more than 5,000 examples of the 1857-S, many of which are incredible, radiant gems. At least eight different varieties of the 1857-S double eagle were identified. The fabulous preservation of these treasure coins is what makes this issue truly great. No other coins from this period can be found in nearly the same condition as the day they left the Mint. **CERTIFIED POPULATION ·** 7,143

On September 12, 1857, the steamship SS *Central America* sank in the Atlantic Ocean, 200 miles off the coast of North Carolina, on the way to New York with treasure fresh from the California gold rush. On board was an incredible quantity of gold bars, gold dust, and more than 7,000 gold coins. Unfortunately, nearly 600 people were also making the trip home from the land of opportunity. When the ship sank below the waves, 425 lives were lost. The story of the SS *Central America* is one the most heart-wrenching episodes of bravery and courage in U.S. history. Because of a Herculean effort on the part of the passengers and crew, 153 passengers survived the ravages of the storm.

The ship and her golden bounty lay on the ocean floor in 7,200 feet of water for the next 130 years. In 1985, a group of explorers and investors formed the Columbus-America Discovery Group to locate the treasure. The wreck was found in September 1986. It was one of the largest discoveries of treasure ever found. Over the next few years, the artifacts were brought to the surface. A legal battle ensued with insurance companies over the ownership of the find. A settlement was reached, and the gold was finally brought to market. The California Gold Marketing Group, headed by Dwight Manley, was formed to market the rare coins and gold bars.

Recently the wreckage of the SS *Central America* has yielded yet more treasure. The shipwreck company Odyssey Marine has been conducting successful dives and the full extent of the lost gold is still being explored.

Nearly all of the 1857-S double eagles from the SS *Central America* are pristine in appearance, and some very choice examples of a few earlier issues—notably 1856-S—were found as well. Prior to the find, double eagles from the 1850s were nearly impossible to locate in higher states of preservation. Now, for a relatively small investment, one can own a tangible piece of this incredibly important chapter of U.S. history.

It has been reported that the movie rights to the fascinating book *Ship of Gold in the Deep Blue Sea* have been purchased by a major movie studio. The story of the SS *Central America* is captivating, and the 1857-S double eagles may one day appear on the silver screen.

The wreck of the SS *Central America* yielded thousands of stunning gold coins.

Designed by James B. Longacre. The obverse features the portrait of Liberty facing left, wearing a coronet, and surrounded by 13 stars. The reverse features an outspread eagle and shield design. Mintage for this issue is 970,500 coins.

HISTORICAL VALUES
Choice Uncirculated

1960: $250	1980: $3,500	1st ed./2003: $8,500	2nd ed./2005: $9,000	3rd ed./2008: $12,000	4th edition: $15,000

1832 "12 STARS" CAPPED HEAD HALF EAGLE

STANDARDS · **Weight:** 8.75 grams. **Composition:** 92% gold, 8% silver. **Diameter:** 23.8 mm. **Edge:** Reeded **RARITY** · Researchers estimate that just five or six coins are known in all grades. **CERTIFIED POPULATION** · 3

The early half eagle series is filled with important rarities, of which the 1832 "12 Stars" half eagle is certainly one. The 1832 "12 Stars" half eagle has only six specimens known in all grades, making it as rare as, or rarer than, each of the two varieties of the 1829 half eagle and the 1815 half eagle. However, because an 1832 half eagle can be more easily acquired with 13 stars, collectors often overlook this much rarer variety. The variety was first widely publicized in 1913 when B. Max Mehl sold the famous Granberg collection. The coin was purchased by the most prolific collector of U.S. coins by die variety at the time: Waldo Newcomer.

This curious variety is an interesting Mint blunder, the result of the engraver punching the stars so widely that there was room for only 12 stars. No new examples of the 1832 "12 Stars" have surfaced in decades.

In the past 10 years, two 1832 "12 Stars" half eagles have sold at auction. The first coin, an attractive Uncirculated specimen from the Byron Reed collection, sold for just less than $300,000 in 1996 (an impressive sum for the time). The coin had been off the market for more than 100 years. By comparison, an EF-45 sold for $159,000 just two years later. The Harry W. Bass Jr. Reference Collection also contains one specimen, which is currently on display at the American Numismatic Association museum in Colorado Springs, Colorado. The Smithsonian example that was part

The standard obverse of the 1832 half eagle featured 13 stars in a ring around Liberty.

of the Lilly Collection is in About Uncirculated condition, but has had a hole expertly repaired.

Designed by John Reich with modifications from William Kneass. The obverse features a large portrait of Liberty surrounded by 12 stars with the date below. The reverse shows an eagle with spread wings, holding an olive branch and arrows. Surrounding the eagle are the inscriptions UNITED STATES OF AMERICA and 5 D., with the motto E PLURIBUS UNUM above the eagle's head.

HISTORICAL VALUES					
Extremely Fine					
1960: $3,500	1980: $45,000	1st ed./2003: $125,000	2nd ed./2005: $135,000	3rd ed./2008: $250,000	4th edition: $300,000

1841 LIBERTY HEAD QUARTER EAGLE

STANDARDS · **Weight:** 4.18 grams. **Composition:** 90% gold, 10% copper. **Diameter:** 18 mm. **Edge:** Reeded. **RARITY** · Between 15 and 18 specimens are known. **CERTIFIED POPULATION** · 14

The 1841 Liberty Head quarter eagle, or "Little Princess," is a legendary rarity and rightly deserving of 100 Greatest U.S. Coins status. Only Proof quarter eagles are believed to have been produced in 1841. Circulated examples exist, but they are probably mishandled Proofs that entered circulation. The origins of the "Little Princess" label are unknown, but some have attributed the name to Abe Kosoff, a dealer who was active from the 1940s until the 1970s. Abe Kosoff was also one of the founders of the Professional Numismatists Guild.

The 1841 quarter eagle has an uncertain history: it was struck in Proof format, but the U.S. Mint did not begin to sell Proofs to the public until 1859, and prior to that, Proofs were only struck for special circumstances. Another curiosity is that no quarter eagle circulation strikes were produced in 1841 per Mint records

(however, these are not always complete). Furthermore, the Philadelphia Mint struck quarter eagles for circulation every year from 1834 to 1862 except for 1841. Why the coin was struck remains uncertain. There may have been no demand for quarter eagles that year, and therefore the Mint only struck about 20 to 25 Proofs. One numismatist speculated that a group of foreign dignitaries visited Philadelphia in 1841 and the quarter eagles were presented as gifts. However, the fact that nearly every 1841 quarter eagle was discovered in the United States refutes that theory. Regardless of how they came into existence, the 1841 quarter eagles have had a storied past in numismatic circles. For many years, it was assumed that only a handful of specimens were known. In fact, one example sold privately for $3,000 in 1930. As more coins surfaced, the coin's value decreased sharply, with one specimen selling for $605 at auction in 1940. Today, it is believed that 15 to 18 are known.

In recent years, the value of an 1841 "Little Princess" has soared. Circulated examples in About Uncirculated condition now fetch over $100,000. The finest we have seen was an NGC PF-65 Ultra Cameo that brought $253,000 at auction in 2004. That coin traces its pedigree to the sale of the Adolph Menjou collection. The National Numismatic Collection of the Smithsonian contains two examples of the 1841 quarter eagle: a gem coin from the original Mint Collection, and a circulated Proof coin that was part of the Lilly Collection.

The Smithsonian Institution's National Numismatic Collection contains two 1841 quarter eagles.

Designed by Christian Gobrecht. The obverse features a bust of Liberty wearing a coronet. The word LIBERTY is inscribed on the headband. The portrait is encircled by 13 stars, with the date at the bottom. The reverse features a spread eagle located in the center with the words UNITED STATES OF AMERICA written at the edge. The denomination 2 1/2 D. is featured at six o'clock.

HISTORICAL VALUES					
Extremely Fine					
1960: $3,500	1980: $20,000	1st ed./2003: $75,000	2nd ed./2005: $85,000	3rd ed./2008: $100,000	4th edition: $100,000

1851 AND 1852 LIBERTY SEATED SILVER DOLLARS

STANDARDS · Weight: 26.73 grams. **Composition:** 90% silver, 10% copper. **Diameter:** 38 mm. **Edge:** Reeded. **RARITY, 1851 DOLLAR** · Very rare. Only 1,300 were struck for circulation, plus an estimated 50 Proof restrikes. The best original circulation strikes cluster around the MS-64 grade (in 1997, an MS-65 realized $57,500). Proof restrikes appear at auction at the rate of about one to two per year. **RARITY, 1852 DOLLAR** · Very rare. Only 1,100 were struck for circulation. Proof and Mint State originals are extremely rare. Proof restrikes are very rare but can usually be found in high grades. **CERTIFIED POPULATION** · 99

Experts recognize two varieties of the 1851 silver dollar: originals made in 1851 for circulation, and Proof restrikes made several years later. Only 1,300 original 1851 silver dollars were made for circulation. Price guides show a complete range of valuations from Very Good to Uncirculated, but mid-range grades are extremely rare. A collector is more likely to find a Mint State 1851 silver dollar than one in Fine condition. A true circulation-strike 1851 silver dollar is an underrated rarity. Proof restrikes are relatively common by comparison, with a surviving population estimated to number around 20 to 30 pieces.

The story of the 1852 silver dollar differs slightly from that of the 1851 silver dollar. The 1852 coins can be found as (1) originals struck for circulation, (2) originals struck as Proofs, and (3) Proof restrikes made years later.

At a mintage of 1,100 pieces, the 1852 circulation strikes are slightly rarer than the 1851 circulation strikes, but the grades of the known examples are distributed more evenly across the grading scale, all the way from Good to full Mint State. Proof originals are exceedingly rare: only one original 1852 Proof silver dollar has appeared at auction in recent years, when a PF-61 example sold for $55,200 in late 2007. Finally, Proof restrikes of the 1852 silver dollar are known in both silver and copper. The 1852 Proof restrike appears at auction almost as often as the 1851 Proof restrike silver dollar, but usually brings a slightly higher price because of its slightly higher rarity.

A subtle difference can be spotted between the 1851 original strikes for circulation and the 1851 Proof restrikes: in the latter, the date is centered in the space between the rock and the rim, whereas it is tight to the rock in the former.

Designed by Christian Gobrecht. The obverse shows Liberty in a flowing gown sitting on a rock. Her left hand holds a staff surmounted by a liberty cap; her right hand steadies a shield and holds a band bearing the word LIBERTY. An arc of 13 stars appears around Liberty, and the date appears at the base of the obverse, below the rock. The reverse shows an eagle with a shield on its chest, an olive branch in its right talon, and a bunch of arrows in its left. The words UNITED STATES OF AMERICA appear above the eagle; the abbreviation ONE DOL. appears below.

HISTORICAL VALUES					
1851, Choice Proof					
1960: $1,500	1980: $7,500	1st ed./2003: $37,500	2nd ed./2005: $42,500	3rd ed./2008: $50,000	4th edition: $55,000
1852, Choice Proof					
1960: $1,500	1980: $7,500	1st ed./2003: $35,000	2nd ed./2005: $38,500	3rd ed./2008: $45,000	4th edition: $50,000

1863 PROOF LIBERTY HEAD QUARTER EAGLE

STANDARDS · **Weight:** 4.18 grams. **Composition:** 90% gold, 10% copper. **Diameter:** 18 mm. **Edge:** Reeded. **RARITY** · Approximately 15 to 20 coins are known today in grades from impaired Proof to PF-66.
CERTIFIED POPULATION · 21

The story of the 1863 quarter eagle begins with its total mintage of only 30 Proof examples. This issue rates in the top tier of quarter eagle rarities along with the 1841, 1854-S, and 1804 "13 Stars." In 1863, quarter eagles were only struck as Proofs, and no circulation-strike coins are known for the date. What's more, of the original 30 that were struck, no more than 20 left the portals of the Mint. Demand for Proof gold was lukewarm at the time, so the Mint melted Proofs year after year. The 1863 quarter eagles were among those melted.

Harold P. Newlin, a famous researcher in his day, corresponded with legendary collector T. Harrison Garrett about the 1863 quarter eagle. In a letter dated September 13, 1883, Newlin wrote: "I have recently secured two pieces which were obtained at the mint in the year they were struck, by the gentleman from whom I got them. They are the gold dollar and quarter eagle of 1863. They are in beautiful proof condition. The former is rare and the latter in my estimation is the rarest of the series of quarter eagles."

Although more specimens surfaced after 1883, the gist of Newlin's message still holds true: the 1863 quarter is one of the rarest of the quarter eagles. There are approximately 15 to 20 coins known in all grades, including several that entered circulation and have been impaired. Author Jeff Garrett sold an example a few years ago that had been heavily polished. The finest seen in recent years has been an NGC PF-66 Ultra Cameo that sold at public auction in early 2007 for $149,500. The Smithsonian's National Numismatic Collection contains two of the known examples for the date. One was bequeathed as part of the Josiah K. Lilly collection; the other specimen is from the original Mint Collection, having been saved at the time of issue.

The combined count of coins graded by PCGS and NGC numbers 21 examples in all grades. This number is exaggerated, however, by coins that have been resubmitted with the tags either

The 1863 quarter eagle struck in Philadelphia featured a modified reverse, with smaller letters and arrowheads than previously. This new reverse was used from 1859 to 1907, but some Philadelphia-struck quarter eagles from 1859, 1860, and 1861 used the old reverse, shown above.

withheld or lost. Several years ago, one prominent dealer made public his hoard of unsubmitted tags from slabs that had been cracked for resubmission of the coin. He held thousands of inserts, and the grading companies took months to bring the databases up to date after they were turned in. Population numbers are a good guide to a coin's rarity, but they must be discounted in many cases. Several U.S. gold coins have combined population numbers that exceed original mintage numbers.

Designed by Christian Gobrecht. The obverse features a bust of Liberty wearing a coronet. The word LIBERTY is inscribed on the headband. The portrait is encircled by 13 stars, with the date at the bottom. The reverse shows a spread eagle located in the center with the words UNITED STATES OF AMERICA written at the edge. The denomination 2 1/2 D. is featured at six o'clock.

HISTORICAL VALUES
Choice Proof

1960: $1,500	1980: $15,000	1st ed./2003: $40,000	2nd ed./2005: $65,000	3rd ed./2008: $85,000	4th edition: $100,000

1819 CAPPED HEAD HALF EAGLES
TWO VARIETIES

STANDARDS · Weight: 8.75 grams. **Composition:** 92% gold, 8% silver. **Diameter:** 25 mm. **Edge:** Reeded. **RARITY ·** Both varieties combined, fewer than 24 half eagles of 1819 are known. **CERTIFIED POPULATION ·** 18

The 1819 half eagle is one of great rarities of the denomination, although it often gets overshadowed by the 1815 and 1825, 5 Over 4 half eagles. There are two distinct varieties known of the 1819 half eagle: the Close Date, Normal 5 and the Wide Date, 5D Over 50. The Philadelphia Mint frequently reused coinage dies. The 1819 "5D Over 50" half eagle exemplifies this, as a blundered die from 1818 was used again in 1819, despite its erroneous denomination marking. Apparently, an engraver carelessly punched "50" into the original die, but he eventually realized his mistake. He then punched the correct "5D" over the first impression, although rather obvious signs of the blunder still remained. The die was finally retired late in the year 1819, probably because of wear or deterioration.

Official Mint records report that 51,723 half eagles were struck in 1819. Considering how scarce 1819 half eagles are, this is difficult to believe. Once again, 1818 obverse dies were probably used until they were worn beyond potential use. Reusing dies year after year led to inaccurate and misleading mintage information, which has occasionally confused researchers. In any event, it is believed that fewer than two dozen 1819 half eagles are known between the two varieties. Although the 5D Over 50 variety is the more famous, the 1819 Close Date, Normal 5 is the rarer of the two, with only six to ten examples known.

The core collection of early U.S. gold coins assembled by Harry W. Bass Jr. is still intact and on exhibit at the American Numismatic Association museum. The 1819 half eagle is represented there, as is nearly every other early U.S. half eagle. The collection also contains the only complete set of $3 gold pieces known, including the unique 1870-S. A visit to the museum is highly recommended while these incredible coins are still available for public viewing.

The finest example of an 1819 half eagle to cross the auction block was a PCGS MS-63 from the Bass collection that sold for the bargain price of just $59,800 in 1999. The coin would bring much more on today's market.

Designed by John Reich. The obverse features a large portrait of Liberty surrounded by 13 stars with the date below. The reverse shows an eagle shown with spread wings, holding an olive branch and arrows. Surrounding the eagle are the inscriptions UNITED STATES OF AMERICA and 5 D., with the motto E PLURIBUS UNUM above the eagle's head.

HISTORICAL VALUES					
Close Date, Normal 5, About Uncirculated					
1960: $1,500	1980: $25,000	1st ed./2003: $45,000	2nd ed./2005: $55,000	3rd ed./2008: $85,000	4th edition: $100,000
Wide Date, 5D Over 50, About Uncirculated					
1960: $1,500	1980: $25,000	1st ed./2003: $35,000	2nd ed./2005: $40,000	3rd ed./2008: $65,000	4th edition: $75,000

GREAT COLLECTORS OF THE PAST
by Michael Berkman and Jeff Garrett

HARRY W. BASS JR.

Harry W. Bass Jr. is regarded not only as a famous collector of U.S. gold coins but also as a student of the series. After starting his collection in the 1960s, Bass acquired some of the greatest rarities in U.S. gold, including such memorable items as the 1870-S $3 piece, an 1875 $3 piece, many of the rare early half eagles, an 1854-S quarter eagle, and countless others. In a style similar to Virgil Brand, Bass did not mind buying multiples of major rarities. In addition, he collected U.S. gold by die combination—something that most numismatists largely ignore. Most of the Bass collection was sold in 1999 and 2000 by Bowers and Merena Galleries, with the balance of the holdings (now known as the Harry W. Bass Jr. Reference Collection) put on display at the American Numismatic Association museum in Colorado Springs, Colorado.

FREDERICK C.C. BOYD

Frederick Boyd was born in New York City in 1886 and began collecting coins at an early age. Although collecting eventually became his main numismatic focus, he dealt in coins for a brief period of time, as demonstrated by a small mail-bid auction he held in 1913. His primary occupation was managing the Union News Company, which maintained newsstands at railroad stations across the United States. With his considerable income, Boyd acquired many premier rarities in the U.S. coinage series, including the 1804 silver dollar and the 1854-S half eagle. When Boyd decided to sell his holdings in the 1940s, the Numismatic Gallery of New York was chosen to be the auctioneer. So spectacular were Boyd's coins that the auctions were held under the name "The World's Greatest Collection."

VIRGIL M. BRAND

The Brand collection ranks as one of the largest and most extensive coin collections—or hoards, some would argue—ever assembled. Virgil M. Brand was born in 1861 in Blue Hill, Illinois. He eventually moved to Chicago, where he formed a highly successful brewing company. Brand began to collect coins in 1879, although he did not begin to record these acquisitions until 1889. Brand recorded each coin purchase in a large leather-bound volume; these volumes

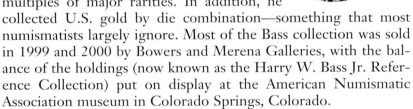

are now in the American Numismatic Society library. Brand was one of the most active rare coin buyers in the United States, adding to his collection at an incredible rate without regard for duplication. For example, Brand owned six 1884 trade dollars—an amazing feat considering that only ten were minted. Equally shocking, he owned five 1792 silver-center cents, three Strawberry Leaf cents, four 1875 $3 pieces, and 30 Stellas. When Brand died in 1926, his collection contained more than 350,000 specimens. The Brand estate was so immense that it took more than six decades to liquidate the collection. Brand's family began to sell the coins in the 1930s, and the last coins were sold by Bowers and Merena in 1984.

JEFF BROWNING

The name Jeff Browning may be foreign to most numismatists, but his collection is now widely known. Browning was a major collector of U.S. gold coins, purchasing many important rarities in the 1960s and 1970s. Among his most important acquisitions were a complete set of U.S. Stellas, an 1804 "13 Stars" quarter eagle, an 1870-CC double eagle, the 1861 Paquet Reverse double eagle, and a 1907 Ultra High Relief double eagle. He is also one of only a few numismatists to have ever owned a complete set of Liberty Head double eagles, including such rarities as the 1856-O, 1870-CC, and 1861 Paquet. His collection was sold in December 2001 as the Dallas Bank Collection in an auction conducted jointly by Sotheby's and Stack's.

JERRY BUSS

Although in this book the coins are ranked Nos. 1, 2, and 7 respectively, the 1804 dollar, the 1913 Liberty Head nickel, and the 1894-S dime are often called the "Big Three" of U.S. numismatics. Only a handful of collectors have ever owned this prestigious trio, of which Jerry Buss can be considered one. A Los Angeles businessman, Buss is widely known for owning the Los Angeles Lakers basketball team. At one point, he also owned the Los Angeles Kings hockey team and the Great Western Forum. In the numismatic world, Buss acquired his three great rarities with the assistance of Superior Stamp and Coin in 1978 and 1979. The same firm later auctioned the coins in 1985.

THE CARTER FAMILY

Amon Carter (pictured on next page) was a prominent Texas businessman whose activities included publishing the *Fort Worth Star-Telegram*, drilling for oil, and cofounding American Airlines. The

Carter collection contained many prominent U.S. rarities, including an 1822 half eagle, an 1875 $3 piece, an 1815 half eagle, and an 1804 silver dollar. After Carter passed away, his son, Amon Carter Jr., managed the collection. His holdings remained totally intact save for one coin: the 1822 half eagle. Josiah Lilly offered $60,000 for the coin, which the younger Carter found too tempting. After Amon Carter Jr. died, the collection was sold at auction by Stack's in 1984.

WILLIAM F. DUNHAM

No discussion of important U.S. collections can exclude the William Forrester Dunham collection, sold in 1941. Dunham was born in Vermont in 1857, but later relocated to Chicago. He was a successful druggist and put much of his earnings toward his fantastic collection. After his death in 1936, Dunham's collection was sold to B. Max Mehl, who, in turn, sold the collection via mail-bid auction in 1941. Interest was so great that 2,500 catalogs were sold for $3 each. Although the collection contained many famous rarities, the 1804 silver dollar and the 1822 half eagle were certainly the highlights. Interestingly, the 1804 silver dollar realized $4,250, while the 1822 half eagle brought $11,575—then a record amount for a U.S. coin.

LOUIS E. ELIASBERG

Louis Eliasberg is widely regarded as "The King of Coin Collectors," and for excellent reason. Although there have been many spectacular collections in the history of U.S. numismatics, Eliasberg was the only individual to own every single major U.S. coin issue. In other words, he owned a complete U.S. coin collection. Born in 1896, Eliasberg moved to Baltimore in 1907, where he established his highly successful banking business. Eliasberg was extremely fortunate in that many fabulous collections came on the market in the 1940s, the period in which he was most active. In 1942, the New York firm of Stack's sold the John H. Clapp collection to Eliasberg in its entirety for $100,000. This transaction alone brought Eliasberg close to completing his collection. After that monumental sale, Eliasberg picked the remaining rarities he needed from sales such as the F.C.C. Boyd collection. A few other coins were acquired via private treaty. Interestingly, it took no more than a decade to finish the collection, which remained intact until 1982. That year, Eliasberg's federal gold coins were sold at auction by Bowers and Merena, although the copper, nickel, and silver specimens were not sold until 1996 and 1997. When the hammer fell on the last coin, the Eliasberg collection had grossed a record $45 million.

KING FAROUK OF EGYPT

The King Farouk collection was a result of the overindulgence and avarice that surrounded Farouk's reign in Egypt. Despite his

seemingly unlimited budget, Farouk never seemed to have a true appreciation for U.S. coinage—he simply enjoyed buying whatever was available at virtually any price. Indeed, the key to success as a coin dealer in the 1940s was to have King Farouk as a customer. Farouk was eventually exiled in the early 1950s, at which point Sotheby's was appointed to liquidate the king's substantial excesses. Unfortunately, many of the coins were lacquered before the auction, and the coins were grouped together sloppily in massive lots. The nearly priceless MCMVII (1907) Indian Head double eagle pattern, for example, was grouped into a large lot of patterns without description. The auction proved to be a field day for U.S. collectors and dealers, who either attended in person or sent representatives to Egypt on their behalf. Many great collections, such as the Norweb and Pittman holdings, were formed with coins from the Farouk sale.

THE GARRETT FAMILY

Regarded as one of the finest collections of coins ever assembled, the Garrett collection was completed by two generations during a span of more than six decades. T. Harrison Garrett, the founder of the Baltimore and Ohio Railroad, started the collection in the late 1870s. However, he was killed in a boating accident, which left the collection to his son Robert Garrett. In 1919, the coins were once again transferred, this time to Robert's brother John Work Garrett (pictured), who proved to be more active in acquiring pieces for the collection. After John Garrett's death in 1942, the holdings were bequeathed to Johns Hopkins University, which decided to liquidate the collection in the late 1970s. Bowers and Ruddy conducted four sales of the Garrett collection, which netted more than $25 million total.

COLONEL E.H.R. GREEN

Colonel E.H.R. Green was the son of Hetty Green, known to many as "the Witch of Wall Street." In 1917, the younger Green inherited massive amounts of money, which he spent on a wide variety of items, including rare coins. Like Virgil Brand, Green owned multiples of many major rarities. In fact, at one point he owned all five 1913 Liberty Head nickels known today! For comparison purposes, Green also owned the entire sheet of "Inverted Jenny" stamps,

which are regarded as the philatelic world's equivalent of the 1804 dollar. Green's massive collection was sold privately in the late 1930s and early 1940s, with the coins sold *en bloc* to major dealers. In order to buy one select rarity, dealers often were forced to buy entire sections of the collection.

EDWIN HYDEMAN

Some collections are known for being particularly extensive or all-encompassing. Edwin Hydeman chose to focus on major rarities. Among his most important holdings were an 1804 silver dollar, a 1913 Liberty Head nickel, and the unique 1866 "No Motto" quarter and half dollar. Hydeman was the owner of a department store and sold his collection through Abe Kosoff in 1961. Although many of the coins met the reserves in the auction, some were retained and later sold by Kosoff via private treaty. Interestingly, both the 1804 silver dollar and 1913 Liberty Head nickel landed in the Jerry Buss collection, which had a similar emphasis on major rarities.

JOSIAH K. LILLY

Most numismatists forget about Josiah K. Lilly's world-class collection—until they walk into the Smithsonian Institution. Unbeknownst to most, one of the greatest collections still intact is that of Lilly, former director of the pharmaceutical firm that bears his father's name. Not only is Lilly's name foreign to most numismatists today, but he also escaped notice during his heyday in the 1950s and 1960s. Most major collectors appeared at conventions, participated in public auctions, or were somehow known to the numismatic world. Lilly, on the other hand, operated in an extremely private manner, despite his substantial appetite and budget for rare gold coinage. Lilly died in 1966, at which point his collection was donated to the Smithsonian to offset an outstanding tax bill.

JOSEPH J. MICKLEY

A true pioneer in U.S. numismatics, Joseph J. Mickley was one of the first major coin collectors in the United States. Born in 1799, Mickley began his pursuit of coins as a teenager, initially focusing on foreign coins from Europe. His tastes shifted later to U.S. coinage, even though there were no coin dealers in the United States. Indeed, the first true full-time coin dealer was Ed Cogan, who did not open for business until 1858. As a result, Mickley's only viable trading partner was the U.S. Mint itself! Mickley was able to purchase many formidable rarities from the Philadelphia Mint, including a Class 1 1804 dollar and many early Proof sets. Mickley's collection was sold in 1867, when his prized 1804 dollar realized $750. Although there were countless major rarities in the sale, U.S. numismatics was still a young field at the time, and thus many scarce coins brought tiny premiums over face value.

WALDO NEWCOMER

Waldo Newcomer, one of the lesser-known major collectors of the 20th century, owned many of the rarest coins in all of numismatics. A banker by profession, Newcomer called Baltimore, Maryland, his home. Among the more important coins in his collection were an 1804 dollar, a Brasher doubloon, and an 1838-O half dollar. Newcomer elected to sell his collection gradually, beginning with a small auction in 1914, another in 1919, and several others into the 1920s and 1930s. Many coins from the Newcomer collection were later sold to John Work Garrett, mostly through Wayte Raymond at the Scott Coin and Stamp Company.

THE NORWEB FAMILY

The Norweb collection was assembled by a husband-and-wife team. R. Henry Norweb, who owned mines in Canada, later became a U.S. ambassador. Interestingly, it was his wife, Emery, who took the most interest in the collection and negotiated many of the acquisitions. She had also inherited part of the collection. Among the notable rarities owned by the Norwebs were an 1827 quarter, a silver-center cent, a 1792 pattern quarter, an 1815 half eagle, a fabulous superb gem 1861 Paquet Reverse double eagle, and many others. The Norwebs owned a Brasher doubloon and a 1913 Liberty Head nickel at one point, but decided to donate the coins to the Smithsonian and the ANS, respectively. Bowers and Merena auctioned a portion of the Norweb collection in 1987 and 1988.

LORIN G. PARMELEE

The Lorin Parmelee collection is undeniably one of the finest assemblages of U.S. coins ever formed. Born in Vermont in 1827, Parmelee moved to Boston in 1849. He accumulated substantial wealth as a bean baker and supplied most restaurants in Boston with legumes. Parmelee became interested in coins by picking large cents out of circulation, which resulted in his special interest in copper coinage. His love of coins extended to all series, and hence he purchased almost every major rarity available to him. He also acquired several major collections intact, including the spectacular Bushnell collection of early U.S. and colonial coinage. Parmelee's collection was auctioned in 1890, although many items were bought back and sold privately at a later date.

JOHN JAY PITTMAN

Not only was John Jay Pittman's collection one of the finest ever assembled, but the story of how he formed the collection is truly fascinating. Unlike many of the collectors mentioned in this text, Pittman was not a particularly wealthy individual. He worked for Eastman Kodak in Rochester, New York, where he held a respectable but not necessarily lucrative position in the chemical department. Rather than focus on major rarities, Pittman acquired coins that were esoteric, rare, and undervalued. Some of his favorite areas included scarce Proof material and early U.S. coinage. Pittman was also extremely careful in how and when he acquired coins for his collection. In 1946, for example, he decided not to participate extensively in the auction of the "World's Greatest Collection" (that of F.C.C. Boyd), as he felt that he could acquire some of the coins for substantially less at a later time. He was correct: many of the coins came on the market two years later and could be had for a fraction of their original selling price. Pittman actually mortgaged his house in order to attend another memorable event, the storied Farouk collection sale in Cairo. This spectacular 1954 auction contained many extreme rarities, such as the 1913 Liberty Head nickel and the 1933 double eagle. Rather than compete on the premier rarities, however, Pittman was an aggressive bidder on the more esoteric items in the sale. Even though Pittman spent less than $100,000 on his entire collection, his holdings were sold for more than $25 million in 1997 and 1998. Many coins were originally purchased for $50 to $100 in the 1940s, yet realized well in excess of $100,000 in the late 1990s. Pittman's collection was a testimony to the investment potential of U.S. coins.

ED TROMPETER

Proof gold coins are regarded as the *crème de la crème* of U.S. numismatics, as they tend to have miniscule original mintages and low survival rates. For many collectors, owning just one specimen is a true accomplishment. Yet Ed Trompeter miraculously assembled a complete set of regular-production Proof gold, which would include coins minted from 1860 through 1915. He also acquired major rarities such as an 1855 Proof gold dollar, the 1872 Amazonian set, a complete set of Stellas, an 1874 Bickford $10 gold piece, a Quintuple Stella, and a 1907 Ultra High Relief double eagle. A portion of his collection was auctioned in 1992, shortly before his death, but the balance of the collection did not appear on the market until 1998. In fact, Trompeter's half eagles, eagles, double eagles, and the Amazonian set changed hands for a record $15,177,500 in the summer of 1998.

GEORGE O. WALTON

George Walton was fairly unknown in current numismatic circles until the 2003 rediscovery of the famous "lost" 1913 Liberty Head nickel. Walton was born on May 15, 1905. Although his name is now closely linked to the 1913 Liberty Head nickel, Walton's collecting interests were vast in scope. When Walton's collection was sold by Stack's in 1963, the total hammer price was $874,836— then a record price for a single collection of coins sold at auction. His collection included nearly every series of U.S. coinage, but his Southern gold collection, including Bechtler coinage, was the finest assembled to that point. Walton was also a serious gun and sword collector; he collected more than 18,000 guns in his career. He was also very active in the prominent numismatic organizations of the time. Tragically, Walton was killed in an automobile crash on March 9, 1962. For many years, the location of his 1913 Liberty Head nickel remained a mystery. Rumors that the coin had been sold or had been lost at the scene of his accident were proven wrong in 2003. After a national search had been announced offering a $10,000 reward for the discovery of the coin's location, Walton's family decided to have the coin they had been told was counterfeit checked out one more time. The rest is numismatic history!

DR. JOHN E. WILKISON

As a group, gold patterns are among the rarest and most beautiful coins in U.S. numismatics. In fact, several of the coins listed in this book are technically gold patterns (1849 double eagle, MCMVII [1907] Ultra High Relief double eagle, MCMVII [1907] Indian Head double eagle pattern, Amazonian set, 1877 Half Union, 1879–1880 Stellas, 1804 eagle, 1907 Rolled Edge eagle, 1874 Bickford $10 gold pattern). These coins are also exceedingly scarce. As one can imagine, assembling a set of gold patterns is a daunting task, but John Wilkison accomplished the extraordinary feat of owning nearly every known gold pattern. His collection was sold intact in 1973 to Paramount International Coin Corporation, and subsequently the set was traded in its entirety to A-Mark Financial. In the late 1970s, individual pieces were sold to various collectors and dealers, including notable rarities such as the MCMVII (1907) Indian Head double eagle pattern and the Amazonian set.

WILLIAM H. WOODIN

William H. Woodin was born in Berwick, Pennsylvania, on May 27, 1868. An eclectic personality, Woodin was involved in numerous activities, ranging from writing children's songs to serving as secretary of the Treasury under President Franklin D. Roosevelt. He was also extremely active in numismatics and assembled one of the greatest and most exotic collections of U.S. coins ever, including major rarities such as the unique 1870-S $3 gold piece. One fascinating story involving Woodin is the history of the 1877 gold Half Unions. These fabulous coins, ranked No. 19 in this text, appeared on the private market for a brief time around 1909. Woodin acquired the two known specimens for $10,000 apiece—a record sum for the time. However, the U.S. government seized the coins, but compensated Woodin with an incredible assortment of rare and unique pattern coinage. Many of the patterns on the numismatic market today likely originated from this transaction. Woodin sold his collection at auction in 1911 through dealer Thomas L. Elder.

PRICE HISTORY OF THE 100 GREATEST U.S. COINS

Asterisks indicate entries new to the fourth edition.

Rank	Description	Grade	In 1960	In 1980	1st Edition	2nd Edition	3rd Edition	4th Edition
1	1804 Draped Bust Silver Dollar	Choice Proof	$30,000	$250,000	$3,000,000	$3,750,000	$5,500,000	$6,000,000
2	1913 Liberty Head Nickel	Choice Proof	$50,000	$250,000	$2,000,000	$3,250,000	$4,000,000	$4,000,000
3	MCMVII (1907) Ultra High Relief Saint-Gaudens Double Eagle	Gem Proof	$20,000	$250,000	$1,000,000	$1,650,000	$2,500,000	$3,000,000
4	1933 Saint-Gaudens Double Eagle	Choice Uncirculated	$25,000	$250,000	$7,500,000	$8,500,000	$5,000,000	$7,500,000
5	1849 Liberty Head Double Eagle	Choice Proof	$100,000	$1,000,000	$7,500,000	$10,000,000	$20,000,000	$25,000,000
6	MCMVII (1907) Indian Head Double Eagle Pattern	Gem Proof	$25,000	$500,000	$7,500,000	$10,000,000	$12,500,000	$15,000,000
7	1894-S Barber Dime	Choice Proof	$15,000	$100,000	$750,000	$850,000	$1,250,000	$2,000,000
8	1885 Proof Trade Dollar	Choice Proof	$15,000	$100,000	$1,000,000	$1,250,000	$2,250,000	$3,000,000
9	1794 Flowing Hair Silver Dollar	Extremely Fine	$6,500	$25,000	$125,000	$150,000	$250,000	$275,000
10	1776 Continental Dollar	Uncirculated	$300	$10,000	$35,000	$60,000	$75,000	$100,000
11	1943 Bronze Lincoln Cent	Extremely Fine	$5,000	$20,000	$50,000	$60,000	$100,000	$200,000
12	1792 Half Disme	Very Fine	$500	$5,000	$35,000	$50,000	$85,000	$85,000
13	1793 Flowing Hair, Chain Reverse Cent	Extremely Fine	$750	$10,000	$25,000	$40,000	$75,000	$100,000
14	MCMVII (1907) Ultra High Relief Saint-Gaudens Double Eagle Piedfort	Gem Proof	$20,000	$250,000	$2,500,000	$3,500,000	$6,500,000	$7,000,000
15	1861 "Paquet Reverse" Liberty Head Double Eagle	Uncirculated	$5,000	$75,000	$350,000	$750,000	$2,000,000	$2,500,000
16	1872 Amazonian Gold Pattern Set	Choice Proof	$15,000	$500,000	$3,000,000	$3,250,000	$5,500,000	$6,000,000
17	1822 Capped Head Half Eagle	Extremely Fine	$25,000	$650,000	$2,500,000	$3,500,000	$5,000,000	$5,000,000
18	1879 $4 Gold Stella, Flowing Hair	Choice Proof	$5,000	$25,000	$75,000	$100,000	$150,000	$175,000
18	1879 $4 Gold Stella, Coiled Hair	Choice Proof	$10,000	$75,000	$250,000	$350,000	$450,000	$650,000
18	1880 $4 Gold Stella, Flowing Hair	Choice Proof	$10,000	$45,000	$125,000	$150,000	$250,000	$300,000
18	1880 $4 Gold Stella, Coiled Hair	Choice Proof	$15,000	$100,000	$350,000	$500,000	$750,000	$1,000,000
19	1877 Half Union $50 Gold Coin, Type 1	Choice Proof	$50,000	$1,000,000	$4,500,000	$7,500,000	$10,000,000	$12,500,000
19	1877 Half Union $50 Gold Coin, Type 2	Choice Proof	$50,000	$1,000,000	$4,500,000	$7,500,000	$10,000,000	$12,500,000
20	1792 Disme	Extremely Fine	$1,000	$17,500	$75,000	$150,000	$250,000	$300,000
21	1915-S Panama-Pacific Exposition $50 Gold Piece, Octagonal	Choice Uncirculated	$2,500	$15,000	$35,000	$50,000	$75,000	$80,000
21	1915-S Panama-Pacific Exposition $50 Gold Piece, Round	Choice Uncirculated	$3,500	$20,000	$45,000	$65,000	$75,000	$80,000
22	1870-S Indian Princess Head $3 Gold Piece	Very Fine	$25,000	$650,000	$2,500,000	$3,000,000	$5,000,000	$5,000,000
23	1909-S V.D.B. Lincoln Cent	Choice Uncirculated	$150	$750	$1,500	$2,500	$2,750	$2,750
24	1794 "Starred Reverse" Liberty Cap Large Cent	Very Fine	$1,500	$10,000	$75,000	$85,000	$125,000	$150,000
25	1792 Birch Cent	Very Fine	$1,500	$35,000	$200,000	$240,000	$350,000	$500,000
26	1876-CC Liberty Seated Twenty-Cent Piece	Choice Uncirculated	$7,500	$50,000	$100,000	$145,000	$275,000	$300,000
27	1838-O Capped Bust Half Dollar	Choice Proof	$5,000	$75,000	$200,000	$300,000	$600,000	$750,000
28	MCMVII (1907) High Relief Saint-Gaudens Double Eagle	Choice Uncirculated	$500	$7,500	$15,000	$20,000	$25,000	$25,000
29	1870-S Liberty Seated Silver Dollar	Extremely Fine	$15,000	$75,000	$200,000	$250,000	$750,000	$850,000
30	1895 Morgan Silver Dollar	Choice Proof	$1,500	$17,500	$25,000	$35,000	$55,000	$60,000
31	1854-S Presentation-Strike Liberty Head Double Eagle	Presentation Strike	$25,000	$250,000	n/a	$2,000,000	$4,000,000	$5,000,000
32	1854-O Liberty Head Double Eagle	Extremely Fine	$500	$35,000	$75,000	$125,000	$300,000	$350,000
33	1798 "Small Eagle" Capped Bust Half Eagle	Extremely Fine	$3,500	$75,000	$250,000	$275,000	$400,000	$500,000
34	1838 Proof Liberty Head Eagle	Choice Proof	$5,000	$100,000	$500,000	$600,000	$1,250,000	$1,500,000
35	1849-C "Open Wreath" Liberty Head Gold Dollar	Extremely Fine	$7,500	$75,000	$275,000	$325,000	$375,000	$450,000
36	1787 Fugio Cent	Choice Uncirculated	$50	$500	$2,500	$3,500	$5,000	$6,500
37	1907 "Rolled Edge" Indian Head Eagle	Choice Uncirculated	$3,500	$40,000	$85,000	$125,000	$175,000	$225,000
38	1893-S Morgan Silver Dollar	Choice Uncirculated	$2,500	$35,000	$125,000	$135,000	$150,000	$175,000
39	1861-D Indian Princess Head Gold Dollar	Uncirculated	$2,000	$15,000	$35,000	$40,000	$75,000	$85,000
40	1792 Silver-Center Cent	Very Fine	$1,500	$25,000	$85,000	$150,000	$250,000	$300,000
41	1933 Indian Head Eagle	Choice Uncirculated	$2,500	$75,000	$150,000	$250,000	$350,000	$450,000
42	1815 Capped Head Half Eagle	Extremely Fine	$2,500	$45,000	$100,000	$125,000	$200,000	$250,000
43	1916 Standing Liberty Quarter Dollar	Choice Uncirculated	$750	$2,500	$7,500	$20,000	$25,000	$30,000
44	1844-O Proof Liberty Head Half Eagle	Choice Proof	$2,500	$75,000	$850,000	$850,000	$1,250,000	$1,500,000
44	1844-O Proof Liberty Head Eagle	Choice Proof	$2,500	$75,000	$1,250,000	$1,500,000	$1,750,000	$2,000,000
45	1834–1837 Proof Classic Head Half Eagles	Choice Proof	$2,500	$25,000	$65,000	$100,000	$150,000	$200,000
46	1866 "No Motto" Liberty Seated Silver Dollar	Choice Proof	$15,000	$100,000	$1,000,000	$850,000	$1,250,000	$2,000,000
47	1817, 7 Over 4 Capped Bust Half Dollar	Extremely Fine	$3,500	$40,000	$200,000	$250,000	$350,000	$350,000
48	1866 "No Motto" Liberty Seated Quarter Dollar	Choice Proof	$25,000	$75,000	$350,000	$375,000	$500,000	$750,000
49	1854 Proof Indian Princess Head Gold Dollar	Choice Proof	$3,500	$35,000	$150,000	$250,000	$350,000	$400,000
49	1855 Proof Indian Princess Head Gold Dollar	Choice Proof	$3,500	$35,000	$125,000	$165,000	$225,000	$275,000
50	1861-S "Paquet Reverse" Liberty Head Double Eagle	About Uncirculated	$1,500	$7,500	$35,000	$45,000	$85,000	$100,000
51	1921 Proof Saint-Gaudens Double Eagle	Proof	n/a	n/a	n/a	n/a	$2,500,000	$3,500,000

n/a: indicates that a coin was either unknown at the date of pricing or not ranked in a previous edition of *100 Greatest U.S. Coins*.

Rank	Description	Grade	In 1960	In 1980	1st Edition	2nd Edition	3rd Edition	4th Edition
52	1804 "13 Stars" Capped Bust Quarter Eagle	Extremely Fine	$2,500	$7,500	$75,000	$85,000	$250,000	$275,000
53	1856-O Liberty Head Double Eagle	Extremely Fine	$500	$35,000	$85,000	$135,000	$275,000	$300,000
54	1798, 8 Over 7 Capped Bust Eagle, 9 x 4 Stars	About Uncirculated	$1,000	$12,500	$35,000	$40,000	$75,000	$85,000
54	1798, 8 Over 7 Capped Bust Eagle, 7 x 6 Stars	About Uncirculated	$2,500	$25,000	$95,000	$100,000	$175,000	$185,000
55	1825, 5 Over 4 Capped Head Half Eagle	About Uncirculated	$2,500	$125,000	$250,000	$275,000	$350,000	$400,000
56	1796 Draped Bust Silver Dollar, 15 Stars	Extremely Fine	$2,000	$15,000	$45,000	$55,000	$125,000	$150,000
56	1796 Draped Bust Silver Dollar, 16 Stars	Extremely Fine	$2,000	$16,500	$50,000	$60,000	$125,000	$150,000
56	1797 Draped Bust Silver Dollar	Extremely Fine	$2,000	$15,000	$45,000	$65,000	$125,000	$150,000
57	1856 Flying Eagle Cent	Choice Proof	$1,250	$3,500	$15,000	$17,500	$18,500	$20,000
58	1870-S Liberty Seated Half Dime	Choice Uncirculated	n/a	$425,000	$750,000	$1,000,000	$2,000,000	$2,000,000
59	1875 Indian Princess Head $3 Gold Piece	Choice Proof	$7,500	$75,000	$125,000	$145,000	$175,000	$200,000
60	U.S. Assay Office $50 Gold Slugs	Extremely Fine	$1,500	$6,500	$15,000	$18,000	$30,000	$50,000
61	1793 "Strawberry Leaf" Flowing Hair, Wreath Reverse Cent	Fine	$2,500	$30,000	$200,000	$245,000	$450,000	$450,000
62	1854-S Liberty Head Half Eagle	About Uncirculated	$5,000	$200,000	$750,000	$1,000,000	$2,000,000	$2,500,000
63	1848 "CAL." Liberty Head Quarter Eagle	Uncirculated	$1,500	$20,000	$45,000	$75,000	$85,000	$100,000
64	1927-D Saint-Gaudens Double Eagle	Gem Uncirculated	$1,500	$150,000	$500,000	$1,100,000	$2,000,000	$2,000,000
65	1873-CC "No Arrows" Liberty Seated Dime	Choice Uncirculated	$25,000	$250,000	$750,000	$1,000,000	$1,500,000	$2,000,000
66	1884 Proof Trade Dollar	Choice Proof	$7,500	$50,000	$200,000	$225,000	$500,000	$750,000
67	1833 Proof Capped Head Half Eagle	Gem Proof	$3,500	$100,000	$500,000	$750,000	$1,000,000	$1,000,000
68	1916-D Mercury Dime	Choice Uncirculated	$750	$3,500	$10,000	$14,000	$17,500	$20,000
69	1804 "Plain 4" Capped Bust Eagle	Choice Proof	$3,500	$50,000	$150,000	$750,000	$3,000,000	$5,000,000
70	1796 Liberty Cap Half Cent, With Pole	Very Fine	$750	$7,500	$25,000	$45,000	$75,000	$85,000
70	1796 Liberty Cap Half Cent, No Pole	Very Fine	$1,250	$15,000	$75,000	$95,000	$150,000	$200,000
71	1796 "No Stars" Capped Bust Quarter Eagle	About Uncirculated	$2,500	$20,000	$75,000	$85,000	$150,000	$175,000
72	1792 Quarter Dollar Pattern	Extremely Fine	$2,500	$30,000	$175,000	$250,000	$500,000	$650,000
73	1836 Gobrecht Silver Dollar	Choice Proof	$1,750	$5,500	$15,000	$25,000	$45,000	$45,000
73	1838 Gobrecht Silver Dollar	Choice Proof	$2,500	$7,500	$40,000	$65,000	$85,000	$85,000
73	1839 Gobrecht Silver Dollar	Choice Proof	$2,500	$7,500	$40,000	$55,000	$80,000	$85,000
74	1955 Doubled-Die Obverse Lincoln Cent	Uncirculated	$50	$550	n/a	n/a	$3,000	$3,500
75	1873-CC "No Arrows" Liberty Seated Quarter Dollar	Uncirculated	$3,500	$75,000	$175,000	$185,000	$250,000	$300,000
76	1796 Draped Bust Quarter Dollar	Extremely Fine	$1,250	$7,500	$17,500	$25,000	$50,000	$50,000
77	1802 Draped Bust Half Dime	Extremely Fine	$2,000	$25,000	$75,000	$100,000	$150,000	$175,000
78	1795 "Nine Leaves" Capped Bust Eagle	About Uncirculated	$1,000	$12,500	$75,000	$100,000	$175,000	$200,000
79	1870-CC Liberty Head Double Eagle	Extremely Fine	$2,500	$25,000	$125,000	$165,000	$285,000	$325,000
80	1801 Proof Draped Bust Silver Dollar	Choice Proof	$4,500	$35,000	$150,000	$225,000	$750,000	$1,000,000
80	1802 Proof Draped Bust Silver Dollar	Choice Proof	$4,500	$35,000	$150,000	$225,000	$650,000	$750,000
80	1803 Proof Draped Bust Silver Dollar	Choice Proof	$4,500	$35,000	$150,000	$225,000	$600,000	$700,000
81	1829 Capped Head Half Eagle, Large Planchet	Uncirculated	$3,500	$50,000	$150,000	$165,000	$250,000	$300,000
81	1829 Capped Head Half Eagle, Small Planchet	Uncirculated	$3,500	$45,000	$125,000	$135,000	$250,000	$300,000
82	1853-O "No Arrows" Liberty Seated Half Dollar	Fine	$3,500	$25,000	$175,000	$185,000	$250,000	$300,000
83	1866 "Small Motto" Liberty Seated Half Dollar	Choice Proof	$20,000	$75,000	$350,000	$375,000	$500,000	$750,000
84	1918-D, 8 Over 7 Buffalo Nickel	Extremely Fine	$375	$1,850	n/a	n/a	$9,500	$10,000
85	1874 Bickford $10 Gold Pattern	Choice Proof	$3,500	$100,000	$350,000	$350,000	$600,000	$1,000,000
86	1918-S, 8 Over 7 Standing Liberty Quarter Dollar	Uncirculated		$525	$6,000	n/a	n/a	$20,000
87	1827 "Original" Capped Bust Quarter Dollar	Choice Proof	$7,000	$40,000	$100,000	$115,000	$175,000	$200,000
88	1974 Aluminum Lincoln Cents*	Uncirculated	n/a	n/a	n/a	n/a	n/a	$500,000
89	1867 Proof "With Rays" Shield Nickel	Choice Proof	$1,500	$5,000	$45,000	$45,000	$60,000	$75,000
90	1854-S Liberty Head Quarter Eagle	Very Fine	$1,500	$15,000	$75,000	$85,000	$225,000	$300,000
91	1864 Proof "Small Motto" Two-Cent Piece	Choice Proof	$1,500	$5,000	$35,000	$45,000	$65,000	$70,000
92	1808 Capped Bust Quarter Eagle	About Uncirculated	$2,000	$17,500	$35,000	$55,000	$95,000	$100,000
93	1842 "Small Date" Liberty Seated Quarter Dollar	Choice Proof	$2,500	$15,000	$85,000	$85,000	$125,000	$150,000
94	1797 "16 Stars Obverse" Capped Bust, Heraldic Reverse Half Eagle	Extremely Fine	$2,500	$50,000	$300,000	$325,000	$750,000	$1,000,000
95	1857-S Liberty Head Double Eagles	Choice Uncirculated	$250	$3,500	$8,500	$9,000	$12,000	$15,000
96	1832 "12 Stars" Capped Head Half Eagle	Extremely Fine	$3,500	$45,000	$125,000	$135,000	$250,000	$300,000
97	1841 Liberty Head Quarter Eagle	Extremely Fine	$3,500	$20,000	$75,000	$85,000	$100,000	$100,000
98	1851 Liberty Seated Silver Dollar	Choice Proof	$1,500	$7,500	$37,500	$42,500	$50,000	$55,000
98	1852 Liberty Seated Silver Dollar	Choice Proof	$1,500	$7,500	$35,000	$38,500	$45,000	$50,000
99	1863 Liberty Head Quarter Eagle	Choice Proof	$1,500	$15,000	$40,000	$65,000	$85,000	$100,000
100	1819 Capped Head Half Eagle, "Close Date, Normal 5"	About Uncirculated	$1,500	$25,000	$45,000	$55,000	$85,000	$100,000
100	1819 Capped Head Half Eagle, "Open Date, 5D Over 50"	About Uncirculated	$1,500	$25,000	$35,000	$40,000	$65,000	$75,000
	Totals		$860,700	$11,261,150	$66,135,000	$90,935,500	$140,073,250	$170,867,750

n/a: indicates that a coin was either unknown at the date of pricing or not ranked in a previous edition of *100 Greatest U.S. Coins.*

TOP 200 U.S. COIN PRICES REALIZED, 1990–2014

Date/Variety	Denomination	Grade	Price	Date	Firm
1794, Silver Plug (B-1, BB-1)	Silver Dollar	PCGS SP-66 CAC	$10,016,875	January 2013	Stack's Bowers Galleries
1933	Double Eagle	Gem BU	$7,590,020	July 2002	Sotheby's/Stack's
1787 Brasher, EB on Breast (B-5840)	Doubloon	NGC MS-63 CAC	$4,582,500	January 2014	Heritage
1804, Original, Class I	Silver Dollar	PCGS PF-68	$4,140,000	August 1999	Bowers & Merena
1804, Original, Class I	Silver Dollar	PCGS PF-62	$3,877,500	August 2013	Heritage
1913, Liberty Head	Nickel Five-Cent Piece	NGC PF-64	$3,737,500	January 2010	Heritage
1804, Original, Class I (NGC#3128352-001)	Silver Dollar	NGC PF-62	$3,737,500	April 2008	Heritage
1913, Liberty Head	Nickel Five-Cent Piece	NGC PF-64 CAC	$3,290,000	January 2014	Heritage
1913, Liberty Head	Nickel Five-Cent Piece	PCGS PF-63	$3,172,500	April 2013	Heritage
1787 Brasher, EB on Breast	Doubloon	NGC EF-45	$2,990,000	January 2005	Heritage
1907, Saint-Gaudens, UHR, LE	Double Eagle	PCGS PF-69	$2,990,000	November 2005	Heritage
1907, Saint-Gaudens, UHR, LE	Double Eagle	PCGS PF-69	$2,760,000	June 2012	Stack's Bowers Galleries
1880, Coiled Hair	$4 Gold Piece	NGC PF-67Cam	$2,570,000	September 2013	Bonhams
1787 Brasher, EB on Wing	Doubloon	NGC AU-55	$2,415,000	January 2005	Heritage
1804, Restrike, Class III	Silver Dollar	PCGS PF-58	$2,300,000	April 2009	Heritage
1907, Indian Head, Rolled Edge, Satin Finish	Eagle	NGC PF-67	$2,185,000	January 2011	Heritage
1927-D	Double Eagle	NGC MS-66	$1,997,500	January 2014	Heritage
1792 Copper Pattern (J-1, P-1)	Cent	PCGS MS-64BN Secure Plus CAC	$1,997,500	August 2014	Heritage
1927-D	Double Eagle	PCGS MS-67	$1,897,500	November 2005	Heritage
1804, Restrike, Class III	Silver Dollar	NGC PF-55	$1,880,000	August 2014	Stack's Bowers Galleries
1873-CC, No Arrows	Dime	PCGS MS-65 Secure Plus	$1,840,000	August 2012	Stack's Bowers Galleries
1907, Saint-Gaudens, UHR, LE	Double Eagle	PCGS PF-68	$1,840,000	January 2007	Heritage
1913, Liberty Head	Nickel Five-Cent Piece	NGC PF-66	$1,840,000	March 2001	Superior
1804, Original, Class I	Silver Dollar	PCGS PF-64	$1,840,000	October 2000	Stack's
1804, Original, Class I	Silver Dollar	PF-63	$1,815,000	April 1997	Bowers & Merena
1796, No Stars on Obv (B-1, BD-2, B-6113, Bass-3002)	Quarter Eagle	PCGS MS-65	$1,725,000	January 2008	Heritage
1920-S	Eagle	PCGS MS-67	$1,725,000	March 2007	Heritage
1861, Paquet Reverse	Double Eagle	PCGS MS-61	$1,645,000	August 2014	Heritage
1839, 9 Over 8	Eagle	NGC PF-67UCam	$1,610,000	January 2007	Heritage
1861, Paquet Reverse	Double Eagle	PCGS MS-61	$1,610,000	August 2006	Heritage
1894-S	Dime	PCGS PF-BM64	$1,552,500	October 2007	Stack's
1796 (B-2)	Quarter Dollar	NGC MS-67+ Star CAC	$1,527,500	November 2013	Heritage
1927-D	Double Eagle	PCGS MS-66	$1,495,000	January 2010	Heritage
1921	Double Eagle	PCGS MS-63	$1,495,000	August 2006	Bowers & Merena
1913, Liberty Head	Nickel Five-Cent Piece	Gem PF-66	$1,485,000	May 1996	Bowers & Merena
1856-O	Double Eagle	NGC SP-63	$1,437,500	May 2009	Heritage
1776 CURRENCY EG FECIT, Pewter (N.3-D, W-8470)	Dollar	NGC MS-63	$1,410,000	May 2014	Heritage
1792 Copper Pattern (J-1, P-1)	Cent	NGC MS-63+BN	$1,410,000	May 2014	Heritage
1792	Half Disme	PCGS SP-67	$1,410,000	January 2013	Heritage
1793, Chain, Periods (S-4)	Cent	PCGS MS-65BN CAC	$1,380,000	January 2012	Heritage
1829, Large Planchet (BD-1, B-6489)	Half Eagle	PCGS PF-64 Secure Plus CAC	$1,380,000	January 2012	Heritage
1797 (O-101a)	Half Dollar	NGC MS-66	$1,380,000	July 2008	Stack's
1796, No Stars (B-1)	Quarter Eagle	PCGS MS-65	$1,380,000	June 2005	American Numismatic Rarities
1855-S (NGC #1578367-003)	$3 Gold Piece	NGC PF-BM64Cam	$1,322,500	August 2011	Heritage
1894-S	Dime	NGC PF-66	$1,322,500	March 2005	David Lawrence Rare Coins
1792	Half Disme	PCGS SP-67	$1,322,500	April 2006	Heritage
1927-D	Double Eagle	NGC MS-65	$1,322,500	January 2006	Heritage
1894-S	Dime	NGC PF-BM66	$1,322,500	March 2005	David Lawrence Rare Coins
1927-D	Double Eagle	PCGS MS-63	$1,292,500	March 2014	Heritage
1792	Half Disme	PCGS SP-67 Secure Plus CAC	$1,292,500	August 2014	Heritage
1797 (O-101a)	Half Dollar	PCGS MS-65+ Secure Plus CAC	$1,292,500	August 2014	Heritage
1874 Gold Pattern (J-1373, P-1518)	Eagle	PCGS PF-65DCam	$1,265,000	January 2010	Heritage
1795, Reeded Edge (S-79)	Cent	PCGS VG-10	$1,265,000	September 2009	Ira and Larry Goldberg
1795 (B-7, BB-18)	Silver Dollar	V CH to Gem UNC	$1,265,000	December 2005	Coinhunter
1907, Saint-Gaudens, UHR, LE	Double Eagle	PCGS PF-67	$1,210,000	May 1999	Ira and Larry Goldberg
1804, Restrike	Silver Dollar	PCGS PF-58	$1,207,500	July 2003	Bowers & Merena
1866, No Motto	Silver Dollar	NGC PF-63	$1,207,500	January 2005	American Numismatic Rarities
1796, Small Date, Small Letters (B-2, BB-63)	Silver Dollar	NGC MS-65 CAC	$1,175,000	April 2013	Heritage
1783 CONSTELLATIO, Stars (B-1102, W-1830)	Pre-Federal	PCGS AU-53 Secure Plus	$1,175,000	April 2013	Heritage
1794 (B-7, C-7)	Half Cent	PCGS MS-67RB	$1,150,000	January 2014	Ira and Larry Goldberg
1792 Copper Pattern (J-1, P-1)	Cent	PCGS MS-61BN	$1,150,000	April 2012	Heritage
1794 (B-1, BB-1)	Silver Dollar	NGC MS-64	$1,150,000	June 2005	American Numismatic Rarities
1907, Saint-Gaudens, UHR, LE	Double Eagle	PCGS PF-68	$1,150,000	February 2003	Ira and Larry Goldberg
1792	Half Disme	NGC MS-68	$1,145,625	January 2013	Stack's Bowers Galleries
1811 (B-1, C-1)	Half Cent	PCGS MS-66RB CAC	$1,121,250	January 2014	Ira and Larry Goldberg
1870-S	Silver Dollar	BU PL	$1,092,500	May 2003	Stack's

Date/Variety	Denomination	Grade	Price	Date	Firm
1921	Double Eagle	PCGS MS-66	$1,092,500	November 2005	Heritage
1852 Humbert (K-10)	$10 Gold Piece	NGC MS-68 CAC	$1,057,500	April 2013	Heritage
1907, Saint-Gaudens, UHR (J-1788, P-2001)	Double Eagle	PCGS PF-58 Secure Plus	$1,057,500	August 2012	Heritage
1879, Coiled Hair	$4 Gold Piece	NGC PF-67Cam	$1,040,000	September 2013	Bonhams
1894-S	Dime	PCGS PF-BM65	$1,035,000	January 2005	Heritage
1921	Double Eagle	PCGS MS-65 PQ	$1,012,000	September 2007	Ira and Larry Goldberg
1885	Trade Dollar	NGC PF-62	$1,006,250	November 2004	David Lawrence Rare Coins
1796, Stars on Obverse (BD-3, B-6114, Bass-3003)	Quarter Eagle	NGC MS-65	$1,006,250	January 2008	Heritage
1885	Trade Dollar	NGC PF-62	$1,006,250	November 2004	David Lawrence Rare Coins
1884	Trade Dollar	PCGS PF-65 CAC	$998,750	January 2014	Heritage
1793, Chain, AMERICA (S-2)	Cent	PCGS MS-65BN CAC	$998,750	January 2013	Stack's Bowers Galleries
1799 (S-189)	Cent	NGC MS-62BN	$977,500	September 2009	Ira and Larry Goldberg
1880, Coiled Hair	$4 Gold Piece	NGC PF-66Cam	$977,500	January 2005	Heritage
1833, Large Date	Half Eagle	PCGS PF-67	$977,500	January 2005	Heritage
1797 (O-101a)	Half Dollar	NGC MS-66	$966,000	March 2004	American Numismatic Rarities
1880, Flowing Hair	$4 Gold Piece	NGC PF-67 Star	$959,400	September 2013	Bonhams
1849 Moffat & Co., Close Date (K-9)	$10 Gold Piece	PCGS SP-67	$948,750	August 2006	American Numismatic Rarities
1852 Moffat & Co., Close Date (K-9)	$10 Gold Piece	PCGS SP-63 CAC	$940,000	January 2014	Heritage
1792, Straight Cap, Thin Leaves (B-4, C-4)	Half Cent	PCGS MS-66BN CAC	$920,000	January 2014	Ira and Larry Goldberg
1802 (B-8, BB-302)	Silver Dollar	PCGS MS-65Cam	$920,000	April 2008	Heritage
1885	Trade Dollar	NGC PF-61	$920,000	May 2003	Stack's
1907, Saint-Gaudens, Small Edge Letters	Double Eagle	PCGS PF-68	$920,000	November 2005	Heritage
1795, Off-Center Bust (B-14, BB-51)	Silver Dollar	NGC MS-66+ Star CAC	$910,625	November 2013	Heritage
1885	Trade Dollar	PF-65	$907,500	April 1997	Bowers & Merena
1796, No Pole (B-1a, C-1)	Half Cent	PCGS MS-65BN CAC	$891,250	January 2014	Ira and Larry Goldberg
1873-CC, No Arrows (B-3365)	Dime	NGC MS-65	$891,250	July 2004	Bowers & Merena
1796 (JR-1)	Dime	PCGS MS-67 CAC	$881,250	June 2014	Heritage
1796 (B-1)	Quarter Dollar	PCGS SP-66	$881,250	August 2014	Heritage
1795, 13 Leaves (BD-5)	Eagle	PCGS MS-65	$881,250	August 2014	Heritage
1794, Head of 1793 (S-18B)	Cent	PCGS MS-64BN CAC	$881,250	January 2013	Stack's Bowers Galleries
1889-CC	Silver Dollar	PCGS MS-68	$881,250	August 2013	Stack's Bowers Galleries
1804, Restrike	Silver Dollar	PCGS PF-58	$874,000	November 2001	Bowers & Merena
1793, Wreath, Strawberry Leaf (N-3)	Cent	NGC F-12	$862,500	January 2009	Stack's
1796, Stars on Obverse (B-6114, BD-3, Bass-3003)	Quarter Eagle	NGC MS-65	$862,500	January 2007	Heritage
1879 Gold Pattern (J-1643, P-1843)	Double Eagle	PCGS PF-62	$862,500	January 2007	Heritage
1879, Coiled Hair	$4 Gold Piece	PCGS PF-66Cam Secure Plus	$851,875	January 2014	Heritage
1803 (B-7, BB-303)	Silver Dollar	PCGS PF-66	$851,875	January 2013	Heritage
1802 (B-8, BB-302)	Silver Dollar	PCGS PF-65Cam CAC	$851,875	August 2012	Heritage
1907, Saint-Gaudens, UHR, LE	Double Eagle	PF	$825,000	December 1996	Sotheby's
1795, 2 Leaves (B-2, BB-20)	Silver Dollar	NGC SP-64	$822,500	August 2014	Stack's Bowers Galleries
1799 (B-5, BB-157)	Silver Dollar	NGC MS-67	$822,500	November 2013	Heritage
1792 Copper Pattern (J-1, P-1)	Cent	NGC MS-61BN+	$822,500	April 2013	Heritage
1870-S	Silver Dollar	NGC EF-40	$805,000	April 2008	Heritage
1921	Double Eagle	PCGS MS-65	$805,000	November 2005	Heritage
1796 (JR-6)	Dime	PCGS MS-68 CAC	$793,125	August 2014	Heritage
1792 (LM-1)	Half Disme	PCGS MS-66 OH	$793,125	August 2013	Stack's Bowers Galleries
1838-O (GR-1)	Half Dollar	NGC PF-BM64 CAC	$763,750	January 2014	Heritage
1870-S	Silver Dollar	PCGS EF-40	$763,750	January 2014	Heritage
1826 (BD-2)	Half Eagle	PCGS MS-66	$763,750	January 2014	Heritage
1849 Pacific Company (K-1)	$5 Gold Piece	PCGS AU-58	$763,750	April 2014	Heritage
1855 Kellogg & Co. (K-4)	$50 Gold Piece	PCGS PF-64Cam	$763,750	April 2014	Heritage
1793 Chain, AMERICA (S-3)	Cent	NGC MS-66BN	$747,500	August 2012	Stack's Bowers Galleries
1921	Double Eagle	PCGS MS-66 Secure Plus	$747,500	January 2012	Heritage
1855 Kellogg & Co. (K-4, B-7921)	$50 Gold Piece	PCGS PF-64	$747,500	January 2007	Heritage
1794 (B-1, BB-1)	Silver Dollar	NGC MS-61	$747,500	June 2005	Heritage
1838-O	Half Dollar	PCGS PF-BM64	$734,375	January 2013	Heritage
1793, Straight Cap, Bunch Leaves (B-3, C-3)	Half Cent	PCGS MS-65BN CAC	$718,750	January 2014	Ira and Larry Goldberg
1796, With Pole (B-2a, C-2)	Half Cent	PCGS MS-65+RB CAC	$718,750	January 2014	Ira and Larry Goldberg
1933	Eagle	NGC MS-66	$718,750	October 2004	Stack's
1870-S	Silver Dollar	PCGS VF-25	$705,698	February 2008	Bowers & Merena
1849 Mormon (K-3)	$10 Gold Piece	NGC AU-58	$705,000	April 2014	Heritage
1783 CONSTELLATIO, Plain Edge (W-1820)	Pre-Federal	NGC AU-55	$705,000	May 2014	Heritage
1803, Large 3 (B-6, BB-255)	Silver Dollar	NGC MS-65+ CAC	$705,000	November 2013	Heritage
1836	Half Eagle	NGC PF-67UCam Star	$690,300	September 2013	Bonhams
1909-O	Half Eagle	PCGS MS-66	$690,000	January 2011	Heritage
1796, Liberty Cap (S-84)	Cent	PCGS MS-66RB	$690,000	September 2008	Ira and Larry Goldberg
1825, 5 Over 4 (BD-2)	Half Eagle	NGC AU-50	$690,000	July 2008	Heritage
1792 Copper Pattern (J-10, P-11)	Cent	NGC PF-62BN	$690,000	July 2008	Heritage

Date/Variety	Denomination	Grade	Price	Date	Firm
1907 Saint-Gaudens Gold Pattern (J-1907, P-2001)	Double Eagle	NGC PF-58	$690,000	July 2008	Stack's
1860 Clark, Gruber & Co. (K-4)	$20 Gold Piece	NGC MS-64	$690,000	January 2006	Heritage
'1742' Lima Style Brasher	Doubloon	NGC EF-40	$690,000	January 2005	Heritage
1907, Saint-Gaudens, UHR, LE	Double Eagle	PF	$690,000	October 2001	Sotheby's/Stack's
1849-C, Open Wreath	Gold Dollar	NGC MS-63PL	$690,000	July 2004	David Lawrence Rare Coins
1835 (B-6506, McCloskey-2-C)	Half Eagle	PCGS PF-67	$690,000	January 2005	Heritage
1839, Type of 1838	Eagle	NGC PF-67	$690,000	September 1999	Ira and Larry Goldberg
1795, 13 Leaves (BD-5)	Eagle	NGC MS-65	$675,625	August 2013	Heritage
1803 (B-7, BB-303)	Silver Dollar	PCGS PF-66	$672,750	February 2007	Bowers & Merena
1804 (S-266c)	Cent	PCGS MS-63BN	$661,250	September 2009	Ira and Larry Goldberg
1870-S (B-3128)	Half Dime	NGC MS-63	$661,250	July 2004	Bowers & Merena
1907, Saint-Gaudens, UHR, LE	Double Eagle	PCGS PF-67	$660,000	January 1997	Bowers & Merena
1879, Coiled Hair	$4 Gold Piece	NGC PF-67Cam	$655,500	January 2005	Heritage
1891	Double Eagle	NGC PF-68UCam Star	$655,200	September 2013	Bonhams
1909-O	Half Eagle	PCGS MS-66 Secure Plus	$646,250	January 2014	Heritage
1795, Reeded Edge (S-79, B-9)	Cent	PCGS VG-10	$646,250	January 2014	Heritage
1851 Baldwin (K-5)	$20 Gold Piece	PCGS EF-45 OGH	$646,250	April 2014	Heritage
1652 New England (N.1-A, W-10)	Sixpence	NGC AU-58	$646,250	May 2014	Heritage
1795, 3 Leaves (B-5, BB-27)	Silver Dollar	NGC MS-65 CAC	$646,250	November 2013	Heritage
1879, Coiled Hair	$4 Gold Piece	PCGS PF-64Cam Secure Plus	$646,250	May 2013	Stack's Bowers Galleries
1828, 8 Over 7 (BD-1, B-6487)	Half Eagle	NGC MS-64 CAC	$632,500	January 2012	Heritage
1870-S	Silver Dollar	PCGS EF-40	$632,500	August 2010	Bowers & Merena
1793, Liberty Cap (S-13, B-20)	Cent	PCGS AU-55	$632,500	February 2008	Heritage
1794, Starred Reverse (S-48, B-38)	Cent	PCGS AU-50	$632,500	February 2008	Heritage
1804, 14 Stars Reverse (JR-2)	Dime	NGC AU-58	$632,500	July 2008	Heritage
1838-O (JR-1)	Half Dollar	PCGS PF-BM63	$632,500	February 2008	Heritage
1652 Willow Tree (N.1-A, Cr. Unlisted, W-7)	Threepence	VF	$632,500	October 2005	Stack's
1861, Original	Half Dollar	VF-35	$632,500	October 2003	Stack's
1838-O	Half Dollar	PCGS PF-BM64	$632,500	June 2005	Heritage
1873-CC, No Arrows	Dime	PCGS MS-64	$632,500	April 1999	Heritage
1880, Coiled Hair	$4 Gold Piece	NGC PF-63	$618,125	July 2005	Superior
1796, No Stars on Obverse	Quarter Eagle	BU	$605,000	November 95	Stack's/RARCOA/Akers
1852, Restrike, Large Berries (B-1-D)	Half Cent	PCGS PF-65RD CAC	$603,750	January 2014	Ira and Larry Goldberg
1854-O	Double Eagle	PCGS AU-55	$603,750	October 2008	Heritage
1792 Copper Pattern (J-2, P-2)	Cent	PCGS VF-30	$603,750	January 2008	Heritage
1884	Trade Dollar	PCGS PF-65	$603,750	November 2005	Heritage
1921	Double Eagle	PCGS MS-65 CAC	$587,500	August 2012	Heritage
1792 Copper Pattern (J-10, P-11)	Disme	NGC PF-62BN	$587,500	October 2012	Heritage
1795, Small Eagle Reverse (BD-1)	Half Eagle	PCGS MS-65	$586,500	June 2008	Stack's
1794	Silver Dollar	Gem BU	$577,500	November 1995	Stack's/RARCOA/Akers
1927-D	Double Eagle	PCGS MS-65	$577,500	May 1998	Akers
1856-O	Double Eagle	NGC AU-58	$576,150	October 2008	Heritage
1920-S	Double Eagle	PCGS MS-66 Secure Plus CAC	$575,000	January 2012	Heritage
1794 (B-1, BB-1)	Silver Dollar	PCGS AU-58+ Secure	$575,000	May 2011	Ira and Larry Goldberg
1880, Coiled Hair	$4 Gold Piece	NGC PF-62	$575,000	January 2009	Heritage
1877 Copper Pattern (J-1549, P-1722)	$50 Gold Piece	NGC PF-67BN	$575,000	January 2009	Heritage
1895-O	Silver Dollar	PCGS MS-67	$575,000	November 2005	Heritage
1907, Saint-Gaudens, HR, Wire Edge	Double Eagle	PCGS MS-69	$575,000	November 2005	Heritage
1927-D	Double Eagle	NGC MS-62	$575,000	July 2004	David Lawrence Rare Coins
1907, Saint-Gaudens, HR, Wire Edge	Double Eagle	NGC PF-69	$573,300	September 2013	Bonhams
1876-CC	Twenty-Cent Piece	PCGS MS-65 Secure Plus	$564,000	January 2013	Stack's Bowers Galleries
1855 Wass, Molitor & Co., Large Head	$20 Gold Piece	NGC AU-53	$558,125	April 2014	Heritage
1849 Mormon (K-4)	$20 Gold Piece	NGC MS-62	$558,125	April 2014	Heritage
1793, Wreath, Vine/Bars Edge (S-9)	Cent	PCGS MS-69BN OGH	$558,125	January 2013	Stack's Bowers Galleries
1933	Eagle	PCGS MS-65	$552,000	January 2008	Heritage
1870-S	Silver Dollar	VF-20	$552,000	October 2007	Stack's
1873-CC, No Arrows	Dime	MS-65	$550,000	May 1996	Bowers & Merena
1838	Eagle	PF	$550,000	May 1998	Akers
1776 CURRENCY EG FECIT, Pewter (N.3-D, H-3-B, W-8460)	Dollar	NGC MS-67	$546,250	January 2012	Heritage
1893-S (NGC #3181273-001)	Silver Dollar	NGC MS-67	$546,250	August 2011	Heritage
1851 Humbert 880 THOUS. (K-2)	$50 Gold Piece	PCGS MS-63	$546,250	August 2010	Heritage
1880, Coiled Hair	$4 Gold Piece	NGC PF-62	$546,250	July 2009	Heritage
1795, 13 Leaves (B-1-A, BD-1, T-1)	Eagle	PCGS MS-64	$546,250	July 2008	Stack's
1933	Eagle	PCGS MS-65	$546,250	January 2007	Heritage
1907, Saint-Gaudens HR, Wire Edge	Double Eagle	PCGS MS-69	$546,250	January 2007	Heritage
1856-O	Double Eagle	NGC SP-63	$542,800	June 2004	Heritage

Note: Stack's and American Numismatic Rarities merged under the Stack's name in 2006. The resultant company merged with Bowers & Merena in 2010 to form Stack's Bowers Galleries.

100 GREATEST U.S. COINS BY TYPE

Denomination	Type	Year	Artist	Mintmark	Notes	Ranking
Half Cent	Liberty Cap, Facing Right	1796	Robert Scot	—	With Pole and No Pole	70
Cent	Fugio	1787	James Jarvis	—		36
Cent	Birch	1792	Robert Birch	—	Pattern	25
Cent	Silver-Center	1792	Robert Birch	—	Pattern	40
Large Cent	Flowing Hair, Chain Reverse	1793	Henry Voigt	—		13
Large Cent	Flowing Hair, Wreath Reverse	1793	Unknown	—	Strawberry Leaf	61
Large Cent	Liberty Cap	1794	Robert Scot	—	Starred Reverse	24
Small Cent	Flying Eagle	1856	James Longacre	—		57
Small Cent	Lincoln	1909	Victor David Brenner	S	V.D.B.	23
Small Cent	Lincoln	1943	Victor David Brenner	—	Bronze	11
Small Cent	Lincoln	1955	Victor David Brenner	—	Doubled-Die Obverse	74
Small Cent	Lincoln	1974	Victor David Brenner	—	Aluminum	88
Two-Cent Piece		1864	James Longacre	—	Proof, Small Motto	91
Half Disme		1792	Unknown	—		12
Half Dime	Draped Bust	1802	Robert Scot	—		77
Half Dime	Liberty Seated	1870	Gobrecht/Longacre	S		58
Nickel	Shield	1867	James Longacre	—	Proof, With Rays	89
Nickel	Liberty Head	1913	Charles Barber	—		2
Nickel	Buffalo	1918, 8 Over 7	James Earle Fraser	D	Overdate	84
Disme		1792	Unknown	—		15
Dime	Liberty Seated	1873	Gobrecht/Longacre	CC	No Arrows	65
Dime	Barber	1894	Charles Barber	S		7
Dime	Mercury Head	1916	Adolph Weinman	D		68
Twenty-Cent Piece	Liberty Seated	1876	Christian Gobrecht	CC		26
Quarter Dollar	Pattern	1792	Joseph Wright	—	Pattern	72
Quarter Dollar	Draped Bust	1796	Robert Scot	—		76
Quarter Dollar	Capped Bust	1827	John Reich	—	Original	87
Quarter Dollar	Liberty Seated	1842	Christian Gobrecht	—	Small Date	93
Quarter Dollar	Liberty Seated	1866	Christian Gobrecht	—	No Motto	48
Quarter Dollar	Liberty Seated	1873	Christian Gobrecht	CC	No Arrows	75
Quarter Dollar	Liberty Standing	1916	Hermon MacNeil	—		43
Quarter Dollar	Liberty Standing	1918, 8 Over 7	Hermon MacNeil	—	Overdate	86
Half Dollar	Draped Bust	1796, 1797	Robert Scot	—	15- and 16-Star varieties	56
Half Dollar	Capped Bust	1817, 7 Over 4	John Reich	—	Overdate	47
Half Dollar	Capped Bust	1838	John Reich	O		27
Half Dollar	Liberty Seated	1853	Christian Gobrecht	O	No Arrows	82
Half Dollar	Liberty Seated	1866	Christian Gobrecht	—	No Motto	83
Dollar	Continental	1776	Elisha Gallaudet	—		10
Silver Dollar	Flowing Hair	1794	Robert Scot	—		9
Silver Dollar	Draped Bust	1801–1803	Robert Scot	—	Proof	80
Silver Dollar	Draped Bust	1804	Robert Scot	—	Originals and restrikes	1
Silver Dollar	Gobrecht	1836, 1838, 1839	Christian Gobrecht	—		73
Silver Dollar	Liberty Seated	1851, 1852	Christian Gobrecht	—	Originals and restrikes	98
Silver Dollar	Liberty Seated	1866	Christian Gobrecht	—	No Motto	46
Silver Dollar	Liberty Seated	1870	Christian Gobrecht	S		29
Silver Dollar	Trade	1884	William Barber	—	Proof	66
Silver Dollar	Trade	1885	William Barber	—	Proof	8
Silver Dollar	Morgan	1893	George Morgan	S		38
Silver Dollar	Morgan	1895	George Morgan	—		30
Gold Dollar	Liberty Head	1849	James Longacre	C	Open Wreath	35
Gold Dollar	Indian Princess Head	1854, 1855	James Longacre	—	Proof	49
Gold Dollar	Indian Princess Head	1861	James Longacre	D		39
Gold Dollar*	Amazonian	1872	William Barber	—	Pattern	16
Quarter Eagle	Capped Bust to Right	1796	Robert Scot	—	No Stars	71
Quarter Eagle	Capped Bust to Right	1804	Robert Scot	—	13 Stars	52
Quarter Eagle	Capped Bust to Left	1808	John Reich	—		92
Quarter Eagle	Liberty Head	1841	Christian Gobrecht	—		97
Quarter Eagle	Liberty Head	1848	Christian Gobrecht	—	CAL.	63
Quarter Eagle	Liberty Head	1854	Christian Gobrecht	S		90
Quarter Eagle	Liberty Head	1863	Christian Gobrecht	—	Proof	99
Quarter Eagle*	Amazonian	1872	William Barber	—	Pattern	16
$3 Gold Coin	Indian Princess Head	1870	James Longacre	S		22
$3 Gold Coin*	Amazonian	1872	William Barber	—	Pattern	16
$3 Gold Coin	Indian Princess Head	1875	James Longacre	—		59

* The Amazonian set shares a single entry in the rankings, but each coin is listed individually here.

Denomination	Type	Year	Artist	Mintmark	Notes	Ranking
$4 Gold Coin	Stella	1879, 1880	Charles Barber / Morgan	—	Flowing and Coiled Hair	18
Half Eagle	Capped Bust to Right	1797	Robert Scot	—	Heraldic Reverse, 16 Stars Obverse	94
Half Eagle	Capped Bust to Right	1798	Robert Scot	—	Small Eagle	33
Half Eagle	Capped Head	1815	John Reich	—		42
Half Eagle	Capped Head	1819	John Reich	—	Two varieties	100
Half Eagle	Capped Head	1822	John Reich	—		17
Half Eagle	Capped Head	1825, 5 Over 4	John Reich	—	Overdate	55
Half Eagle	Capped Head	1829	John Reich	—	Large and Small Planchets	81
Half Eagle	Capped Head	1832	John Reich	—	12 Stars	96
Half Eagle	Capped Head	1833	John Reich	—	Proof	67
Half Eagle	Classic Head	1834–1837	William Kneass	—	Proof	45
Half Eagle**	Liberty Head	1844	Christian Gobrecht	O	Proof	44
Half Eagle	Liberty Head	1854	Christian Gobrecht	S		62
Half Eagle*	Amazonian	1872	William Barber	—	Pattern	16
Eagle	Capped Bust	1795	Robert Scot	—	Nine Leaves	78
Eagle	Capped Bust	1798, 8 Over 7	Robert Scot	—	Overdate, two varieties	54
Eagle	Capped Bust	1804	Robert Scot	—	Plain 4	69
Eagle	Liberty Head	1838	Christian Gobrecht	—	Proof	34
Eagle**	Liberty Head	1844	Christian Gobrecht	O	Proof	44
Eagle*	Amazonian	1872	William Barber	—	Pattern	16
Eagle	Indian Head	1907	Augustus Saint-Gaudens	—	Rolled Edge	37
Eagle	Indian Head	1933	Augustus Saint-Gaudens	—		41
$10 Gold Piece	Bickford	1874	Bickford / William Barber	—	Pattern	85
Double Eagle	Liberty Head	1849	James Longacre	—		5
Double Eagle	Liberty Head	1854	James Longacre	O		32
Double Eagle	Liberty Head	1854	James Longacre	S	Presentation strike	31
Double Eagle	Liberty Head	1856	James Longacre	O		53
Double Eagle	Liberty Head	1857	James Longacre	S		95
Double Eagle	Liberty Head	1861	Longacre/Paquet	—	Paquet Reverse	20
Double Eagle	Liberty Head	1861	Longacre/Paquet	S	Paquet Reverse	50
Double Eagle	Liberty Head	1870	James Longacre	CC		79
Double Eagle*	Amazonian	1872	William Barber	—	Pattern	16
Double Eagle	Indian Head	1907	Augustus Saint-Gaudens	—	Pattern	6
Double Eagle	Saint-Gaudens	1907	Augustus Saint-Gaudens	—	Ultra High Relief	3
Double Eagle	Saint-Gaudens	1907	Augustus Saint-Gaudens	—	High Relief	28
Double Eagle	Saint-Gaudens	1907	Augustus Saint-Gaudens	—	Piedfort	14
Double Eagle	Saint-Gaudens	1921	Augustus Saint-Gaudens	—	Proof	51
Double Eagle	Saint-Gaudens	1927	Augustus Saint-Gaudens	D		64
Double Eagle	Saint-Gaudens	1933	Augustus Saint-Gaudens	—		4
$50 Gold Coin	U.S. Assay Office "Slugs"	—	Wright/Humbert	—		60
$50 Gold Coin	Half Union	1877	William Barber	—	Two varieties	19
$50 Gold Coin	Panama-Pacific Exposition	1915	Robert Aitken	S		21

* The Amazonian set shares a single entry in the rankings, but each coin is listed individually here.   ** The 1844-O half eagle and eagle share a single entry in the rankings, but the coins are listed individually here.

GLOSSARY

About Uncirculated—a coin close to Uncirculated or Mint State condition, with slight traces of wear on the high points

adjustment mark—a file mark caused when metal was removed from the planchet to bring it down to the proper weight

alloy—a blended mixture of two or more metals used to make a coin

bimetallic—consisting of two metals in an unmixed or unalloyed state

bullion—any form of gold or silver traded for its metal value

bullion dealer—a trader in bullion

bust—a portrait on a coin consisting of the head, neck, and part of the upper body

circulated—a coin that is worn from use in general commerce

circulation strike—a coin made for circulation or use in general commerce

coin press—the machine used to stamp or strike a coin

commemorative—a coin struck to honor a place, event, or person

counterfeit—a fake or false coin

denomination—the stated value on a coin

denticles—toothlike projections around the outer rim of a coin

die—the cylindrical piece of steel used to stamp a coin

double eagle—a U.S. $20 gold piece

doubloon—a Spanish gold coin weighing approximately 420 grains (.875 troy ounces or 27.216 grams)

eagle—a U.S. $10 gold piece

electrotype—a counterfeit coin made by joining electroplate impressions from a real coin

error—a mismade or defective coin

Extremely Fine—a well-preserved circulated coin with excellent details and a trace of original luster

fineness—the purity of gold, silver, or any other precious metal

fusible alloy—an alloy of copper and a small amount of silver used to make the 1792 one-cent pieces

gem—an exceptionally well-preserved Uncirculated coin

Good—a heavily worn coin that retains very little of the original detail

grain—a unit of weight measuring 1/480 of a troy ounce, or .065 grams

greenback—the United States' paper money, first introduced around the time of the Civil War

guinea—a British gold coin from the 1700s, slightly larger than a U.S. quarter dollar

half eagle—a U.S. $5 gold piece

heraldic eagle—an eagle with outstretched wings and a shield on its chest

legend—the wording on a coin

lettered edge—the edge of a coin that has been impressed with words

liberty cap—a brimless cap of soft cloth; also known as a freedman's cap or a Phrygian cap

luster—the brilliant or "frosty" surface quality of an Uncirculated (Mint State) coin

Matte Proof—a Proof coin with a dull, sandblast finish

mint—any of the official government buildings where coins are made

mintmark—a small letter or other mark on a coin, indicating the mint at which it was struck

mintage—the number of coins that were made in a given year for a particular denomination

Mint State—a condition that is brand new or uncirculated (also called Uncirculated)

monetize—the official act of making a coin into legal tender

numismatics—the study of coins

numismatist—a collector and student of coins

obverse—the front of a coin

overdate—date made by superimposing one or more numerals on a previously dated die

overstrike—an impression made with new dies on a previously struck coin

pattern—a coin made to test new designs for possible use on coins made for circulation

pedigree—the chain of ownership of a particular coin

piedfort—a specimen or medal struck on a planchet that is at least twice the normal thickness

planchet—the metal blank that eventually becomes a coin

population—the number of certified examples of a coin, as reported by certification and grading services, frequently inflated by unreported resubmissions of previously certified coins

presentation strike—a coin made expressly for presentation to a VIP or government official

Proof—a coin specially made for collectors or investors, not for general circulation, and usually with reflective, mirror-like surfaces

prooflike—an Uncirculated coin that looks like a Proof

quarter eagle—a U.S. $2.50 gold coin

rarity—a determination of how rare or common a particular coin is

reeding—ridges on the edge of a coin

restrike—a coin struck from genuine dies at a later date than the original issue

reverse—the back of a coin

series—a set of one coin of each year of a specific design and denomination issued from each mint

superb—a coin that is nearly perfect Uncirculated

type set—a collection of all the major design types in a denomination or series of coins

Uncirculated—a coin that has no wear or friction (synonymous with Mint State)

undertype—traces of the original coin that remain after being struck again by different dies

variety—minor or major differences between coins of the same design

Very Good—a coin that is very worn but still legible

SELECTED BIBLIOGRAPHY

In addition to the following reference works, auction catalogs from the following firms are useful sources of information: American Numismatic Rarities, Bowers and Merena Galleries, Heritage Numismatic Auctions, Ira and Larry Goldberg Coins and Collectibles, Mid-American Rare Coin Auctions, Paramount Rare Coins, Sotheby's, Stack's, Stack's Bowers Galleries, and Superior Galleries.

Akers, David W. *United States Gold Coins: An Analysis of Auction Records, Volume I: Gold Dollars.* Englewood, OH: Paramount Publications, 1975.

———. *United States Gold Coins: An Analysis of Auction Records, Volume II: Quarter Eagles.* Englewood, OH: Paramount Publications, 1975.

———. *United States Gold Coins: An Analysis of Auction Records, Volume III: Three Dollar Gold.* Englewood, OH: Paramount Publications, 1976.

———. *United States Gold Coins: An Analysis of Auction Records, Volume IV: Half Eagles.* Englewood, OH: Paramount Publications, 1979.

———. *United States Gold Coins: An Analysis of Auction Records, Volume V: Eagles.* Englewood, OH: Paramount Publications, 1980.

———. *United States Gold Coins: An Analysis of Auction Records, Volume VI: Double Eagles.* Englewood, OH: Paramount Publications, 1982.

———. *United States Gold Patterns.* Englewood, OH: Paramount Publications, 1975.

Bowers, Q. David. *United States Gold Coins: An Illustrated History.* Wolfeboro, NH: Bowers and Merena Galleries, 1982.

Breen, Walter. *Walter Breen's Encyclopedia of United States and Colonial Proof Coins, 1722–1977.* New York: FCI Press, Inc., 1977.

———. *Walter Breen's Complete Encyclopedia of United States and Colonial Coins.* New York: Doubleday, 1988.

Dannreuther, John, and Harry W. Bass Jr. *Early U.S. Gold Coin Varieties: A Study of Die States, 1795-1834.* Atlanta: Whitman Publishing, 2006.

Dannreuther, John, and Jeff Garrett. *The Official Red Book of Auction Records 1994–2007: U.S. Gold Coinage.* Atlanta: Whitman Publishing, 2008.

———. *The Official Red Book of Auction Records 1994–2007: U.S. Small Cents to Silver Dollars.* Atlanta: Whitman Publishing, 2008.

———. *The Official Red Book of Auction Records 1994–2007: Colonials, Early Copper, Commemoratives, Territorials, Patterns, Cal. Gold, and Miscellaneous.* Atlanta: Whitman Publishing, 2008.

Guth, Ron. *Coin Collecting for Dummies.* New York: Hungry Minds, 2001.

Logan, Russell, and John W. McCloskey. *Federal Half Dimes 1792–1837.* Manchester, MI: John Reich Collectors Society, 1998.

"The NGC Population Report, July 2014." Sarasota, FL: Numismatic Guaranty Corporation.

"The PCGS Population Report, July 2014." Newport Beach, CA: The Professional Coin Grading Service.

Pollock III, Andrew W. *United States Patterns and Related Issues.* Wolfeboro, NH: Bowers and Merena Galleries, 1994.

Vermeule, Cornelius. *Numismatic Art in America: Aesthetics of the United States Coinage*, 2nd ed. Atlanta: Whitman Publishing, 2008.

Winter, Douglas. *New Orleans Mint Gold Coins 1839–1909.* Wolfeboro, NH: Bowers and Merena Galleries, 1992.

Winter, Douglas, and Lawrence E. Cutler. *Gold Coins of the Old West: The Carson City Mint 1870–1893.* Wolfeboro, NH: Bowers and Merena Galleries, 1994.

Yeoman, R.S. *A Guide Book of United States Coins*, 68th ed. Atlanta: Whitman Publishing, 2014.

INDEX